Playing in a New League

The Women of the American Basketball League's First Season

Sara Gogol

with photography by John Todd

MASTERS PRESS

Published by Masters Press
A Division of Howard W. Sams & Company
2647 Waterfront Pkwy. E. Drive, Indianapolis, IN 46214

Printed in the United States of America.

98 99 00 01 02   10 9 8 7 6 5 4 3 2 1

Library of Congress Cataloging-in-Publication Data

Gogol, Sara.
    Playing in a new league: the women of the ABL's (American Basketball League) first season / Sara Gogol.
        p.   cm.
    Includes bibliographical references.
    ISBN 1-57028-199-8
    1. Women basketball players --- United States -- Biography. 2. Women coaches -- United States -- Biography. 3. American Basketball League.   I. Title
GV884.A1G63   1998
796.323'092'273--dc21   97-47714
[B]   CIP

To the women and men of the American Basketball League

Credits:

Cover design by Debra Wilson & Suzanne Lincoln
Cover and interior photos by John Todd
Proofread by Pat Brady

Table of Contents

Introduction ❖ 1

A New League ❖ 5

A Founding Player ❖ 23
Katy Steding

An Unofficial Founding Player ❖ 43
Christy Hedgpeth

Veterans of Play Overseas ❖ 60
Val Whiting and Linda Godby

Two Western Conference Coaches ❖ 83
Jacquie Hullah and Lin Dunn

Home at Last ❖ 99
Stacey Ford and Adrienne Goodson

Two Different Seasons ❖ 117
Kirsten Cummings and Trisha Stafford

Back to Basketball ❖ 133
Coquese Washington, Falisha Wright, and Lisa Harrison

The Australia Connection ❖ 154
Shelley Sandie and Debbie Black

College Stars ❖ 176
Kate Paye, Jennifer Jacoby and Natalie Williams

Playing in a New League

Players, Coaches, and More   ❖   199
Sheila Frost, Tonya Alleyne and Tara Davis

Two Eastern Conference Coaches   ❖   218
Kelly Kramer and Lisa Boyer

The Second Oldest Player   ❖   240
Valerie Still

A Future for the Women's Pro Game   ❖   260

Epilogue   ❖   278

Appendix: Sources   ❖   287

Acknowledgements

Writing this book would not have been possible without the players, coaches, and other personnel of the American Basketball League who took time from their busy lives to share their experiences with me. My deepest thanks to Tonya Alleyne, Debbie Black, Lisa Boyer, Kirsten Cummings, Tara Davis, Lin Dunn, Stacey Ford, Sheila Frost, Linda Godby, Adrienne Goodson, Molly Goodenbour, Lisa Harrison, Christy Hedgpeth, Jacquie Hullah, Jennifer Jacoby, Kelly Kramer, Michelle Marciniak, Kate Paye, Shelley Sandie, Trisha Stafford, Katy Steding, Valerie Still, Coquese Washington, Linda Weston, Val Whiting, Natalie Williams, and Falisha Wright. I wish I could have included all your stories in my book.

Thank you to American Basketball League co-founders Gary Cavalli and Steve Hams for their support for this book and their invaluable information about the history of the ABL and their personal involvement in the league. Others who provided useful information for this book include Cathy Aiken, Barbara Bell, Patti Huntley, Gary Lavender, and Tara VanDerveer.

Current and former media directors throughout the ABL assisted me during this project. My thanks go to Tonya Alleyne, Shana Daum, Cindy Fester, Jeff Johnson, Dean Jutilla, Steve Racznski, Linda Reid, Debbie Rosenfeld, Kirk Sampson, Jim Day, and most of all to Kevin Toon, media director for the Portland Power, who was helpful on numerous occasions.

At Masters Press, I'm grateful to acquisitions editor Ken Samelson for believing in this book. And my special thanks to senior editor Holly Kondras, for her enthusiasm for this project and her patience with all my revisions.

Thank you to my brother, Edward Gogol, and my parents, Rose and Sam Gogol, for their help in getting me to the ABL All-Star weekend in Orlando, Florida. And thank you to Marsha Smith, who carefully transcribed numerous interviews.

My thanks go to Julie Allen and Mark Wood for their friendship and their encouragement with this project. And special thanks to Elaine Carter for her daily support and caring, for sharing the many ups and downs of this book project, and for listening to approximately a million stories about basketball players.

And finally, I want to add a note of appreciation to the Colorado Xplosion mascot, the X Bear, whoever you may be inside that bear suit. Thanks for the backrub you gave me while I was sitting at a media table watching the ABL All-Star game.

Introduction

I first met Katy Steding at The Hoop, a mega-gym specializing in basketball in a suburb of Portland, Oregon. My first impression of her was that she looked like a basketball player: tall, with a long stride and a confident air. She greeted me in a friendly way, then led me to an office with "Katy Steding Basketball Academy" emblazoned on the door. Despite the grandiose sound of "Academy," the office was big enough — barely — for two small desks, and three secretarial chairs.

Even though Katy Steding was young enough to be my daughter, I had been nervous about this interview. Katy had just won an Olympic gold medal, which made her the most famous person I'd ever talked with. But she quickly put me at my ease. She was down to earth, articulate, and had a good sense of humor, and she was not self important in the least.

My initial reason to speak with Katy was that I planned to write a children's book. Katy, who was playing on the Power (the American Basketball League team in Portland), had agreed to meet with me but was a little confused about my project. Was my book to be about the whole team, she asked me.

I told her I wanted to write her biography for children. "You might wonder why I chose you," I said. "I think you've done a lot."

"Thank you," Katy said simply. She heard my compliment, acknowledged it, but didn't make too much of it. She was, I quickly learned though our conversations, simply a good person who was a fantastic basketball player. And at 29 years old, she had lived a basketball player's life. That is, the kind of life many women basketball players have experienced in many years.

As we talked about what to include in my book, Katy told me about her childhood experiences as one of the few girls in a boys' basketball league. She told me about playing for high-powered coach Tara VanDerveer at Stanford University and about being faced with a hard choice after college: as a woman player, she could either go overseas to play in women's professional leagues or give up top-level basketball. She went on to tell me about her journey when she returned to the U.S. again—to play on the 1995-96 U.S. National Team, win a gold medal at the Olympic games in Atlanta, and help start a professional basketball league for women in the United States, the first in a number of years, the American Basketball League.

As I spoke with Katy, learned about her life and basketball and read up on the history of the women's game, I got more and more interested. I began to imagine a larger book I could do about women in the new league. What were their lives like? How had they come to be involved with this level of basketball? How did they feel about living out a piece of history by participating in the first year of a new pro league?

When I first approached players and coaches on the Power, I was warmed by their enthusiasm for the project and their willingness to share a glimpse of their lives with me. I spoke with women from the Power and the Seattle Reign, both within easy distance of my home. After games in Portlan, I talked briefly to players and coaches from visiting teams as we stood around in the narrow corridor outside the visitors' locker room, but there wasn't time then to do the kind of in-depth interviews I needed. The women were tired and hungry, ready to talk for five minutes—they were all used to media attention—and then eager to head off quickly for barbecue, or pizza, or just time to kick back. So I began to do a number of my interviews over the telephone. I was afraid that my inability to talk with some of the women face-to-face would be a major obstacle. But despite the hundreds of miles between us, I often had a feeling of genuinely connecting with the women as they told me about their lives.

Kelly Kramer, the Columbus Quest assistant coach, and I only met over the telephone. Yet by the end of our conversation, we felt like friends. "Come say hello at a game next year," Kelly said to me when we were wrapping up our interview. I assured her that I would.

Of course, I wasn't really a part of any of the women's lives, but I felt connected to their world. The women had shared feelings and memories with me. They had given me a piece of their lives, and I appreciated the gift. I came to respect all of these women; they were not only talented athletes but strong people, gutsy women who would face challenges head on. Many of them had coped with injuries, years overseas, and other hardships associated with their sport. All of them had worked hard to get where they were. And they understood that they were helping to make history with the new league.

As I continued speaking to the women involved with the ABL, in person or on the phone, I learned more and more about their lives. And I came to understand something else as well—why I was so interested in women's basketball.

I have to look back in time to find the whole answer to that. I'm 49 years old now. Over thirty years ago, as a preteen and a teenager, I used to shoot baskets in a hoop attached to the garage of my house, just the way countless other young women have. In my case, the hoop wasn't set at regulation height. My father hung it where it happened to fit on the garage. The basketball I used wasn't inflated correctly, and my brother and I sometimes used the same ball for our games of kickball in the alley. But none of that deterred me.

I shot free throw after free throw, letting the ball bounce off the garage wall and back to me. I shot from other angles too. Once in a while I played with my brother and his friends, but mostly my basketball games were played alone. In cold Chicago falls and winters, I discovered that shooting baskets warmed me enough that I could take off my heavy coat and hang it over the fence. Fortunately, from where I stood, my mother couldn't see me shooting baskets without my coat on.

Aside from my alley workouts, I played basketball in gym classes. It was a half court game at the time, with one roving forward and one roving guard. I liked to play the roving guard position—at 5' 4" I didn't aspire to be a forward—so I had the freedom to run up and down the court.

There were no teams for girls at Mather High School in Chicago, where I went from 1962 to 1966. The boys had football, basketball, track, baseball, tennis, swimming, and even golf. Girls were limited to intramural play with the Girls Athletic Association (G.A.A.) teams within the high school. But "team" wasn't really an accurate label for the loosely-organized activities. Girls had to find other girls to join their teams. There was no coaching at all, and only a very limited number of games. I remember playing — and losing — one G.A.A. volleyball game. I don't remember playing G.A.A. basketball, although I surely would have wanted to.

I played a few informal games after college, occasionally making a surprisingly good outside shot. The years I spent shooting baskets on my own had given me a good aim. But that was the extent of my basketball "career." I didn't even watch the game much until the early nineties in Portland when the Blazers were an exciting team who went to the NBA finals two out of three years. I watched Blazers like Clyde Drexler and Terry Porter and enjoyed their high-flying exploits, but it didn't occur to me to wish that I could watch their female counterparts out on the court as well.

But then, when I was in high school I didn't think about the fact that boys had lots of sports teams and girls didn't have any. That was simply the way things were. However, as I spoke with Katy Steding and the other women in the league, I began to think more about my own personal history.

It wasn't that I thought the world had lost a great athlete. I might have made a high school basketball team or run track, but surely my athletic career wouldn't have gone further than that. Maybe I wouldn't have made either team. Still, I wish I'd had the chance to try. I might have had the experience of making and missing shots, of winning and losing games, of playing my heart out along with a group of other girls.

I can't go back in time and change the way things were to how they could and should have been. But the chances I never had, the opportunities that lots of other girls didn't get either, go a long way toward explaining why I'm an enthusiastic fan of the American Basketball League. And why the stories of the women in the league both interest and move me.

The women who played and coached in the first year of the ABL are pioneers whose sweat and hustle affect more than their own lives. A women's pro league like the ABL, and the WNBA as well, makes it possible for fans like me to watch top women basketball players. It means that girls and boys can have top women athletes as role models. It means that girls can dream about being like their heroines on court, the best in the game.

A New League

On June 24, 1996, less than four months before the American Basketball League's first season was scheduled to start, Linda Weston began her new job as General Manager of the Portland Power. To say that getting ready for the season was an uphill battle is something of an understatement. When she started work, Linda didn't yet have an office to go to. And when she did get her new office space—a small room in a cluster of small rooms—there was no usable office furniture. There weren't any pens, pencils or pads of paper either. Linda had to make a personal shopping trip for essential office supplies because the only other staff positions that had been filled at that time were the head coach and his assistant.

A slim, fair-complexioned woman in her early fifties, Linda Weston always seems to be alert, ready to deal with whatever situations arise. She's a smart, articulate person who definitely doesn't possess a laid back personality despite coming from Eugene, Oregon, which some people regard as the "hippie capitol" of the state.

Linda's background — eighteen years in the visitor industry in Eugene, culminating with a position as CEO of the Visitor's Association — had been excellent preparation for her new job with the American Basketball League. Nonetheless, Linda knew she was taking on a challenge. How much of a challenge? Well, as she describes what her new job has been like: "It's been the most exhausting, most stressful, most chaotic, most challenging, most exhilarating, exciting thing I've ever done."

It's also a job that Linda has no regrets about taking on. When

Steve Hams, one of the ABL's founders, contacted her about the position, Linda knew it would not only involve plenty of work but also mean taking a big risk. She could probably have retired in the job she left as head of the Eugene Visitor's Association. The ABL, on the other hand, was definitely a start up venture. "There was scepticism last year," Linda remembers, "about whether or not we'd ever play our first game, let alone complete a season."

Linda was prepared to take the risk. "I didn't want to miss my chance to be a part of history," she says. Her own life history, in fact, had shown her why the league mattered so much.

Linda's daughter Wendy, whose framed photograph sits on the desk in Linda's office, is twenty-five years old. Although she chose not to accept an athletic scholarship for college, she played basketball, soccer, ran track, and was voted the "outstanding athlete," male or female, in her senior class in high school. Some of Wendy's physical abilities could have been inherited from her father, Linda's ex-husband, who played minor league baseball. Did Wendy's athletic talent come from her mother as well? Her daughter will never know for sure because Linda Weston, like so many other girls and young women, never got the chance to explore how far she could go with sports.

At Linda's high school in Eugene, there were no athletic teams for girls. Linda had grown up playing games of Horse in the driveway of her home along with her big brother. As a girl, she fought with her brother over the sports page rather than the comics. But at school, where teenage boys had their choice of various teams, Linda — along with all the other girls — had their athletic opportunities limited to PE classes and the rally squad. "I didn't get the benefit of the opportunities that my daughter had," Linda comments. "Or that these young women who are playing (in the ABL) have had."

Linda Weston describes herself as someone who's "always been a basketball junkie." An avid fan of the NBA, as well as men's and women's college basketball, she used to joke that her dream job would be as a director of marketing for an NBA team. Now she was going to take on a job in women's professional basketball that she might not have imagined existing a few years ago.

She didn't travel far in miles from her home in Eugene. The drive north to Portland is only two hours long, an easy trip up Interstate Five. It was a drive Linda had made many times before, to see friends or for business or to take in a Blazers game. But when Linda left

Eugene at 5:30 on a Sunday evening in June, she embarked on a major life change. She was headed for total immersion in the world of women's professional basketball.

That new job and new world began the very next morning. Initially, Linda had to work out of the small apartment in downtown Portland where she was living temporarily. That afternoon, Linda, the head coach, Greg Bruce, and his assistant, Debbie Gollnick, took a trip to the Memorial Coliseum, the future home of their team and the past home of the Trail Blazers. They wanted to inspect the space which would become their new offices.

The scene they encountered was discouraging, to say the least. "There was furniture that wasn't put together," Linda recalls. "There were big holes in the walls. Lighting fixtures just kind of hanging by wires from the ceiling. It was a mess."

The only working telephone was left over from the Trail Blazers' stay-in-school program. Linda and Greg could make outgoing calls on the phone, but if someone called in, the situation got interesting. If Linda or Greg were already on the telephone, their incoming call would be transferred to the Blazers' voice mail system, which neither Linda nor Greg could access.

A less determined person might have decided to quit. Instead Linda made her shopping trip that evening, purchasing paper and pencils, paper clips, a fax machine. The second morning, after she, Greg, and Debbie carried in Linda's purchases, they started putting together their new office. Literally. Assisted by workers from the Coliseum, they bolted together pieces of desks, gradually setting up their work space.

That was only the beginning of the jobs Linda faced. She had to hire her staff, a process that wasn't completed until the middle of August, only two months before the season opened. She had to sell tickets, obtain sponsorships, and create an awareness about her team. She spoke to Rotary clubs, and business associations, and whoever else would listen to her, plugging both the team and women's professional basketball. And then on weekends she hunted for houses in Portland or drove down to Eugene, where she was packing up her possessions and getting her house there ready to be sold. She didn't move into her new home, a bungalow in a quiet Northeast Portland neighborhood, until the Saturday before opening night.

It must have been hard to stay focused on the big picture when there was so much to be done in such a short time. But Linda Weston knew what she was working for. She knew what the American Basketball League was all about. "I'm really proud," she says, "to have been involved in what is truly a history making movement."

The American Basketball League, which began its inaugural season in October, 1996, represented the first serious attempt at a professional women's basketball league in the United States for many years. Even though the women's college game had grown phenomenally in recent years, many people felt that there simply wasn't enough interest in women's basketball to support a professional league.

The American Basketball League was started by a group of outsiders. They weren't from the NBA. They weren't working at Division One colleges, although one of the ABL founders had previously been employed at Stanford University. They were mostly from the Silicon Valley of Northern California, rather than the traditional media and corporate centers of the East Coast or the Los Angeles area. Initially, they didn't have the corporate sponsors they needed, or the TV contracts, or anything that would inspire most people to take them seriously. But they shared a vision about women's basketball, the same vision that Linda Weston has.

Women's basketball deserved respect and attention, they felt. Top women players in the United States deserved a professional league of their own in their native country. American fans should be able to watch these top women players without digging out passports and taking trips to Japan, or Turkey, or Italy, or Brazil, or the numerous other countries American women were forced to travel to if they wanted to play professional basketball after college. And girls and boys deserved the kind of role models that these top players could provide if they were able to play at home in a professional basketball league.

"It's a Whole New Ballgame" and "The Time is Right for the ABL" are two of the ways the American Basketball League describes itself in the league publication, *ABL Courtside*. In the same magazine, the league's own narrative of how it was developed shows a strong sense of history. "On September 26, 1995, the day the American Basketball League announced its plans for a first-class basketball league in the U.S., skeptics looked on much the way nay-sayers must have snickered before the Wright Brothers launched their dream skyward."

The sense of history didn't seem misplaced. Something different really did seem to be happening with women's basketball. After years of relative obscurity, years of suffering from the handicaps of restrictive rules and insufficient funds, women's basketball was finally achieving much wider public attention than it ever had The times at last did seem right for women's basketball. But the change had been a long time coming.

Basketball was invented in 1891 by James Naismith, and in 1892, Senda Berenson Abbott, a pioneering figure in basketball for women, introduced the sport to students at Smith College. A small gym at Smith, in Northampton, Massachusetts, was the location for the first women's college basketball game, in 1893, when the freshman and sophomore teams competed. Not long afterwards, in 1896, the first West Coast intercollegiate women's basketball game featured the University of California-Berkeley against Stanford University, and the University of Washington against Ellensburg State. Basketball soon became increasingly popular for girls and women. As well as on college campuses and in other school settings, basketball was played in settlement house gyms, industrial leagues, and in many other locations.

There were mixed reactions, however, to the female interest in basketball. During the late nineteenth and early twentieth centuries, there was a growing awareness that sporting activities for women could promote both health and beauty, and new-fangled garments, such as the bloomers worn by female cyclists and basketball players, increased the ability of girls and women to participate in sports. At war with these new attitudes though were beliefs in female physical limitations. Overly strenuous exercise, it was widely thought, could overstrain delicate female bodies, interfere with the female reproductive system, and even, according to the most extreme view, produce biologically and socially abnormal individuals.

Such beliefs—which seem laughable today—strongly influenced the development of girls' and women's basketball. Senda Berenson Abbott and others developed special rules for female basketball, with the basic goal of making the game more ladylike and less strenuous. Among other changes, the basketball court was divided into three and later two parts, with players restricted to one section of the court. No grabbing of the ball from opposing players was allowed; dribbling was restricted; and halves were shortened from 20 to 15 minutes to put less physical strain on females. High-level competition was often discouraged in favor of intramurals or play days where the emphasis was on recreation, enjoyment, and good sportsmanship.

Grace Fern Sullivan Bell was one of the many largely unknown female basketball pioneers. Her daughter Barbara Bell remembers Grace as a phenomenal athlete: "There wasn't any sport that she didn't like and she was damn good at all of them." Born in 1903, Grace grew up on a farm in Southern Oregon and enjoyed outside work such as going on horseback to round up the cows. Only two pounds when she was born—her father would say to her, "I used to carry you around in a cigar box,"—the outdoors work strengthened her. At high school in Lakeview, Oregon, Grace played on the girls' basketball team, and may have played other sports as well.

At the University of Oregon, which Grace attended from the fall of 1921 until she graduated in the spring of 1925, Grace majored in physical education and competed in basketball, field hockey, and softball. Only 5'4" tall, she played forward in basketball and was nicknamed "Cyclone" by her coach for the speed and energy of her play. The clippings from University of Oregon newspaper articles of the time, which Grace carefully preserved in a scrapbook, testify to just how good a basketball player she was.

An account of a competition between Hendricks hall and the Oregon club team includes a glowing description of Grace's contributions. "Grace Sullivan, forward, was again the star for the winning team. Of the 25 points annexed by Hendricks hall, 20 were due to her accurate shooting and the ease with which she netted the baskets was decidedly worthy of praise." In another game, a competition between sophomores and juniors, an article describes "Grace Sullivan, playing up to her usual high standard, made 37 of the 39 points scored against the juniors."

In spite of these athletic successes, in spite of her innate athletic gifts, Grace Sullivan, like many other female athletes of her time, had far fewer opportunities than women today. Athletic competition was between halls or houses, between upperclassmen and underclassmen, and sometimes between teams from the perennial rivals, the University of Oregon and what was then named Oregon Agricultural College, and later became Oregon State University. An article from the University of Oregon newspaper describes the attempt to take women's basketball in an even less competitive direction: "Inter-house competition in women's sports may be abolished." Women's sports at Oregon, many felt, "is placing the emphasis upon competition when it should be upon spontaneity and love of the sport for its own sake."

Grace Sullivan Bell didn't share the belief that competitive sports were bad for women. She chafed at the restrictions placed on her as a basketball player, the half court games and cumbersome uniforms, and also saw the contradictions between the treatment of women's basketball and some other sports for women. "It didn't make any sense," Grace's daughter Barbara remembers her mother saying. "There we were playing that short court stuff (in basketball) and we have to wear those darn bloomers. And then we go outside and play field hockey, which is much more dangerous, and we're playing a full field."

"Those darn bloomers" gradually became a thing of the past for women's basketball, but the restrictions on play continued. It wasn't until the 1930s that guarding was permitted. In the early 60s, the introduction of a roving forward and guard began to open up the two-court game, and in 1966, unlimited dribbling was allowed. Not until 1971 was the modern full-court, five-player game instituted.

More limiting rules weren't the only handicaps female basketball players faced. Although some states developed strong traditions of girls' basketball, public attitudes were still mixed about females participating in strenuous sports. And while tennis, golf, and field hockey, for example, had the advantage of being associated with upper class women, basketball was often seen as a more working class sport, a sport open to all income levels and races, and thus a sport which was less socially acceptable. Female athletes also had to deal with misgivings about whether a girl or woman could be athletic and still feminine. The beauty contests held at some basketball competitions attempted to resolve the supposed contradiction between athletic abilities and femininity.

Then Title IX came to the aid of girls' and women's sports. Passed by Congress in 1972, and rescued by Congress in 1988 from attempts to narrow its scope, Title IX basically states that discrimination based on sex will not be allowed in educational programs receiving federal funds. As it turned out, Title IX has had its biggest impact in the area of athletics, where the inequities between male and female sports programs were glaringly obvious. Title IX didn't change things overnight—it wasn't a magic wand—but over time the picture for girls and women's sports brightened considerably. In 1971, there were only about 300,000 girls playing high school sports, but in 1996, more than 2.4 million high school girls participated in sports.

At the collegiate level, in the early seventies women's sports were held to a starvation diet, with typical expenditures for collegiate women's sports less than two percent of the total athletic budget. Nowadays, money allocated to men's and women's college sports is still not equal. A recent NCAA study of Division One colleges revealed that only a third of college athletic scholarships go to female athletes, and that male athletic programs receive three times as much funding as their female counterparts. However, this still represents significant progress.

Along with stronger programs has come greatly increased attention paid to women's sports. In 1975, the first regular season women's college game was nationally televised, and in 1978, NBC televised the women's collegiate national championship game. Although women's games formerly drew very low attendance—perhaps a few hundred supporters—in 1990 more than 16,000 fans came to watch the NCAA championship in which Stanford played Auburn, and the game was also nationally televised by CBS. Even more recently, women's college basketball games shown on NBC and ESPN have drawn substantial viewing audiences, with millions watching a broadcast of the 1997 women's NCAA championship game.

Yet no matter how much the women's college game flourished, there was still a gap in the sport—a significant one—the lack of a women's professional basketball league in the United States. It wasn't as if the idea had never occurred to anybody. In the 1940s and 1950s, the All-American Red Heads and Hazel Walker's Arkansas Travelers toured the United States, often playing against men's teams. In the late seventies, the Women's Professional Basketball League, often abbreviated as the WBL, took to the court and played until 1981. The first WBL game was held on December 9, 1978, when the Milwaukee Does competed against the Chicago Hustle.

Like the ABL, there were eight teams in the league's first year. Close to 6,000 spectators attended the championship game, and many observers agreed that the quality of play in the league was high. Nevertheless, as Mary Jo Festle describes in *Playing Nice*, the conditions for players in the WBL often contradicted the word "professional" in the league's full name. Player salaries were low, often under five thousand dollars. When teams travelled, often locker rooms for visiting teams were in such bad shape that players would opt to change and shower in their hotel rooms.

All first year WBL teams lost money. In the WBL's second year, when financial problems worsened, players were sometimes paid late or even not at all. And throughout the league's three seasons, media coverage was spotty at best. Festle quotes a sports writer from the Chicago Tribune giving a tongue-in-cheek explanation of why the Chicago WBL team, the Hustle, was getting little attention in the paper: "There hasn't been much coverage of them because news space is needed to report on the hangnails of male athletes."

Since basketball was still widely perceived as a masculine sport, the WBL tried to appeal to both fans and the media by portraying their players as feminine women. A few teams actually scheduled exhibition games against Playboy Bunnies! Players on the California Dreams were sent to a five-week modeling course. Ultimately, however, these ploys failed, as did the league itself after three seasons. It was killed by a combination of insufficient fan interest and funding, some incompetent management, and media scepticism.

During the last year of the WBL, still another new league, named the Ladies Professional Basketball Association, was formed. That league, which only played four games before folding, was built on even shakier foundations than the WBL. The league had teams in Albuquerque, Oakland, Phoenix, and a city in southern California, but other proposed team locations didn't work out. As an article in the *Phoenix Gazette* reports, a proposed team in Tucson lost financial support and a potential San Jose team couldn't go forward because the city council wouldn't approve play in the city's arena.

Cathy Aiken, who was a hot-shooting forward, can still remember what it was like to play in the LPBA. When Cathy graduated from Arizona State and ended her collegiate basketball career there, she was drafted by both the WBL and the LPBA. She chose to become a member of the Phoenix Flames because she wanted to stay in Arizona. During the four games she played for the league, Cathy remembers the competition as good and the hotels for road trips as actually pretty nice. But like other players in the league, she never received a single paycheck. Coaches and the hotels where players stayed were never paid either.

At the end of that greatly truncated season, players took away shoes, and basketballs, and uniforms. Cathy still has the orange and yellow jersey she wore for the Flames. Not getting paid for her efforts didn't matter all that much to her back then. Her main reason for joining the league had simply been to go on playing. It was quitting the sport she loved which was difficult. "Putting down the basketball," she recalls, "and realizing you had to go do something else, after you lived and breathed (basketball) for like fifteen years. It was hard. It was like, now what do I do?"

Many American women who ended their college basketball careers have had to ask the same question. After the failure of the WBL especially, the more viable of the two leagues, it may have seemed that women's professional basketball would never become a reality in the United States. The very brief existence of the Liberty Basketball Association, which played an exhibition game in 1991, didn't brighten the outlook for women's pro ball. Instead, it may have made the women's game seem more like comic relief than a real sport. The Liberty Basketball Association made gimmicky changes such as lowering the basket, shortening the court, and outfitting players in skin-tight lycra unitards.

Ironically, it was the U.S. women's disappointing bronze-medal finish at the 1992 Olympics which helped pave the way for a women's professional league. After the '92 Olympics, and a loss to Brazil in 1994 at the World Championships, USA Basketball went to corporate sponsors like the NBA for funds to launch an experiment in women's basketball. A small group of top women basketball players would be paid to spend a year touring with a U.S. National Team which would generate more attention for women's basketball, and, organizers hoped, win a gold medal at the 1996 Olympics in Atlanta. In 1995, the team was formed. As the team toured the United States and international locations, winning every one of its games, many people's eyes were opened to just how good women's basketball could be.

Gary Cavalli, CEO of the American Basketball League and one of the league founders, first saw the light about women's basketball from two perspectives. The positions Gary held at Stanford University provided one set of vision-altering lenses. From 1974 to 1979, he was Sports Information Director at the university, and from 1979 to 1982, Associated Athletic Director. Those were interesting times to be involved with collegiate athletics, with Title IX enacted in 1972, and Stanford, according to Gary, was one of the first universities to actively promote women's athletics.

Gary can distinctly remember how change started to happen. In the early 70s, when he was a sports information director, he describes a typical audience for a women's basketball game as composed of "two boyfriends and two parents" and occasionally a reporter from the campus newspaper. That may have been a little understated, but there was no denying that by the late 1980s and early 1990s, times had definitely changed. "All of a sudden there's five, six thousand people at every game," Gary remembers.

At Stanford University, Gary Cavalli had a front row seat on the historic changes in women's sports. But he also had a perspective that was much more personal. His second set of vision-changing lenses were given him by his daughters, whom he coached in basketball and softball in various leagues. "I really had an opportunity to see this whole explosion of interest in women's sports," Gary says. "The look of excitement and enthusiasm, not only in my own daughters' eyes but in the eyes of the (other) girls that I was coaching, really told me that something was happening in this country with girls and women in athletics."

Gary can rattle off the statistics, about 1 in 27 high school girls involved in sports in the early 1970s versus about 1 in 3 currently participating. But this isn't just an academic matter for him. Working at Stanford University, and coaching his three daughters—Erin, Kelly, and Alyssa—Gary felt a personal connection with those numbers.

Gary left Stanford to form a sports marketing, public relations and event management company which became known as Cavalli and Cribbs, with Anne Cribbs, a former Olympic swimmer who had won a gold medal at the 1960 Olympics, joining Gary as a partner. He thinks it was about 1993 or 1994 when the topic of a women's professional basketball league came up in conversations between himself and Ann. "We never really did anything about it," Gary recalls. "We just talked about it and wondered if it would happen and if we'd be a part of it in any form."

On February, 1995, Cavalli and Cribbs received a phone call from Steve Hams, the man whose idea for a professional league would become the ABL. Steve had been an executive with Hewlitt Packard and after that with a new software company called General Magic, but perhaps most important, like Gary Cavalli, Steve Hams was also the father of three daughters, Lauren, Brett, and Taylor. In its genesis, one could say, the American Basketball League was a daughter-powered league.

It was Lauren who may have first started the ball rolling. From the age of ten, she'd been excited about basketball. She and her father Steve went to all the women's basketball games at Stanford, and all of that got Steve thinking. "It just seemed crazy to me," he says simply, "that we didn't have a professional league in this country." After college, elite women basketball players in the United States basically had to choose between going overseas or giving up playing top-level basketball. Steve wanted to change that situation. As a father, he would love to have professional women basketball players as role models for his daughters.

When Steve decided that he wanted to be involved in starting a league, he assumed that with the growing interest in women's basketball, other people would already be working on the idea. Since he didn't find that to be true, he put together an advisory committee and began working on a plan. That plan was still in its in early stages in February of 1995, when Steve read an article in the *San Jose Business Journal* about Anne Cribbs—her personal sports background and her advocacy for women's sports—and about the firm of Cavalli and Cribbs' involvement in sports. After Steve Hams called, Anne went to a committee meeting and returned with a concept document for Gary Cavalli to examine and an invitation for Gary to attend the next meeting.

Instead, Gary Cavalli, Anne Cribbs, and Steve Hams, who became the three co-founders of the ABL, went out to breakfast at a small restaurant in Palo Alto. "It was kind of a fateful breakfast," Gary recalls. And the meeting went well from Gary's perspective. "I really liked Steve," Gary comments, "I liked his enthusiasm, his vision for what he wanted to accomplish."

Gary agreed to help with press releases and advertising, yet he tempered his own enthusiasm with a healthy dose of scepticism. At the time the ABL had no major sponsors and no recognizable names in sports involved. "My honest appraisal at that time," Gary remembers, "was that this thing had absolutely no chance to succeed." After that first breakfast with Steve Hams, Gary filled in colleagues at Cavalli and Cribbs about Steve Hams' idea. "What do you think the chances are?" someone asked. "About .01 percent," was Gary's estimate.

Perhaps it helped that Gary and Steve and Anne were all residents of California, a state where dreams seem to become reality more easily than in more hard-nosed locales like Nebraska or Vermont. So the trio of founders, Gary and Steve and Anne, along with the ABL advisory committee, began discussing and revising key elements of the proposed league. Gary liked the cities under consideration, but added the idea of having players with ties to a specific region assigned to that area so they could build on already developed fan recognition. He didn't like the initial idea of the season starting in August right after the Olympics the first year, and then in May for the following year. The league, he thought, should play its games during the traditional basketball season.

Then a piece of luck entered the picture, luck combined with a small amount of manipulation on Gary's part. Cavalli and Cribbs was given the job of arranging the Stanford Athletic Hall of Fame dinner in June of 1995, with Jennifer Azzi, who was a former Stanford basketball player and a current member of the U.S. National Team, one of the players to be honored. Since Gary Cavalli was to be presenter for another award recipient, he would be seated at the head table with other presenters and winners of awards, including Jennifer Azzi.

Gary seized the opportunity. He arranged the seating so that he sat next to Jennifer Azzi and he bent her ear about the plan for a new league. During the course of the dinner and presentations, he discussed how a professional women's basketball league could take shape. By evening's end, in spite of Jennifer's initial scepticism—other people had talked to her about ideas for leagues as well—she was enthusiastic about the idea Gary presented to her. She gave Gary a hug and told him she wanted to help. "I'm really excited about this," Jennifer said. "Keep me informed, and anything I can do to help I will."

Jennifer was the first high-profile female basketball player to express an interest in the league but not the last. Both Jennifer and Steve Hams spoke with Teresa Edwards and she too got excited about the league. Jennifer and Teresa spoke with other players, as did Steve Hams, and little by little, most of the U.S. National Team players committed themselves to the ABL.

The players' support was crucial, and Anne, Steve and Gary were increasingly optimistic about their new league's chances. The U.S. National Team, they knew, would get great publicity as they played basketball around the United States and overseas and, everyone hoped, won a gold medal at the Olympics in Atlanta. With the members of the U.S. National Team behind them, the new league had a good chance of actually making it. "We would springboard right into our first season," Gary envisioned, "using those players as kind of the lynch pins . . . for the league."

In September, 1995, when the American Basketball League called a press conference to publicly announce its founding, nine of the eleven U.S. National Team members were there at the press conference. The Founding Players of the league, they wore ABL T-shirts and spoke about their support for the league. Everyone was present except Rebecca Lobo and Katrina McClain; Sheryl Swoopes even joined in via teleconference. "All of us have had this dream of having a league in our own country," Jennifer Azzi said at the conference. "Women's basketball is really ready for this," Teresa Edwards added.

At that point the players had signed a one year Letter of Intent (which eventually proved not to be a legally binding contract) committing them to promote and represent the ABL and eventually to play for the league. In December, Steve Hams made a tour of potential ABL cities and also talked to people he hoped to get involved, such as potential sponsors, general managers, and TV people. He met with some discouraging responses. Many people thought the league was a good idea, but agreeing to commit money was another matter. "I'm not comfortable making an investment this early," people would tell Steve. "I think it's too risky." Potential sponsors wanted to wait for TV deals; TV possibles wanted to wait for sponsors. It was the kind of catch-22 many new ventures meet up with.

Nevertheless, the league founders went ahead with their plans. Although the original idea had been to start with twelve teams in twelve cities, that came to seem too large a size to start with, and in February the ABL publicly announced the eight cities which would make up first-year teams. San Jose, Seattle, Portland, and Denver would be the four Western Conference cities, and Columbus, Richmond, Hartford, and Atlanta would be the Eastern Conference cities.

Not a single game had been played yet, but even coming that far was quite an accomplishment. For one thing, even though Steve Hams hadn't run into them when he first looked into starting a league, it turned out that other people besides the ABL founders had recognized the growing interest in women's basketball and had seen the opportunity for a women's league. "The landscape was really cluttered back in 95," Gary comments, about all the wannabe league founders. When the ABL people went to Nike to speak with Sue Levin, then the Manager for Women's Sports Marketing, she mentioned that the ABL was not the first but the sixth or seventh group to speak to her about a women's league.

Fortunately for the ABL, the other groups all proved to be weak competitors. A group in Tennessee had gotten a half page write-up in *USA Today*, but when Gary checked it out, the group seemed less than fully legitimate. "Press A if you want to buy vitamins," their phone message said, "press B if you want to participate in our seminar; press C if you're calling about basketball." An Idaho group promoted itself as having already made arrangements for three arenas, one in San Jose, but when Gary talked to San Jose people, he found that the arrangement didn't actually exist. Other groups included a business women's group, a group in New York, and the WBA, a low-budget Midwestern league with eight teams who played in high school gyms and only paid their players $50 a game.

All the groups attempting to start a league were invited to take part in a panel discussion about the future of women's professional basketball held in March of 1996 at the women's Final Four and sponsored by the Women's Basketball Coaches Association. The other groups had all basically faded away by then, however, leaving the ABL as the only group left on the panel and the apparently legitimate inheritors of the crown. Things were definitely looking up for the ABL. The media overall had remained sceptical—an October, 1995 *Sports Illustrated* article on the ABL, for example, wondered if the league would attract any fans and described Steve Hams as having a "brazenness" that "seems kind of ditzy" for not including "Women's" in the league name. Yet the league had the commitment of most of the players on the US National Team and a number of other top players.

Corporate sponsorships were starting to come together. At the 1996 Final Four, both Nike and Reebok made a commitment to sponsor three ABL teams each.

Then in late April, an event happened that could have been the death knell of the ABL. David Stern, head of the NBA, announced that the NBA would start a women's league of its own which would begin play in the summer of 1997. The ABL could have given up the fight at that point, decided that they were bested by a competitor with far deeper pockets. But Steve Hams, Gary Cavalli, and Anne Cribbs were determined to go ahead with the ABL.

However, some things did begin to unravel. An article in the *Los Angeles Times* mentioned three potential players for the women's NBA league, the WNBA, Sheryl Swoopes, Lisa Leslie, and Rebecca Lobo. All were members of the US National Team, and two out of three had previously committed themselves to the ABL. The deal with Nike eventually fell apart, with the official explanation being that the ABL hadn't secured a TV contract. The actual reason, Gary Cavalli is convinced, was connected to the NBA's intention to create a league.

While ABL co-founders were all, undoubtedly, crossing fingers and toes, they continued to have some good fortune. Reebok, which had agreed to sponsor three teams for the ABL, decided to take on a fourth team after Nike bowed out. And most important, many of the US National Team players remained firm in their commitment to the ABL.

In late May and early June, the ABL took a giant step towards actually starting play by holding its first tryouts at Emory University at Atlanta. The league had decided to ask players interested to pay a $200 entrance fee because, as Gary Cavalli puts it, "we wanted to make sure these were serious people as opposed to anybody who could just dribble a basketball." Even so, a logistically daunting more than 570 players came to the tryouts, a kaleidoscopic mix of former and recently graduated players from small colleges, players from Division One universities, women who had played overseas for years, women who hadn't played in several or more years but wanted their chance to try again. And the ABL was going to give them that chance. The league wouldn't shut anyone out. "This league is really all about hopes and dreams and opportunities," Gary Cavalli comments, "and so we wanted to give as many people a legitimate opportunity as possible."

The league tried its best, in spite of the logistical nightmare. Appropriately enough, two women ran the show. One was a former player from Stanford who had been involved in the league from early on, Christy Hedgpeth, who had the title of Director of Player Development and who contacted numerous players about the tryouts. The other was a woman who had played at Boston College, had been on the 1980 Olympic team which never got the opportunity to compete, and who became the General Manager in Atlanta the first year, Debbie Miller-Palmore.

Linda Weston attended the tryouts along with the other general managers and first year coaches. In Atlanta that late May and early June, the tryouts were held in an air conditioned gym which contrasted with the steamy heat outside. It was just plain cold inside the gym, Linda remembers. Even players, who had the advantage of plenty of physical exercise, were often seen putting on sweat shirts. But the main thing Linda recalls was the need to make quick decisions about so many talented players. "Wait a minute, who's number 379?" is a typical question Linda remembers as coaches and general managers tried to figure out who they would pick.

The ABL had brought together a rich harvest of female basketball players. The level of talent was impressive, but the process of sorting through that talent was a real headache. Linda Weston describes the feeling as "almost overwhelming" because there were "so many players to keep track of."

As the first ABL draft in June, 1996 followed the tryouts, as some players opted not to play in the ABL after all, some of them deciding to wait for the WNBA, and as other players were signed to teams, there were plenty of players who shared at least some of the scepticism about the ABL held by many of the agents who represented top women basketball players. Yet the women were hopeful as well. They liked the unapologetically ambitious goal of the new league. As Gary Cavalli puts it, "The goal was to bring America's players home and to develop a league in this country that would give them a chance to pursue their careers professionally, here where basketball was invented."

Across the country, in the eight ABL cities, training camps started in September of 1996. On Friday, October 18 in San Jose, California and Hartford, Connecticut, the ABL's first two games were played. On Saturday the 19th, the second two games took place in Portland, Oregon and Columbus, Ohio.

The women who competed in those first games, or waited their turn on the team bench, or coached the players, or did other jobs for the ABL, were a diverse group. They differed from each other in terms of race, age, sexual orientation, ethnic, class, and geographic background. They came from college campuses, from college coaching jobs, from fields unrelated to basketball, and many came from the sometimes lucrative and often lonely professional leagues in countries as varied as Italy and Israel. But all of their personal journeys had brought them together for a pioneering year in women's basketball.

Linda Weston will never forget the opening game for her own ABL team, the Portland Power. They had expected a crowd of about five or six thousand. Linda had feared that even with all the tickets sold, people would decide not to come. The almost 9,000 fans who showed up for opening night took the Power staff by surprise. "We were stunned," Linda recalls.

Linda was nervous as well. "I was a wreck," she says, laughing at the memory. But she was also excited, and proud of the players and the staff, and of all the fans who had come to see something new in women's basketball.

"I remember the tremendous energy in the arena and how excited people were," Linda describes. She also recalls the introductions of the players, the fireworks as the players ran onto the arena floor, the roar of the crowd. When the team mascot, a person-sized "parrot," punched a fist through a paper mache egg with jagged seams velcroed together, "the crowd went wild," Linda describes. "They really never were quiet after that on opening night."

Before the game began, Linda Weston spoke to the players in the Power locker room. She talked about how hard everyone had worked to make this night happen. She talked about how the players were making history. As she felt the emotion build in the locker room, saw players looking a little teary eyed, and felt teary eyed herself, she realized she couldn't end her speech that way just before an important game.

"So let's just go out there and kick ass," was the next and last thing Linda said. Everyone laughed and "then everything was fine," Linda remembers.

Then the players took the floor. The ball was tipped off and the game began. A spectator now, Linda Weston alternately sat at the end of the team bench or paced near the bench and along the path to their locker room, a walking route which would become familiar to her during the season. When the final buzzer sounded, Linda's team had won their home opener and Linda felt "elated." Her first season of women's pro basketball was off to a wonderful start!

A Founding Player

By the end of the first American Basketball League season, Katy Steding was tired. She was like a marathon runner who has hit the wall and pushed past it—with grit and desire and muscles trained for the long haul—and who finally finishes the long, body-and-mind-stretching race.

Katy had played game after game with the U.S. National Team, one of a group of talented women on a basketball high. They pounded opponents around the United States and in many different countries, playing hard even when an opposing team didn't challenge them, never significantly lowering the high standard of basketball they'd set. At the 1996 Olympics in Atlanta, the U.S. women won again—eight more games—hitting the boards and hitting shots while competing against top international opponents. After the final game, the U.S. women were both exhilarated by their victory and relieved that their long basketball journey was over.

Katy wore her gold medal on the plane ride back to her hometown, Portland, Oregon. But unlike most of her Olympic teammates, she didn't take a break. Instead she spent her days working with girls in the basketball camp and school she owns and runs, teaching them the fundamentals of basketball. After that she started on the last long leg of her basketball marathon, a race which she knew she was running both for herself and for many others.

Katy is a strong person, used to persevering towards difficult goals. Although the ABL allowed the Founding Players, all members of the 1996 Olympic team, to skip training camps if they wanted to, Katy was there from the very start. She understood the significance of the league, of course. But it was also that she didn't want to be put on any kind of a pedestal. She didn't want her new teammates to think that she expected special treatment because she was an Olympian.

In September, Katy went to the gym and started working out with her teammates on the Portland Power. At The Hoop in Beaverton, Oregon, the large, new-looking basketball floor has a spacious feeling with several basketball courts on it. It may have given players an expansive feeling, suggesting the possibilities in front of them. In October, possibilities turned to realities as the team began its forty game season, with practices, road trips, and several games a week.

It was a schedule that demanded a great deal of both players and coaches. And the ABL, as a new league, also asked its personnel to make large numbers of public appearances, to speak at functions that varied from school assemblies to Rotary clubs. In Portland, as a local girl and a recent Olympian, Katy Steding was in high demand. Because she wanted the league to succeed, and because she's simply a nice person, she practically always said yes to the requests for her time.

By the time the Portland Power played their last game for the year, Katy was definitely ready for some time away from basketball. And yet nothing had changed her enthusiasm for the sport. Or the strong feelings she has for women's professional basketball. "We're starting something that's going to last," Katy says. Twenty years from now, she expects "to be able to look back and say, I was part of that."

Katy's own basketball journey has taken her many places. The easily visible surgical scars on both her knees are evidence of the dues she's paid to the sport. She turned 29 during the first ABL season, and there haven't been too many years in her life that haven't involved close encounters with a basketball and a hoop. For most of her life, Katy has been in training for the role she's playing now.

Katy grew up in Lake Oswego, Oregon, a suburb of Portland where there was plenty of room for neighborhood children to play all kinds of sports. When Katy was in third grade she wanted to play basketball in a YMCA league, but there weren't any girls in the league at the time.

Katy's mother, Patti Huntley, has always been one of Katy's strongest supporters. With the encouragement of her mother, Katy found a couple of friends, both girls, who would join the league along with her. Katy was the only girl on her team, though, and by sixth grade about the only girl left in the whole league. But the times were changing for girls in sports, and both the boys in the league and the adult male coaches essentially accepted Katy's role as a player, which was the same attitude she had herself. "I guess I kind of took it for granted," she says about playing in the league. "Nobody told me I couldn't do it. Or that I was weird for doing it."

But moving into traditionally male turf, even a pre-pubescent version, took a little getting used to. There was a rougher, more physical style of play in the YMCA league, and initially Katy held back, playing by "rules" more commonly followed by girls than boys. She seemed a little timid on court. She didn't want to hurt anyone's feelings. In her first game, the boys often grabbed the ball from her hands.

Katy cared as much about winning, however, as any of the boys she played with or against. After the first game, which her team lost, Katy hid behind an armchair in her family's living room and cried. The boys were "so mean," she complained to her mother.

Katy's mother could have told her daughter that boys' games were too rough for little girls, a message lots of girls have received. Instead, Patti Huntley encouraged her daughter not to give up. If she wanted to play in the league, Katy's mother told her, she would have to learn to play the boys' way.

A head taller than most of the boys, Katy did learn. She hadn't played for very long in the YMCA league when she had her moment of basketball inspiration. As she guarded a boy who was shorter than her, the boy held the ball up over his head. All of a sudden a young Katy spotted the basketball opportunity. "I could see the light come on in her head," Katy's mother recalls, "and she thought 'hey,' and she grabbed it."

Katy kept on grabbing basketballs, in one way or another, throughout her childhood and teenage years. Although her mother and father got divorced when she was five years old, they both encouraged her sports abilities. Her father hung up a basketball hoop for her and played basketball with Katy and her older sister Julie. The girls and their father made wild and crazy shots, hanging part way out of the garage or shooting from part way up the outside steps. Katy's mother didn't shoot baskets—women her age usually didn't—but she drove Katy to basketball practices. Early Saturday morning during late fall and winter, in often unheated gyms, Patti

Huntley would sit watching her daughter play.

Katy's relationship with her sister Julie, who was four years older, helped foster an interest in sports. Julie was a gifted athlete who played volleyball and basketball in high school, and then went to Oregon State University on a volleyball scholarship. Katy aimed to do as well as or better than her talented sister. "She was very inspiring to me," Katy says about Julie. "Since she was so into athletics and very successful at it, I wanted to be successful at it too."

And then there was NBA basketball, the men's game. In Portland, the Trail Blazers were the only top-level professional team in town. In 1977, when Katy was nine, the Blazers won their one and only NBA championship, and the parade for the winning team packed city streets. Fans celebrated. Local kids collected autographs from their heroes. Katy was among the star struck fans.

Bill Walton, the tall, red-headed Blazers center, was Katy's favorite player. As she shot hoops in her driveway, Katy sometimes daydreamed about being a Blazer herself. She wore a T shirt with Bill Walton's number as she drove to the basket or leaped into the air to make shots. Her career goal was to be a professional basketball player, she told her fifth grade class.

The other kids laughed, and Katy laughs too at that childhood story, which she thinks has gotten blown out of proportion. "I didn't say," Katy emphasizes, "Well dang it, everybody laughed at me in fifth grade. I'm going to go out there and show them."

Katy didn't dwell on what she'd said to her classmates, yet some part of her hung on to the dream, the vision of excellence in sport that Bill Walton and his teammates had given her. As a girl, she was already showing that she had what it took to excel. The joy she has always taken in basketball, the drive that has consistently pushed her to be better at the sport, was already evident. No fair weather player, she was out in her driveway in the cold and rain—and western Oregon has lots of that kind of weather—shooting hoops with gloves on to keep her hands warm.

In junior high school, she played in an interscholastic girls basketball league. High school basketball was, of course, a natural for her too. She was already five feet eleven when she entered Lake Oswego High School. With her height plus her natural athletic ability, Katy was a freshman player any coach would notice. But her high school basketball coach, Gary Lavender, remembers that rather than seeking the limelight, Katy would hide from him on the bench.

Once again she didn't want to hurt feelings. She felt bad about taking the place of a senior.

Katy's basketball skills were so strong, however, that she became a starter soon. "She was an impact player from the middle of her freshman year on," her former coach told a reporter. "She may be the best pure shooter I've ever seen."

Katy was also one of those hardworking kids whom coaches love. She would get the keys to the gym from her coach and practice shooting on her own. In games she worked hard too, setting a rebounding record for Oregon high school play and a scoring record for Lake Oswego High School as she helped her team, the Lakers, to reach the semi-finals at the state championship three times. In her sophomore, junior, and senior years, she was named an All State player. Her senior year she was also named Oregon Class 3A Girls' Basketball Player of the Year, as well as a Converse All-American.

Even now, with many more basketball accomplishments to list on her resume, Katy is definitely not someone blown up with self-importance. That was true for her as a teenager as well. Until the letters from colleges started coming, Katy hadn't expected that she'd receive a college basketball scholarship. Then in her sophomore year, a letter arrived from Stanford, from the coach who was Tara VanDerveer's predecessor. Katy showed it to Gary Lavender, the high school coach who was also something of a father figure to her. "Am I good enough?" she asked.

"You can go anyplace you want, Katy," he told her. "You've got that much talent."

Stanford was where Katy decided she wanted to go. A top basketball school with a solid academic reputation, Stanford was a name which Katy could mention with confidence at a post-college job interview. At that point in her life, Katy assumed she'd have to do something aside from basketball after college. Tara VanDerveer, the new women's basketball coach at Stanford, talked to Katy on the phone. She and an assistant coach made a visit to Lake Oswego and met Katy and her family. Katy was Tara VanDerveer's first recruit. Without knowing it at the time, Katy had begun a basketball relationship that was to be crucial for her sports career.

Tara VanDerveer was in the process of building one of the top women's college programs in the country. Women's basketball was well funded at Stanford, unlike at many colleges across the U.S., and Tara VanDerveer and her players were going to help show the country just how good women's basketball could be.

Katy would have an important role in that women's basketball movement. But she didn't start out at Stanford with an overabundance of self-confidence. "Oh my God," she said to herself, "everyone is going to be so much better than me." Actually, Tara VanDerveer had also had a moment of doubt about Katy. Tara had signed Katy after seeing her play but without Amy Tucker, Tara's assistant coach and usual scout, evaluating Katy first.

When Amy did watch Katy play in a high school game, Amy painted a gloomy picture. "Katy looked terrible," Amy reported. "She did nothing in the game."

"I was panic stricken," Tara told a reporter. But her assistant coach was only playing a practical joke on her. In fact, Katy had done very well in that high school game, and her strong play continued in her freshman year at Stanford. Among other achievements, she earned the coach's unofficial title of "garbage collector" for pulling down so many rebounds. Tara's instincts had been right about Katy's basketball abilities.

Both Tara's and Katy's judgments were tested the following year. Katy's sophomore year was the really tough one for her, a time she still refers to as the "ugly year." A bigger, stronger freshman, Trisha Stevens from Philomath, Oregon, took Katy's accustomed place as an inside player. Tara moved Katy outside, to the three position or small forward spot.

Katy realizes now that Tara knew exactly what she was doing. Tara saw the big picture and understood that Katy wasn't large enough to be a post player at the top college or international level. Without the change of position Tara insisted on, Katy couldn't have gone nearly as far as she has with her sport.

Tara VanDerveer tells it the way she sees it, to reporters and to her players. "Get outside," she told Katy. "Start working on your three."

The women's three-point shot had just been added to the college game. Katy could run and rebound well and she was a good shooter, a logical choice for a long-range gunner. But nothing about her role switch on the court felt natural to Katy at first. "I'd done things differently all my life," she recalls. All through her sophomore year, Katy struggled with her own play and with her coach as well. Tara would tell Katy what she was doing wrong. Katy would resist her coach's comments. She had a bad attitude that year, Katy admits.

Some players would have given up in frustration, decided that they weren't going to be able to fill the bill for a demanding coach. Katy, however, used the approach that has served her well throughout her athletic career: she cranked up the gears; she worked harder. She stayed at Stanford to train over the summer, and the extra effort paid off. By her junior year, things were clicking for Katy, and for other Stanford women players as well. When Katy had first arrived at Stanford, their women's basketball program didn't have a national ranking. Heads up play by Katy and teammates such as Jennifer Azzi helped Stanford reach the NCAA Sweet 16 in Katy's sophomore year. In Katy's junior year, they went to the NCAA regional final, then the final eight where they lost to Louisiana Tech.

Once again Katy worked hard over the summer. Her senior year, her last chance at college basketball, was coming up, and Katy knew she wouldn't feel right if she gave it anything less than her best. That year Katy and her teammates recovered collectively from their season-ending loss. They seemed to share in a kind of collective magic, in fact, as they won game after game. In post-season play, they reached the NCAA quarterfinals, then the semi-finals, then the championship game.

Before the final game, Tara gave this simple piece of advice to Katy: "If you don't shoot threes, you're coming out." It was Katy's last college game and she wanted to be out there playing. She ended up taking eighteen three-point shots and made six of those shots, setting a new NCAA record for a championship game.

Katy's teammates did their utmost too. But their opponent, Auburn, was tough at well. The lead seesawed as the Stanford team lost an eleven-point lead, then fought their way back. At the half, the score was tied, 41-41. In the last minute or so, Stanford had the lead and the other team kept fouling for possession. Katy could only watch as Sonja Henning, the Stanford point guard, went to the line.

Time slowed down for Katy then. She was mentally on her toes, poised to jump for a rebound. She watched Sonja Henning, a small intense woman, hit free throw after free throw, making seven out of ten. "I remember thinking," Katy describes, "that that was the longest 20 seconds in my life. That you could actually watch the clock click."

When the interminably long seconds were over, Stanford was the new national champion, winning the game 88-81. Katy cried, hugged her teammates, and took her turn at cutting down the net from the rim. "I'm so glad that this is the way everything has worked out," she thought. "All of the hard work and all of the effort—conditioning as a freshman, and practically being in tears on the track because you're so tired, all the countless hours in the weight room." It had all paid off. With dividends, you could say.

But there was still a bittersweet feeling for Katy to that season finale. She'd made close friends with her teammates and considered them her personal basketball sorority, "Kappa Kappa Basketball." Now she'd played her last game with those 11 women. And as far as she knew, her last basketball ever.

If Katy had been only ten years or so older, it might have been true. Basketball might have become something in the past tense for her, as it has for many other women, a sport she used to be good at. She might have watched from the sidelines and wished she could be out on the basketball court again. But when Katy graduated from college, times were continuing to change for female basketball players. A former Stanford men's basketball player who was playing professionally in Japan mentioned Katy to his coach, who was interested enough to pass the word to another coach.

Opportunity didn't knock. As Katy describes it, "It fell into my lap." Until her senior year, she hadn't even known that women could play overseas. Before long, she had signed a contract to play basketball in Japan for the Bank of Tokyo. The money was good enough to inspire her to put other plans on hold, and she was able to go on with the game she loved.

Of course basketball in Japan wasn't exactly the same, but Katy still speaks enthusiastically about her time in Japan. "I loved the people. I loved my teammates. They were great," she says. "I just had a blast over there. I loved it." Actually, the whole picture was more complicated than that. Katy was often homesick at first. Japan was too foreign, too far away. She missed her family, friends, and life in the United States, but at the same time she enjoyed making new friends and learning about a very different culture.

Basketball in Japan was a step forward for Katy. The Bank of Tokyo made her a professional basketball player. But it was while playing for her team there, the Golden Eagles, that Katy suffered her first serious injury. It happened in the third game of the season, her first year in Japan. She was going for a breakaway layup and took off wrong, putting too much pressure on her knee. That one quick awkward movement tore Katy's anterior cruciate ligament in her right knee.

The physical pain she experienced was intense but short-lived. The mental and emotional pain lingered. Motions which had come so naturally to Katy became impossible. She couldn't run down the court or sky for a rebound.

An ACL tear is a season-ending and potentially career-ending injury, but Katy was determined not to have that second category apply to her. She went back to Stanford where she knew a doctor, had the surgery, and stayed around Stanford for a while to work on her knee. Then she came back to Oregon to continue the six-month rehabilitation which she describes without exaggeration as a "long, painful, and sometimes very tedious process." She stretched and strengthened muscles. She worked out on the stairmaster, pedaled miles on a stationary bike.

The Japanese company who sponsored Katy's team was supportive, paying her the whole time and telling her how much they were looking forward to her return. Determined to be back on the basketball court, Katy still left herself an escape clause in her personal basketball "contract." "If it happens again," she told herself, "I'm done. Game over. I'm hanging em up and I'll find something else to do."

The following year, and the year after that, Katy played in Japan again. Although she had spoken no Japanese when she arrived in the country, she took lessons the whole time she was there and became somewhat fluent. And she found increasing enjoyment in hanging out with her Japanese teammates, going shopping and cooking dinners with them, forming friendships that bridged the barrier of language and culture. One Christmas, when Katy's mother and stepfather came over, the players made a party for them. Everyone sat on the floor, in Japanese fashion, and ate traditional Japanese food.

In May of '92, after her second season in Japan, Katy returned to the United States to try out for the Olympic team. It was an ambitious goal, which Katy's ex-coach, Tara VanDerveer, had encouraged Katy to shoot for. But although Katy and her former Stanford teammate, Jennifer Azzi, were among the final players considered for the team, they were cut on the last day. That in itself was an accomplishment, although Katy didn't see it that way at the time.

The disappointment was tough for her. A grown woman now, she still cried when she called her mother to tell her the bad news. But Katy has always had a natural resilience, an ability to bounce back from setbacks. A couple of days later, when she spoke with her mother again, she told her mother that she was fine. She had a new goal now: a spot on the 1996 Olympic team.

Meanwhile Katy's overseas basketball career continued. After her third year in Japan, when the country banned foreign players in the interest of developing players of their own, Katy had to move on. Her agent found her a place on a team in Madrid, Spain.

Katy describes Madrid as a beautiful city, but playing in Spain remains an unpleasant memory for her. Perhaps the time away from the United States, away from friends and family, was adding up, just as it has for so many other American women forced to play overseas in order to continue with basketball after college. Katy mentions feeling "out of touch" with her peer group. "All my friends were moving on with their lives," she adds.

Then another injury ended Katy's season. Once more she tore an anterior cruciate ligament, this time in her other knee. Desperately upset, and seriously considering giving up the sport she loved, Katy phoned her mother first but couldn't reach her. She talked to a friend and then called Tara VanDerveer, who was by then her basketball mentor. Katy told Tara about her injury, the second time she'd torn an ACL. The physical and emotional pain Katy felt must have transmitted itself through the telephone wires loud and clear.

Tara wasn't just Katy's ex-college coach. She was someone who knew and cared about Katy, as a player and as a person. And Tara had enough experience with basketball to understand what Katy was going through. "It's awful right now," Tara sympathized, "but it'll be okay. You'll get through it."

Tara helped keep Katy focused on her basketball future. "You're a great shooter," Tara told her. The upcoming USA Basketball team, which Tara would coach, needed Katy. "That helped a lot," Katy recalls.

Katy left Spain and returned to Oregon to undergo major knee surgery for a second time. Once again she went through the hard, painful work of rehabbing a knee. While she was still recovering, in the fall of '94, she coached a high school freshman boys' team, becoming the only woman to coach a boys' basketball team in Oregon. Predictably, some of the freshman boys were sceptical, but Katy won them over with her knowledge of the game and her leadership skills. Her coaching success, however, didn't change her personal goal. She wanted to play again. And she wanted a place on the U.S. National Team, the team which would play in the 1996 Olympics.

Katy didn't know if she could achieve that goal, but she knew she had to try. And just as during her college days, she was willing to pay the price in sweat. January of 1995 was when Katy's personal marathon really began. She started training hard for the May team trials. She worked out on the track, in the weight room, and played at least two hours of basketball every day. As it turned out, all her hours of work paid off. This time she and Jennifer Azzi weren't among the players cut. In May 1995, both women were named to the U.S. National Team.

At about the same time, corporate America seemed to suddenly notice Katy and her teammates. Katy received an endorsement deal with Converse. Other players made similar arrangements with shoe companies. Corporations such as the NBA, ESPN, and Nike were all involved in some way with the team.

Corporate interest meant that top women basketball players were finally being taken seriously. In the eyes of corporate America, women's basketball was a real sport at last. But Katy Steding and her teammates still had plenty of hard work ahead. The U.S. National Team had two missions: to win gold at Atlanta, and to win national and international attention for women's basketball. According to Katy, they essentially went "everywhere" to fulfill that goal. At least it must have seemed that way to the players.

As their marathon basketball tour began, they played some college teams first. Against one team, Colorado, Katy ended up with a game-high 22 points, making a solid 8 out of 11 shots. Then she and her teammates embarked on a trip to Italy and Lithuania. In the fall they went on a college tour where they played in twenty cities in two months. While traveling and playing, they also made lots of public appearances, talked to the media, signed innumerable autographs. While male athletes could simply be athletes, the women on the team had to present themselves as women America could be proud of.

On the strictly basketball front, top colleges like Stanford could challenge the U.S. National Team, at least for a while. But Katy and her teammates were very talented, fierce competitors, and they had a tough coach in Tara VanDerveer who wouldn't let them slack off. Against the University of Connecticut, Katy remembers proudly, "we struggled in the first half, then came out and beat their butts in the second half." Together, the U.S. women played red hot basketball.

Winning was the name of the game for Katy and her teammates—

winning individual games and winning respect for women's basketball. The cast of characters, including women's basketball greats like Katrina McClain and Teresa Edwards, was well equipped to do just that. After finishing with their round of college opponents, the U.S. team headed for international competition. In January they went to Siberia, not the most seasonable time for a visit.

They landed at an airport covered with snow. Snowdrifts were banked high against buildings. High temperatures were around zero. Even wearing bulky parkas and boots, the U.S. women could feel the cold. On the basketball court, the women were hot — playing and beating a Russian club team — but team members sitting on the bench had to put on parkas and gloves to stay warm.

More touring, more college games, more training camp followed. The U.S. women went to China in March, to Australia in May. They saw the Great Wall and the Great Barrier Reef. They had a "team bonding night" in a hotel in China where all the players spontaneously came together to drink coffee and hang out. They endured the "flight from hell" back from Australia when their quite large airplane was blown around in a frightening fashion. Finally in June the Olympic team itself was named, with Katy among the dozen women on the roster.

They'd hung tight as a team, supported each other through all the travel and other stresses, gone shopping and to movies with each other, and formed themselves into a basketball family. They had "great chemistry" and hadn't lost a single game so far, but the greatest test was still to come. The Olympics represented an international arena for women's basketball, as all over the world attention was focused on the women players. The best of the best would be competing in Atlanta.

For the U.S. women, proving themselves was both an opportunity and a necessity. If they won the gold, that would be a step forward for the U.S. women's game. It could help launch the new professional league. Anything less than gold at Atlanta, though, would be perceived as a disappointment.

Starting their Olympic moment was exciting for all the players. Katy remembers walking out on the Georgia Dome Arena floor for the first time, looking around the massive facility. "I got a little emotional," Katy told a reporter. "I was a little starry-eyed."

Katy's role all along had been to come off the bench—although she'd usually played half the available minutes—but as the Olympics continued, playing minutes shrank for Katy and other bench players. Katy's biggest and best game was the opening one, against Cuba. "The bench was the key in that game," Katy says. "We were kind of the spark."

Katy's own play definitely fanned the flames. The starters were nervous, she remembers. Katy was nervous too, but she didn't show it in her play. She made a layup, then hustled for a loose ball, then stole a pass. She ran without the ball on the fast break, then hit a three-point shot at the end of a 10-0 U.S. team run which gave the U.S. a 23-21 lead. In the first half she pulled down five rebounds and ended up with a solid 11 points, helping her team to the win.

Naturally, Katy wanted to play more than she did in some other Olympic games. It wasn't easy to sit on the bench during the Olympics. But Katy knew part of her role on the team, part of everyone's role really, was to accept Tara VanDerveer's decisions. Whenever Katy was out on the floor though, she gave the game her best shot. She put into practice her personal philosophy: "If you get in there for five minutes or twenty, you just try to play your guts out."

When the U.S. women had collectively done just that, and won their final game, against a strong Brazilian team, by a decisive 111 to 87 margin, Katy Steding stood with her teammates on the podium. One by one, gold medals were hung around each woman's neck. "You felt like you're being knighted," Katy recalls.

The women were given bouquets of flowers too. The national anthem played, and the women linked hands as they stood there. It was a proud, emotional moment for all of them. "That was the culmination of everything," Katy says. "It was all worth it."

It was a moment which would make a wonderful finale for a women's basketball movie, a last scene that would leave the audience misty eyed as they left the theatre. But in Katy's real life it wasn't curtains for basketball. And she no longer had to choose between basketball overseas or a more ordinary, less high flying life at home. The American Basketball League would soon begin its opening season.

Katy was one of the first players to officially sign a contract with the new league. Her connection with the league, though, started quite a bit sooner. Founding Players like Katy had been involved early on in the planning of the ABL. In the summer of '95, most of the women on the U.S. National Team met to discuss basketball details which might seem unimportant or arcane to an outsider.

What were the dimensions of the basketball court to be? Would the ball the ABL used be the smaller woman's NCAA basketball or the standard sized ball used in international play? Would the league allow zone defense? Would there be a 24 second shot clock? A 30 second clock?

The Founding Players were the ones who made that kind of decisions. They weren't just handed a set of rules. Instead, they had a lot to say about how the women's professional game would be played. They took ownership of the new league, you could say. Their presence at the press conference in September, 1995 when the ABL was officially announced lent a badly needed legitimacy to the new venture. In the fall of 1996, the new league began its first season.

Katy has vivid memories—probably most players do—of the opening game. The Portland Power played at home against the Atlanta Glory. Memorial Coliseum, the no frills arena the Blazers had used before their new state-of-the-art arena was constructed, was packed with fans. The game had to be delayed so that all the spectators could find their seats, but somehow that seemed fitting.

After all, this wasn't just an ordinary game. It was the start of something that mattered. There were speeches about the league, fireworks and loud applause as the players on the home team were introduced—applause that reached its peak of volume when Katy Steding's name was announced. Smoke hung in the arena air, and at times the fireworks seemed to flare dangerously close to players. That too seemed appropriate. New ventures aren't entirely safe.

Katy wasn't playing it safe either. Even if it hadn't been the season opener, she might have remembered the game. She was playing with her nose taped up. It had been broken in practice less than a week before and needed more time to heal. But Katy was the hometown heroine and this was the opening game. She had to play, Katy felt.

The Portland fans were loud and enthusiastic. Players were too pumped, a little nervous at first, and missed some easy shots before they settled down. It was "a very good feeling" to be out there, Katy says. It was after all the first game for her of the league she'd helped to start.

The opening game wasn't all high fives and exhilarating fast breaks for Katy. In the second quarter, she took a ball hard in the face. For a moment she stood unmoving on the court, covering her face with her hands. Then she left the game with tears running down her cheeks.

Her recently broken nose was painful enough that she considered staying out for good. After all she'd started the game, done her thing for the hometown fans. But she had to go back in, she realized soon. For this opening game, she had to be back out there in the middle of the action.

Katy Steding

"I said a little prayer before I went out on the floor," Katy remembers. "Just let me be able to hang in there and just not concentrate on pain or on what people are thinking or anything like that. Just let me play the way I'm supposed to play."

Katy's inner strength helped her do just that. She hit a three-point shot and the crowd roared. She made a layup, then a tricky reverse layup. Katy's team, the Portland Power, won the game. Katy finished with solid numbers, sixteen points and seven assists.

For Katy and her teammates, the new league was launched in a satisfying fashion. But time didn't stop of course. Many more games had to be played. The Power lost their second and third games, then won their fourth.

The forty-game ABL season moved along, bringing both high and low moments for all ten women on the Portland Power. There were long road trips and back-to-back games. All the ABL teams were loaded with talent and played heads up, physical, exciting basketball. But every team was new as well. The Power struggled with team chemistry, a problem the U.S. National Team had never had. They suffered through an eleven-game losing streak, the longest in the ABL.

The ABL players had all competed on top teams. None of them were accustomed to losing. Maybe a game here or there, but not eleven in a row. In the entire month of November, which included a weeklong trip east, the Power didn't win a single game. "I got very depressed sometimes," Katy admits. "It's no fun to lose and especially when you're not used to it."

"We definitely hit rock bottom," Katy adds. "I think we kind of scraped along the bottom for a while."

Katy is the kind of player who thinks about games afterwards, about what she did and what she could have done better. As the former Olympian, the hometown girl, and one of two premiere players for her team, Katy was in a difficult situation. Many people expected her to put up big numbers every game, even though throughout her career, certainly since high school, that hadn't been her role. She'd excelled as a complementary player, as the one to hit an outside shot, such as one of her trademark three pointers, if a post player was tightly guarded. Yet knowing that didn't end the pressure she felt from others and that she put on herself.

The long losing streak, of course, was tough on everyone, Katy tried to encourage her teammates. "It's not going to be this way forever," she would say. The team did hang together, kept on trying, and by and large avoided the temptation of blaming each other. Fan support stayed strong. Finally the long string of lost games ended. In early December, Portland beat Seattle at Portland, 77 to 60. "They were so hungry to get a win," Seattle coach Jacquie Hullah said about Portland to an *Oregonian* reporter. "It was like a shark smelling blood."

After the game, players raced onto the court, hugged teammates, waved towels to signal the victory. "It feels like we won the championship," Katy told the same reporter. "It feels like a big weight has been taken off us."

But another kind of weight was still affecting Katy and her teammates. All along, ever since training camp and preseason games, tensions had flared between head coach Greg Bruce and many of the players. Greg had been a successful coach for the women's basketball team at Portland State University. PSU, however, had played in Division II, and Greg Bruce admitted that coaching elite athletes was new and different for him. Some players on the Power began to question Greg's leadership.

As the co-captain of the team and a member of the Players' Advisory Board for the league, Katy was stuck in the middle between other players and the coach. She helped mediate disputes and tried to keep the situation from getting out of hand. She tried to help maintain a positive atmosphere on the team. But that effort took its toll on her. Playing the role she was forced to play increased her mental fatigue. It "burnt me out really fast," is how Katy recalls it.

That year on the Power, Katy struggled at times with her game as well. "Katy's going to look good in a system," is her former coach Tara VanDerveer's assessment. "She's going to look good when people are screening for her, when there's an offense that is not free wheel but more set."

The Power offense often didn't work that way though. It often didn't involve running plays for Katy so she would get the ball where she could shoot her best. Rather than blame her teammates or coach, Katy looked inward. "I'm frustrated with myself for not hitting shots," Katy told an *Oregonian* reporter shortly before she left for the ABL All-Star game. "I'm supposed to be a shooter, so shoot the ball, Steding. There's a lot of pressure that I put on myself."

Katy's salary as a premiere player and a Founding Player was $125,000, the most an ABL player could earn. Her individual statistics—an average of 10.6 points, 3.2 assists, and 6.4 rebounds—were decent but lower than most of the other premiere players. Those statistics didn't tell the whole story. They didn't measure the tight defense Katy played, the savvy passes she made, the way she steadied her team and hustled back on defense. Yet statistics did matter to many people, and clearly Katy was under pressure to earn her large salary, to expand her role as a player. "I don't think I've lived up to the job," she also commented to the reporter.

Many of Katy's teammates didn't agree with her somewhat negative self assessment. Jennifer Jacoby, in fact, loaded on the compliments when she described Katy. In Jennifer's opinion, Katy is a "great leader" on and off the court, and someone who "works the hardest of anybody on the team." According to Jennifer, Katy is "a great shooter," someone who "plays great defense," and overall an incredible athlete."

In spite of her teammates' support, the pressures of myriad expectations, combined with the load of fatigue she carried, could get Katy down at times. Fortunately, one big change on the Power helped take some of the weight off Katy. In January Coach Bruce resigned and a new coach, Lin Dunn, took over the head coaching spot. All the Power players were enthusiastic about the new coach. She brought fresh energy, clear leadership, as well as a much needed sense of humor to the team.

There were still ups and downs to come, and for Katy there was one more change. In late January Lin Dunn replaced Katy as a starter and had her come in off the bench. It was a shift which some people assumed Katy would view as "some major slight."

But Katy is not the kind of basketball player whose main goal in life is to hog the limelight. Teammates and coaches describe her as essentially a team player—"a total team player" Tara VanDerveer says—and that's also the way Katy describes herself. She wanted to do what was best for the team. As several teammates reported, Katy's attitude remained the same whether she was a starter or a reserve. She wasn't going to sit on the bench and sulk. Instead, she was going to accept the coach's judgement, cheer her teammates on, try her best whenever she was out on the court, and work as hard as ever.

Katy did just that as the season continued. In early February the Power lost a close game in Richmond, coming back from 15 points down to lose by a disappointing margin of only one point. Katy missed a shot with less than a minute left then made a layup. In the fourth quarter, she scored eight points, to help bring her team back.

Later in February, the team lost again, this time in Atlanta. Still coming off the bench, Katy put up solid numbers, ending with 11 points. "Katy played as well as I've seen her play since I have been with the team," Coach Dunn told a reporter.

Lin Dunn knew that Katy was very tired—exhausted really—just as all the 1996 Olympic players were. Katy admitted the same about herself and the other Founding Players. "Everyone I've talked to is burnt out," she said. "But we all kind of feel like we've got to just suck it up and keep going." Founding Players knew what the ABL meant. For the sake of the new league, they would keep giving the game all they had.

Fatigue did affect Katy though. Lin Dunn describes her as one of the best three-point shooters in the ABL, but during the season, she had lost some of her confidence, some of her sweet shooting touch. She started to second guess when she should or shouldn't take her shot. Basketball is too fast a game to do that, of course, and in the ABL the action was lightning quick. If a player hesitated on court, the opportunity was usually lost. Katy was in a shooting slump for a while. "Take the shot, Katy," Lin Dunn could be heard shouting sometimes. She encouraged Katy to go ahead and shoot when she was open.

In the next-to-last game of the season, when Portland again played Seattle, Katy showed some of her stuff as a shooter and an all-around player. In the second quarter she made two mid-range jumpers, looking sharp as she aimed and shot. She beat the shot clock buzzer with a close basket. By the end of the game she'd hit a three-pointer, shot perfectly at the line, made three steals and put up fourteen points total, all in only 17 minutes of play.

The long season still wasn't quite over yet. That Wednesday afternoon the Power players met at The Hoop, for their last full practice of the season. Katy was "mentally tired," she admitted after the almost three hour practice. But as a basketball professional, a veteran in the best sense of the word, she did her best, paying close attention to the coach's instructions.

The floor vibrated from dribbled basketballs. Katy ran to the basket, made a crisp pass to a teammate. "Nice pass," Coach Dunn shouted. "Where is the best place to make a lob pass?" she asked a few minutes later.

Katy's expression was deadpan. She may have been bored by the question. But she almost instantly pointed to the right spot.

The players took a short water break. Then the practice continued. Patches of sweat stained the players' jerseys. Katy ran into a solid pick. No big deal, her body language said, as she kept moving on the court. A little later, she shouted that she was open, then drilled a three. When the practice ended, Katy still hung in there. "Good job!" she said to teammates. "Way to finish hard!"

Katy's own end to the season was something of an anticlimax. She didn't play a huge number of minutes or make any spectacular plays. But she was very much in the game, working hard on defense, passing to open teammates, cheering on her team.

Then the last game was over, ending with a win for the Power. As spectators slowly filed out of the arena, Katy signed autographs, talked to fans. She had finally reached the finish line of her basketball marathon.

Katy was definitely ready for a break. Her personal longest "season" ever had taken its toll. In addition to touring with the U.S. National team, playing in the Olympics, and playing through the ABL season, Katy had made a record number of appearances for the league, averaging over two public appearances a week. "I probably beat anybody in the league by about twice," is her own assessment.

Katy made all those appearances to help her team and the league, not because she's the type of person who craves attention. Private time, time for family and friends, is important to her. And in the aftermath of the ABL's first season, Katy's internal compass turns for a while away from sport and towards her personal affairs. In

May, 1997, she takes an important life step that has nothing to do with basketball. She and her fiance, John Jeub, finally walk down the aisle together after postponing their wedding for both the Olympics and the first ABL season.

But basketball remains a central focus for Katy. And when she talks about the ABL, Katy is very enthusiastic. The league is "for the future, and not only for five years down the road but for ten, fifteen, twenty years. Girls that are growing up now and going to camps have something to look forward to."

Katy most definitely has a sense of history about being one of the founding players in the ABL, yet she doesn't want to take too much credit. "The real pioneers," she says, "are the people who came before us that didn't really get much recognition." She mentions women's basketball greats of the recent past like Cheryl Miller, Ann Meyers and Nancy Lieberman-Cline.

Women like Katy Steding are keeping that basketball movement going. "You're seeing women's basketball take off at a level that has never been experienced before," Katy says. There were and are plenty of doubters. But women's pro basketball is happening, and for Katy Steding that means a lot.

"It's kind of schmaltzy," she says about her view of the ABL. "But it's not just for us, it's for the people coming after us too."

An Unofficial Founding Player

Christy Hedgpeth's coach, Jacquie Hullah, has called Christy a "founding player," but officially Christy doesn't qualify. Technically, she can't be listed as part of this small and illustrious group because she wasn't a member of the 1996 Olympic women's basketball team.

But if anyone deserves to be made an honorary founding member, it is surely Christy Hedgpeth. A friendly woman whose southern accent seems to soften her words, Christy's history with the ABL started long before the first season began. Long before the Seattle Reign drafted her as a shooting guard. Actually, she was the first player directly involved with the league. She was the one who spoke with many other players about the ABL. Only 24 years old during the ABL's first season, Christy shouldered more responsibility in starting the league than many people twice her age could have handled.

Christy's personal sports success story started in Thomasville, North Carolina, the "Furniture Capitol" of the state and home of the world's largest chair, a giant-sized 30 or 40 feet high. Perhaps this larger-than-human-scale piece of furniture helped inspire large aspirations in Christy from an early age. When Christy was only five years old, she watched a friend's older brother shooting baskets. "I can do that," a young Christy confidently asserted.

"Yeah, yeah kid, whatever," was the predictable older brother response. But Christy must have insisted because they finally let her try shooting. As the boys watched skeptically, Christy put the basketball through the hoop. Then she did it again, and again. "I made the first three baskets I ever tried," she recalls.

Even the boys were impressed.

"I was just really strong," Christy describes her five-year-old self. As a girl, she used and developed that strength in sports. After her parents put up a basketball hoop in their driveway, Christy would spend hours out there shooting. When she was six, Christy became the only girl member of a YMCA basketball league, although later some other girls followed her example.

Christy didn't mind being the only girl or one of only a few. What did get to her was some of the attitudes about her playing. "I was better than most of the boys," Christy recalls. Apparently, that gave some people in Thomasville trouble. "Why is it so amazing to people," Christy still wonders, "that I'm the best player in the league and I'm a girl?"

Christy continued running up against stereotypical attitudes during those early years. She still gets annoyed by another misconception. "My least favorite comment," she asserts, "is 'you don't throw like a girl.'" Christy's reply? "You know I am a girl, and this is how I am throwing."

Or serving, or dribbling, or volleying. As a child, Christy had a superabundance of energy which she channeled into sports. She started tennis lessons when she was nine and played tennis year round, going to all the junior championships. In steamy, hot southern summers, and in temperate southern winters, Christy would be out on the tennis court. She developed into a promising junior tennis player, winning the state championship for girls in her age bracket when she was ten.

At Westchester Academy, the private school which Christy attended, she started basketball in the seventh grade, and she kept playing all through high school. Like many athletically gifted youngsters, she was pulled by more than one sport. "I think there was always this duality between tennis and basketball for me," she remembers. She liked the team play basketball involved, and the excitement of the sport, and the way it used her natural athleticism.

But tennis was a far more established route to athletic success for girls and women. Both of Christy's parents had played the sport and they gladly spent weeks on the road with her going to tennis tournaments. As a teenager, Christy's tennis skills were good enough that she could have gone to a tennis academy in Florida. She would have had to leave her family to do that, and yet the payoff could have been a professional tennis career.

Tennis had women role models—players like Billie Jean King, Chris Evert, and Martina Navratilova. Basketball, on the other hand, seemed like much more masculine turf. When Christy was growing up, there were hardly any women players on TV. Christy watched male college players like Michael Jordan, who competed in the Atlantic Coast Conference. "I didn't have any women basketball players to look up to," Christy says simply. At the time, women's college basketball still received very little coverage.

For most of Christy's high school years, she wavered between an allegiance to basketball and to tennis. Tennis was what she typically spent her summers playing. But in her junior year in high school, an AAU coach asked her to play basketball that spring. Christy's team ended up winning the state AAU championship.

Christy starred for her high school basketball team—averaging 30 points a game—but since her high school was a small one, the AAU experience was the real turning point for her. It was her play for the AAU team which brought her to the attention of college recruiters. The summer after her junior year, Christy's mailbox was suddenly full with hundreds of letters from colleges across the country.

The prospect of playing college basketball excited Christy. She thought seriously about the University of North Carolina, which had a good basketball program and was close to home. If she went somewhere else, Christy thought, it would have to be really special, "somewhere so incredible I couldn't pass it up."

Stanford University turned out to be that special somewhere. Christy liked the coach for one. When Tara VanDerveer visited Christy and her family in North Carolina, Tara struck Christy "as someone who was no frills," who was simply "down to business," not the sort of person who would fawn over a potential recruit or make false promises. Christy liked Tara's determination and her straightforward manner. "Our goal is to win a national championship. We want you to be a part of it," Tara told Christy.

That was heady stuff for a high school senior to hear, a dream fizzy with champagne bubbles which included her. And Tara's ambitious vision was about to come true. When Christy visited Stanford, in the fall of 1989, their women's basketball team was headed for Stanford's first national championship. Of course, Christy didn't have a crystal ball which would show her that, but she did see a lot that she liked. Future ABL players Sonja Henning, Jennifer Azzi, and

Katy Steding were all at Stanford then. The women on the team worked hard both scholastically and on the basketball court. They were friendly young women—successful academically, talented athletically, but not "stuck up." They were the kind of people Christy enjoyed being around, the kind of players she thought would help to improve her own game.

Christy's mind was made up. The next year she was going to head west. The day after she visited the college, Stanford had a big earthquake, but Christy wasn't worried. "It didn't deter me," she says laughing.

Christy's senior year in high school was an eventful one. First, there was the basketball championship she won at her high school. Her school had a tradition of being successful with girls' basketball, and Christy wanted to help continue that tradition. She played several different positions and posted impressive individual statistics of 32 points, 12 rebounds, 5 steals, and 6 assists per game. Not surprisingly, her team won the state championship. "I was ... on a mission to win," Christy remembers.

Her excitement about basketball continued when she went to see the NCAA Women's Final Four in Knoxville, Tennessee. She sat in the stands, leaning forward in her seat sometimes as she watched Stanford win the championship. It was an exciting game, with an extra excitement for Christy. "Oh my gosh," she thought. "I'm going to go to that school and they're winning the national championship." Then a disturbing thought occurred to her. "Do they really want me?"

A basketball future was still something of a new idea to Christy. While devoting so much time to tennis, she hadn't pictured herself playing college basketball at one of the top Division One schools. But she didn't want to back out of the opportunity either. She watched the Stanford players lose a lead, then come back to tie the score at half-time. She saw the team playing together, teammates excited when someone made a good play. "I just really want to be a part of that," she thought.

Christy knew she would be joining a high-level, demanding basketball program. She was excited about that, and also scared. Fear helped motivate her to work hard over the summer. She lifted weights, ran, biked, climbed stairs. She worked on basketball skills. "I had gotten the scholarship," she felt, "and I was going to be as ready as I could."

Christy arrived at Stanford in better shape than some of the returning players. As she focused solely on basketball, she showed that she did indeed belong in a top college program. She started at shooting guard about 80 percent of the time her freshman year, her starting position a vote of confidence from Tara VanDerveer. Christy was a team player, which fit with the more team-oriented women's game. "I've never been some huge flashy player," Christy says. But she knew her strengths. She was a "great finisher on the break," Tara told her. In the *1991-92 Stanford Basketball Guide*, Tara praised Christy further. "She is very motivated, and is extremely competitive," Tara said. "Christy is a great shooter," Tara added.

In Christy's sophomore year, the 1991-1992 season, the Stanford women's team was loaded with talent, including current ABL players Val Whiting and Molly Goodenbour. After dominating the Pac-10, they went on to the NCAA Final Four. In the semi-final game, they beat the University of Virginia, Dawn Staley's team. The game ended up as a basketball cliff-hanger, a one point victory. Then in the final game Stanford blew out Western Kentucky by a large margin. Christy played long minutes, putting in 17 points in the championship game.

Christy's solid play continued her junior year, when she was second on her team in scoring. But it was in her senior year that Christy felt her team was headed for another national championship. Their team chemistry, that intangible factor which means so much in basketball, was as good as it had been in '92, Stanford's last championship year. "We were destined to win it again," Christy felt.

Then in post-season play, high expectations ended abruptly. The Stanford women were upset at the regional final by Purdue University. It was a tough loss, a defeat that still stings. The regional final was played at Maples Pavilion, Stanford's home court. In a way, that made the outcome even worse. While the Stanford band played and loyal Stanford fans cheered and shouted their support, the Stanford women in their white home game uniforms faced up against the Purdue Boilermakers in bright yellow and black shorts and jerseys.

The Stanford women wanted the win. There was no doubt about that. But wanting and trying weren't enough this time. The team played, Christy feels, "the worst game we played all year."

Stanford was forced to foul at the end, but the last ditch tactic didn't make a difference. When the game was over, the Purdue Boilermakers celebrated. The Stanford women sat in their locker room and cried. Even the Stanford coaches, Christy remembers, "were in shock."

Everyone had expected to go on to the Final Four in Richmond, where they would have played North Carolina. Christy's whole family had planned to be there. Then her and her teammates' dreams crashed into a bitter reality.

Even now, Christy can't bring herself to watch tapes of the game. She describes the loss as "devastating" for her personally. "It was my senior year," she recalls, "and it was at that point the end of my career, the last game I was ever going to play."

Christy had reached another turning point in her life, a place where her personal athletic career could have ended. Although she considered going overseas, she'd heard about players who were badly treated or homesick or never got paid. Also, Christy wasn't a post player, who were always in higher demand, and she didn't have the national recognition of someone like former Stanford player Jennifer Azzi, who had been named National Player of the Year her senior year.

"I'd heard too many horror stories," Christy says, as she explains her decision not to try overseas play. "And it wasn't like I was going to get some huge contract. So I just decided it was time to go on."

She wasn't quite ready to give up basketball though. She tried out for a USA Basketball team that summer, ending up as a finalist for the B team, and then another shooting guard was chosen over her. "That was the worst," Christy recalls. "That was just the final blow." Christy cried after not making the team. She wondered what she would do now. In the summer of 94, it seemed as if her basketball career was really over.

"I was 22 years old," Christy remembers, "in the best shape of my life... really learning the game." Yet with no pro league yet in the United States, she faced the same wrenching decision so many other women have confronted. "What am I going to do now?" she wondered. What would her life be after basketball?

While she tried to stay in shape, she also accepted an internship in event management for the Stanford Athletic Department. That was where she was in the fall of '94 when she received the phone call that would change her life.

Steve Hams phoned Christy and then took her out to dinner, along with his teenage daughter, Lauren, to talk about his idea. "It's a crime," Steve said with conviction, "that American women can't play in their own communities, that American women just reaching their prime have to stop."

Steve had been talking to a few other people, including former women's stars like Ann Meyers. He wanted to know what Christy thought. Did she think a new league could work? Would she want to be a part of it?

Christy immediately liked Steve. And she liked what he was saying about how American women players could be role models of achievement. Christy of course hadn't had women basketball players to look up to when she was a girl—most U.S. women her age hadn't either—but Steve's ideas sounded great to her. Steve Hams was for real, she thought. He wanted to start a new league for good reasons: not to exploit women athletes but to give them a chance.

Steve wanted to move forward with his idea, and Christy agreed to be on an advisory committee made up of people from the area, including many business people. In early 1995 she went to meetings about the new league, the first player to be involved in what was still much more of an idea than a reality.

Their baby needed a name, and members of the advisory committee batted around ideas. What about the Women's American Basketball League? People had different opinions, but Christy was clear about what she thought. She didn't want the W in the name. The NBA, after all, didn't call itself the Men's National Basketball Association. The majority agreed with Christy, and American Basketball League became the official name.

Christy was still working for Stanford University—she wasn't yet being paid by the ABL—but Steve Hams asked her if she would contact some players about the league. As Christy began making phone calls, she thought about her own future. Her Stanford internship would end in June, 1995.

"I didn't know how far this whole idea was going to go," Christy remembers. It was still anyone's guess if the ABL would really happen. Christy wanted to play basketball again, but she hedged her bets by applying for coaching jobs. Coaching seemed like the second best thing to being out on the court herself.

An obviously bright young woman who was good with people, a graduate of one of the top college basketball programs for women, Christy was offered an assistant coach's position at the University of San Francisco. She could have accepted that and been launched on a coaching future in which she would undoubtedly have done well. But another possible future, a road which headed in a different direction, complicated her decision.

Early in the summer of '95, Steve Hams offered Christy a job with the ABL. Christy was well aware of the drawbacks. The ABL was a start up venture with an uncertain future. The league didn't have much money and couldn't pay as much as USF was offering Christy. She had to make a hard choice. Should she go with a more secure position or take a gamble on the new league? She searched her soul to find the answer. "Do you believe in it so much that it would be worth it to you to be a part of it?" she asked herself.

Christy's answer was yes. She shared the vision of a women's professional league; she saw what it could mean for women's basketball. At the same time, Christy fully understood just how iffy the ABL still was. She laughs about that now. "You couldn't even say it was a league yet," she remembers. "It wasn't." The ABL was more of an idea than a reality, a dream about what women's basketball could become.

Christy was going to go for the dream. She officially started working for the league in July, 1995, an exciting time for women's basketball. The U.S. National Team had recently been named and would play both internationally and across the United States. People all over America, Steve Hams thought, "were finally going to open their eyes" to just how good top women's play could be.

The plan was for the ABL to begin play in the fall of '96, soon after the Olympics. The new league would build on the basketball momentum that players like Dawn Staley and Teresa Edwards had set in motion. A lot of hard work, however, and some luck as well, was needed if that was to happen.

Christy did quite a bit of that work. "My job was on the phone," she recalls. "I just called and called and called players." She spoke with women all over the country, playing a role that someone like Steve Hams, as much as he believed in the league, couldn't perform as well. Christy had been a player on a top college team. She'd been at tryouts for USA Basketball teams. Other players knew her, had played against her, or at least had heard of her. When Christy talked about the ABL, players listened.

Of course that didn't mean there weren't plenty of skeptics. "Who's backing it?" was a question Christy heard numerous times. What kind of money did the league have behind it? For a while, that question must have been hard to answer.

On the day the league reached a major milestone, Christy and Steve Hams gave each other a big hug. They had just got the news of their first major investment in the new league, from Bobby Johnson of Atlanta, who ended up being one of the league's co-founders. It was "probably the biggest hug I've ever given anyone other than my family," Christy recalls.

No matter how skeptical some people were, Christy kept on believing in the dream. She spoke with players and anyone else who might sign on to or otherwise help the league. Aside from her basketball experience, her friendly yet unassuming personality must have helped a lot. And Christy had enough self-confidence to call up a women's basketball great like Teresa Edwards and tell her about the ABL. Actually, Christy downplays the difficulty of that. She'd met Teresa Edwards and many other players. "They're just like my peers," was Christy's assessment. Calling up even top players was "no big deal."

It still was a big deal, though, to get a new league started. When Christy looks back now on the early days of the ABL, she reminds herself that "this all started in an office with a small group of people." She knows how many obstacles that core group had to overcome. Getting money for the new league, of course, was a major difficulty. Then there were players to be signed media people to be convinced that the league was something to take seriously.

Christy was there at the press conference the league held in September, 1995 to announce its founding. She was there alongside the league co-founders—Steve Hams, Gary Cavalli, Bobby Johnson, Anne Cribbs—as well as most of the Founding Players from the U.S. National Team. Now the ABL was officially a going concern. "That was a huge day," Christy recalls.

The hard work of forming a new league continued. While Gary Cavalli and Anne Cribbs worked with marketing and sponsorships, Christy and Steve Hams were responsible for communicating with players and doing facility research. Christy made still more phone calls to gather information about facilities. The fledgling league had to make important decisions. What cities were best to place teams in? What cities were most likely to support a new professional women's team?

The ABL tryouts, held in late May and early June, 1996, were another major step for the league. By then Christy had the official title of Manager of Player Development, a responsible sounding title which was well deserved. She spent about two months helping to organize the tryouts, contacting colleges about interested players, designing an application, preparing a participant packet, speaking to players who needed help or information, and doing whatever else it took to get the tryouts off the ground.

When the tryouts finally happened, Christy was the co-director of what could be described as an exercise in organized chaos. With the ABL's open-door policy for its first year tryouts, and about 570 women showing up in Atlanta, Christy's job must have been something like trying to plan schedules for almost 600 new students on the first day of school. So what did she actually do as co-director? "Oh my God, what didn't I do," is her first response.

Lots of people were interested in the league, even women in their later thirties. There were women from Division II and Division I colleges and women who hadn't played in years. At the tryouts, they all wore ABL jerseys as they shot and passed, dribbled and ran the court, hustled and sweated. Naturally, everyone wanted a chance to be seen by coaches and general managers. The ABL did its best to have that happen within the six days of the tryouts. "It was a huge responsibility," Christy remembers.

Players bombarded Christy with questions. Where can I stay? When do I need to be at whatever location or practice? And then there were all the other important details to deal with, such as who had paid their tryout fees and who had signed medical waivers.

Predictably, not everyone was happy with the way the tryouts were set up or with players' chances of getting a place in the league. Forty players, including the Founding players, had already been signed by the league before the tryouts. "A lot of people were resentful that we'd signed that many people," Christy recalls. As co-director of the tryouts, Christy heard those players' complaints.

Much as Christy sympathized, she also knew that many of the women at the tryouts couldn't fully understand the league's position. The ABL badly needed credibility. Signing top players like college stars or the Olympians was, Christy thought, "a huge plus" for the league. Also, the league had originally planned to have teams in twelve cities, which would have meant a total of 120 women playing for the league, but the ABL ended up starting with only eight teams and 80 women.

Christy was one of the forty players already signed. All along, of course, she'd been hoping to play in the new league, to have another chance at playing basketball. As it turned out, the decision that meant such a lot to Christy was made in an informal way. "I asked Steve if he wanted to sign me," Christy recalls with a smile, "and he said that he did."

On draft day, Christy didn't have to wear all her official hats. All she had to do was wait to be drafted. A small group of women were already assigned as regional players to a particular team, but Christy wasn't among them. She waited to see who would choose her.

San Jose was her first choice. She had roots there, had worked for the league in the area. But she wasn't disappointed when she was drafted by Seattle in the sixth round. She already was acquainted with Jacquie Hullah, the Seattle head coach, from an Olympic sports festival. And going to Seattle instead of San Jose had another plus for Christy. It meant she wouldn't be playing behind Jennifer Azzi in the shooting guard position. Anyway, the main thing was that she was now on the roster of an ABL team. "Very very happy" was the main thing she felt.

When training camp started in September, Christy's job description changed. She switched from working for the whole league to doing her job as a player on the Seattle Reign. Once again she was starting something new, and once again it wasn't easy. It was everyone's first year with the Reign. Players and coaches were all in a new situation. The players, Christy thinks, "were all like freshmen, not knowing what to expect."

Kate Paye, the young Seattle point guard, was a familiar face. She'd graduated from Stanford just a year after Christy, so Christy knew a lot about Kate's basketball moves. But she had to work hard to get a feeling for the other Seattle players, as they went through drills and scrimmages together.

Then the first ABL season—a season which Christy had helped to make possible—officially began. The Reign played its first three games on the road, against Colorado, San Jose, and Portland. It was their home opener, however, on October 27, which Christy remembers most vividly.

Tickets to the game were sold out. The small, homelike Mercer Arena, where tiers of seats rise in a rectangle around the basketball court, was packed with 4,591 fans. A band played, adding to the festive atmosphere, and no one could fail to notice that this was the home court of the Reign. At both ends of the court, orange letters spelled out "Seattle Reign." An orange basketball with sunlike rays adorned the center of the court.

The energy the basketball sun seemed to radiate mirrored Christy's own energy and enthusiasm. She started at the off guard position, and her shooting was on the mark. She hit a variety of shots, including a three pointer in the third quarter, and ended up with a solid total of 17 points. The final score was 83-70, in Seattle's favor, not a landslide victory but not a nail biter either. Afterwards, Christy celebrated with her team. "This is . . . everything I'd hoped for and more," she remembers thinking. No way was she sorry she'd linked her future to the league's.

Just as at Stanford, Christy wasn't the flashiest player on her team. But all along, her energy and effort made a difference. In late November, when the Reign played the Richmond Rage, Christy was on the court much of the time. She played in-your-face defense, running out to cover a Richmond player, then moving in quick sideways steps to guard another player. By the end of the game, she was Seattle's leading scorer with 18 points. But that impressive statistic didn't tell the whole story. It didn't describe her hustle and heart, the way she raced down court the instant a Seattle player grabbed a defensive rebound.

Christy always played hard. But by the time the halfway mark of the season had come and gone, there had been lows as well as highs for Christy and the other Seattle Reign women. There were tensions between teammates, games that got away. And then there was Christy's personal low point of the season. It was on Friday, January 17, when the Reign played Colorado at home. In the fourth quarter of that game, Christy went down with a serious injury.

She can still remember exactly how it happened. In reality, the sequence of events must have been lightning fast, but as Christy recalls it, everything seems to unfold in slow motion. Christy drove the lane and caught a pass from Kate Paye. She twisted to avoid a Colorado player and the ball got caught on her hip. She twisted back towards the right to get the ball. At the same time, she planted her left foot solidly on the floor.

Too many contrasting forces pulled at Christy's body. Too many strong muscles contracted in different directions. Something had to give, and in this case it was Christy's knee. She fell to the court in a lot of pain. She lay there hurting in front of the suddenly quiet Seattle fans. Right away she knew something was wrong. Something had shifted in her knee, she felt.

Suddenly Christy's knee went numb. She felt a moment of hope. "Well maybe I'll be okay because it doesn't hurt too bad," she thought. But that turned out to be a false hope. The numbness in Christy's knee was due to the fact that her anterior cruciate ligament was completely torn, and nerves had torn as well.

All at once, Christy's season was over. She'd personally experienced the major injury that hits far more female than male basketball players. Among women athletes overall, basketball players have the second highest rate of ACL tears. Only women in soccer suffer more of them.

For Christy, the injury was tough mentally as well as physically. She'd been at the top of her game, after working hard to get in great shape. She'd done so much to help start the new league, and now she was forced to sit on the sidelines, no longer able to help her team. Reconstructive surgery was in her future, as soon as the swelling went down in her knee.

Christy definitely expected to play again. Numerous players have come back from the identical injury and surgery. ABL players Katy Steding and Jennifer Jacoby have been through that experience twice. But there was always an element of uncertainty. Could Christy really get back to the same level of play? How hard would it be for her to get there?

The forced inactivity really got to Christy. "I feel like I'm on a leash," she said in the aftermath of her injury. She could do some work with weights. She could shoot a little bit, but without pivoting or shifting her weight or jumping. That was about all. She walked on crutches to keep weight off her knee.

One thing she could do—something that certainly raised her spirits—was travel with her team. She still hadn't had her surgery yet when the Reign went on a ten-day road trip towards the end of January. Christy went along, partly so she could keep on working with Robin Moore, the Seattle trainer, and partly because she just wanted to be around basketball. On the road with the Reign, Christy could cheer her teammates on and hang out with them off the court. With extra time on her hands, Christy did something else as well: she kept a journal of her and her teammates' experiences on the road.

On Monday, January 20, the day before an away game, the Reign left Seattle for Philadelphia en route to Hartford, Connecticut. Since the ABL has teams from coast to coast, travel times can be long. The Reign left Seattle mid-morning, but it was about nine o'clock in the evening when they arrived at the Hastings Hotel in Hartford. By the time they got there, Christy wrote, "nearly everyone was on an unstoppable mission to find food. The local Taco Bell was like an oasis in the desert."

The next day, a game day, the players' focus shifted to basketball. But the team's trip to the practice arena involved one small problem, the type of problem that no doubt would never happen in the cash-rich NBA. Reign personnel made a total of 14 people, and waiting for them was a ten-person van. Everyone crammed into the van, crunching long legs and tall bodies together. Nobody was very comfortable. "Next time you pick us up, could you also bring along a Pinto or something!" Reign forward Tari Philipps joked to the driver.

At the game that night, Christy didn't have to be just a spectator. She kept track of some statistics and encouraged her teammates. But she still had a "helpless feeling" as she sat on the bench. She watched her team play without much emotion and lose the game by 8 points, and she couldn't do anything to stop that. Losing, of course, was tough on everyone. After the game, it was very quiet in the locker room.

The very next day the Reign flew to Richmond. There the team's spirits were raised by what Christy labeled their "best restaurant of the year." At least that was her born-and-raised-in-North Carolina perspective. The Southern-style food choices included fried chicken and black eyed peas. Chowing down on tasty food could be one of the good points of a road trip.

But that night Christy had trouble sleeping. As she lay in bed, she thought about her knee. About the way her injury could affect her basketball career and perhaps her whole life. She thought about how important being an athlete was to her. Would she really be able to return to a high level of play, she wondered.

The next day, Christy joined her teammates at a local YMCA. She could only shoot the ball in an awkward, stiff-legged way, but she went ahead and shot some hoops while her teammates joked that she was faking her injury. "It felt good to touch a ball, to shoot, to dribble, to smell the gym," Christy wrote. But that night's game ended in another loss, and once again Christy had a hard time watching the defeat. The loss, she felt, showed an ongoing problem. Though out the year there had been a discrepancy between the huge amount of talent on the Reign and the way all those talented players performed. "We had major chemistry problems," is how Christy summed it all up after the season.

There was one high point for Christy that night. Dawn Staley, one of the Founding Players and the point guard for Richmond, walked over to the Reign bench to give Christy a high five, the way Dawn normally would have done if Christy had been out on the floor as a starter. It was a simple gesture, yet one that meant a lot to Christy. Dawn Staley recognized Christy as a player, even though she couldn't be one at the moment.

The morning after the game, the alarm rang at 7:40 in the hotel room Christy and teammate Linda Godby were sharing. Early morning departures for flights after games the night before are a fact of life in the ABL. Players and other personnel take commercial flights instead of traveling in the cushy private jets many NBA teams enjoy. Six foot and over players still scrunch themselves into coach seats.

On the van ride to the airport, the mood was far from upbeat. The loss last night still hung over the team. Christy worried about the team's mood, especially since they had to play a game in Atlanta that very evening. But a pre-game, players-only meeting energized the Reign and they ended up with a win.

Seattle played one more game on the road, a loss to Columbus. Then the Reign finally flew back to Seattle. Everybody was glad to be heading homeward. The team flew from Columbus to Pittsburgh, changed planes, and then took one last flight to Seattle.

Nine days after the team returned, on February 7th, Christy had her surgery. "I was really scared," she recalls. "You hear so many horror stories about ACL's." She'd never had a really serious injury before. Sprained ankles, broken fingers, and a broken nose didn't count, from Christy's athlete's perspective, as anything that major.

Her surgery went well, and the surgeon felt confident. Then after about a week, Christy's knee started hurting her more and swelling up. The doctors thought Christy might have overdone her exercises in the weight room. They waited to see if the knee would improve. Putting a needle in to check would create the risk of infection.

When doctors did finally take fluid from Christy's knee, it came out filled with pus instead of a healthy clear color. The verdict was that Christy needed another surgery. Right away. She had very little time to prepare herself mentally because the surgery was scheduled for that same night. The infection in her knee was dangerous. It could cause arthritis or destroy the graft the surgeons had made.

In the second surgery, the doctors scraped away all the infected tissue. Christy's prognosis was still good, but having more surgery would probably set back her recovery time. "It was just very unsettling and disheartening," Christy commented, about a week and a half after the second surgery. She was angry and depressed about her injury and about the physical limitations it gave her.

She had a hollow line in her arm that ran through her veins to her heart. Three times a day, she flushed the line with a saline solution, then slowly injected an antibiotic, then flushed with saline again. "It's just so complicated," Christy the Stanford graduate complained. She resented the way her injury complicated her life. As well as injecting the antibiotic, she had to ice her knee and spend time with the injured knee in an electrical stimulating device. About all she could do to exercise at the moment was to lift weights on one side of her upper body.

Christy tried to stay upbeat but it wasn't easy. At an ABL game, she ran into Jennifer Azzi, the Founding Player and shooting guard for San Jose whose season also ended early when she separated her shoulder. "Don't you think it's a little unjust," Christy asked Jennifer, "that two of the people who helped to start the league are the ones sitting there with their butts on the bench?"

But Christy isn't someone who stays down for long. She has the positive spirit, the resiliency, the high goals for herself that so many ABL players possess. By mid April, after the first season has ended, she is definitely on the mend. Her knee is coming along well and the doctor is happy. Christy would like her recovery to go even faster but she's feeling much more positive than before. She can do leg presses, and ride a stationary bicycle, and work out on a stair machine, although she has to keep the resistance at fairly low levels. She can swim, she can shoot a basketball close in, she can lift weights. And most important, she can picture herself back on the basketball court.

Christy isn't blindly optimistic about the league she helped to start. She knows about the problems the ABL has faced, such as with media coverage. During the first season, media treatment of the Reign in Seattle was good but across the country reporting on the ABL was spotty at best. Christy gets indignant when she speaks about that.

"In a democracy you're not supposed to ignore"—she repeats "ignore"—"an entire league where thousands and thousands of people are coming to watch."

But Christy has no doubts that the women of the ABL are worth watching. And she's glad to be a part of women's pro basketball. The girl who grew up without any women basketball players as role models has become one of those role models. The girl who couldn't watch women basketball players on TV now sometimes has TV cameras focused on her.

Veterans of Play Overseas

American women have wowed basketball fans all over the world—in Japan, Italy, Sweden, France and many other countries. Sometimes they earned six-figure salaries; sometimes they didn't get paid. Sometimes they were treated well, sometimes not. American women who wanted to play after college have paid the price as basketball exiles, living and working much of the year in foreign countries. And their families, friends, and potential fans in the U.S. paid a price too. The women they loved or loved to watch were far away.

That was the way it was until the ABL changed the game. Come home and help start a new league. That was the chance the ABL offered to a number of women. Players and agents were sceptical about the new league. ABL salaries could be lower than salaries on teams overseas. How long the league would last was a big unknown. And yet, here was the chance many women had been waiting for. The chance to play at home at last.

Among the eighty women on first year ABL teams, many were drawn from the ranks of American basketball exiles. Almost sixty percent were veterans of basketball overseas in countries as diverse as Israel and Brazil. They brought a richness of experience—in basketball and in life—to their respective ABL teams. Val Whiting, who played for the San Jose Lasers in the league's first year, and Linda Godby of the Seattle Reign, are two of these basketball expatriates who've come home to play.

Val Whiting

Val Whiting went to Italy and then Brazil to play basketball, instead of going to medical school. She was accepted into the medical program at UC San Francisco, but instead of poring over Gray's Anatomy and peering through microscopes, she went to a town in Italy named Viterbo, which the foreign players located there referred to, unlovingly, as Vi-terrible.

Val is a strong-looking woman who looks the part of the athlete she is. She's 6'2" tall and solidly built. Her leg muscles especially are strong and well defined, showing years of workouts, years of running on basketball courts. She has a serious, focused expression which is often on her face when she's out on the basketball court. Going up strong for a rebound or driving past defenders to make a tough shot. Yet her face can soften to a warm smile when she's talking with a teammate or telling someone about her dog Snoopy.

At 25 years old, Val is beyond the need to constantly tell the world about her basketball achievements. Yet by the end of her college career at Stanford University, she'd won many personal honors—including twice being named a Pac-10 Player of the Year, a Kodak All-American, and a member of the NCAA All-Regional Team. Her 2,077 points had made her the leading scorer at Stanford, and she also had the highest number of career rebounds. With all those basketball achievements, after Val had finished her degree in February 1994, it made sense for her to think about playing basketball overseas.

Going or staying wasn't an easy decision. Val wanted to go on playing. Making some money from basketball appealed to her. Then again, she'd heard about plenty of bad experiences for American players overseas.

"Your agent says one thing and you go over there and it's a totally different situation," Val had heard. "You don't get paid, or you don't get paid on time and people treat you like dirt." In the end, Val decided to give basketball overseas a try. She went to Viterbo, Italy, a town near Rome. Like her former Stanford teammate, Jennifer Azzi, Val was less than thrilled with her Viterbo experience. She doesn't mince words. "I hated it," is her main comment.

The negative stories she'd heard came true for Val. She found Viterbo to be a not very friendly, smallish town. Her experience at Stanford had prepared her for the strong fan support which simply wasn't there in Viterbo. Val had also hoped for decent treatment from her new team's management, but in fact she wasn't paid on time. When she complained, the team front office would tell her agent, "Well she got paid. She's lying."

Val's life in Italy wasn't all bad. She fought back against linguistic alienation by hiring a private tutor and learning some Italian. And basketball itself in Italy could be fine. There was "great competition" on the court, Val remembers, with many top American players in Italy. "But it's hard to play well if you're not happy," Val found. She left before the end of the season, after a couple of months in Vi-Terrible with a sour feeling about her whole Italian experience. Like many other American women who played overseas, she never did receive the money that was owed her.

In the spring of 1995, after her Italian "vacation," Val went to Colorado Springs to try out for the U.S. National Team. Going into the tryouts, she had high hopes. "I was in the best shape of my life," she remembers. And that wasn't the only reason for her high expectations. A player with some connection to the committee which would choose the U.S. National Team had relayed to Val a message from one of the committee members: "All you have to do is come in shape and you'll be on this team."

Val did her part. She trained hard for the tryouts. However, with the mix of political pressures and basketball judgments and corporate influence that ultimately affected who was chosen and who wasn't, somehow Val's stock wasn't high enough. "I should have been on the team," Val insists. "Everybody says that. I believe it." But the end result was that she wasn't selected. Instead, she was designated as an alternate on the team.

To say Val was disappointed is an understatement. She'd given her basketball dream everything she had and the bubble had burst on her. "I was crushed," she says simply. And she was left with a lingering sense of injustice about the whole situation.

Perhaps it would have been a good time for Val to have moved on to Plan B for her life, her medical school future. She could have switched from a basketball jersey to a crisp white lab coat or a faded green scrub suit. It was a dream she'd had for a long time. Being a doctor, Val says, "is something I've always wanted to do ever since I was younger, and I really can't imagine myself as anything else." But could she see herself putting away her basketball dreams for good?

Sports had long been part of Val's life. Growing up in Wilmington,

Delaware, Val and her sister Tina played kickball, dodge ball, tag, and lots of other games with neighborhood boys. She was seen as a tomboy, as so many other athletic girls have been. To Val, sports were simply part of who she was.

When she started basketball in seventh grade, though, it wasn't love at first sight. Actually, Val's original goal had been to make the cheerleading squad. "Back then it still wasn't considered feminine to be an athlete. . . ." Val explained to a reporter. "You want the boys to like you, so I thought being a cute little cheerleader, even though I wasn't little, was the thing to do."

When Val was cut from the cheerleading squad, she switched to basketball at a teacher's suggestion. At first she didn't like having to remember all the rules and plays. But she was a tall, athletic girl, well built for the sport, and so she kept on playing. By the eighth grade she liked basketball better. By the time she was in tenth grade, she began working hard at it.

At Ursuline Academy, Val's high school basketball team won four state championships. Val's efforts and energy on court were a big part of why. She averaged 16.1 rebounds, 3.5 blocks, 4.7 assists, 3.5 steals, and an especially impressive 30.3 points per game. Not a one-sport athlete, she also competed on her school's track team and earned two state shot put titles.

In the summer, Val played AAU basketball and went to basketball camps. She also may have spent some time filing away assorted basketball honors. Before her senior year in high school, Women's Basketball News Service and *Parade Magazine* chose her as a First Team All-America. *USA Today* and *Street & Smith's* followed suit, naming her a Third Team All-America and Fourth Team All-America. Her list of accolades included recognition as the Delaware State Player of the Year and the Naismith Player of the Year in her home state.

Sports were never the whole picture for Val. She wrote poetry; she painted; she enjoyed listening to jazz and playing the piano. But not surprisingly, considering all the awards she received, basketball was the activity which brought her scholarship offers from colleges all over the country.

She hadn't even heard of Stanford before she received their letter. But she "fell in love with the campus" when she visited there with her parents. "I had this fascination with California," she admits. The girl from the east coast fell under the spell of the golden west. She liked the Spanish architecture on the Stanford campus, the sunshine, the palm trees. And since Stanford was a top school academically, going there would be a step on the road to medical school.

Val majored in biological sciences, but her other unofficial major was basketball. She became the "sixth man" on her team, as she refers to it, the first player off the bench during her freshman year. After that freshman year, more honors came her way—Pac-10 Freshman of the Year and the Women's Basketball News Service National Freshman of the Year. That summer, she was the West Team's top scorer and rebounder at the U.S. Olympic Festival held in Minneapolis. Back at Stanford, as a sophomore, Val was Stanford's top rebounder.

In the *Stanford Basketball Guide* from 1991-92, Tara VanDerveer describes Val as "an intense player" who "plays aggressive defense. . . is very competitive" and "really wants to win." That was high praise from Tara, who is known as a demanding coach.

In 1990, Val's freshman year, the women's basketball team at Stanford won a national championship. In 1992, Stanford went all the way again. Winning the championship "felt good," Val says simply. "It was kind of like a relief," she adds with a laugh. The pressure to win a second NCAA title must have been intense at a top program like Stanford. Then relief turned to disappointment Val's senior year. Some people expected Stanford to win still another championship, but it didn't turn out that way.

The Stanford disappointment was probably only matched in intensity by Val's failure to receive a place on the U.S. National Team which would become the 1996 Olympic team. It's a testament to how much basketball means to her that afterwards, she decided to give basketball overseas another try. It would be somewhere far away from Italy and slick-talking Italian front offices. That faraway place turned out to be Paulinia, Brazil, which was where Val played for the 1995-96 season. After Italy and Colorado Springs, she was due for a positive experience. Luckily she got it.

Paulinia is a town an hour away from the city of Sao Paulo. It has a tropical climate, with palm trees growing in and around the town, and an equally warm atmosphere. The townspeople there ride around on horses and take the time to chat with each other in the markets. Val remembers the Brazilians she met as "warm and loving," the kind of people who "want to make you happy."

Best of all, Brazilian fans enthusiastically supported women's basketball. In Brazil, women's basketball was second only to men's soccer in popularity, and it was actually more popular than men's basketball. Women players were well taken care of. Her team "provided me with a maid," Val recalls, "someone who would wash my clothes, clean the house, cook. They spoiled me."

Even living the good life in Brazil, Val still missed family and friends. She missed her native language too. "No one spoke English because it was a such a small town," Val remembers. Learning some Portugese, which she did on her own, was a necessity. She had plenty of time to practice the new language with her Brazilian teammates. Their team travelled by bus around the state of Sao Paulo.

In February of '96, Val returned from Brazil to make one tour with the U.S. National Team. While Carla McGhee was injured, Val travelled to China with the U.S. team. In Hollywood movie style, China might have been Val's golden opportunity to make a spot for herself on what was to become the Olympic team. In June of the same year, a twelfth player was going to be added to the team. But it proved very difficult for Val to join a team which had been playing together for nearly a year. She had to learn offenses at lightning speed, fit herself into an already established team chemistry. "It's hard," Val describes, "coming onto a team that they've been together and they've worked together, had lousy practices together and (been) yelled at together. They were bonded."

According to Val, the coach, Tara VanDerveer, didn't help matters by giving Val mixed messages. Talking on the phone to Val, asking her to go to China with the team, Tara had told her not to worry about pressure, that she was "just going to have fun." But perhaps because Tara was under tremendous pressure of her own to produce a team which could win gold at the upcoming Olympics, when Val did join the team, Tara's communications with her were significantly less mellow. "You need to play better. You're fighting for an Olympic spot," were the kind of comments Tara now made to Val.

Val ended up regretting the China trip, trying to forget it. "It took me a while to get the confidence back that I lost on my trip," she says. Nevertheless, she was talked into going to Colorado Springs one more time, for the final tryouts for the Olympic team. That upcoming team needed at least one more post player, and Val might have filled the bill. But the timing wasn't right for her. The last time she'd been to the trials, she'd been in top shape. This time she was coming from a vacation in Brazil, where instead of working out she'd enjoyed dancing in the streets of Paulinia during the festival of Carnival.

Carnival is a warm memory for Val, but she'd be happy to erase her second try for the Olympic team from her memory bank. "I knew I wasn't at my best and I shouldn't have gone (to the trials)," she says. "I don't like doing anything when I'm not 100 percent Val." In the end, she didn't make the team. Venus Lacy, a taller and bulkier player, was chosen instead.

Softening the blow was the fact that another basketball future, a future which would begin after the Olympics, was already opening up for Val. In the spring of '95, just before the National Team tryouts, when she was training at Stanford. Anne Cribbs and Gary Cavalli had approached Val about the ABL. "I was excited," Val recalls. She liked the idea right away. But she was also sceptical. "I didn't know how serious they were because there have been many attempts (at leagues)."

In spite of her doubts, she was definitely interested. Unlike Italy, Brazil hadn't been a bad experience for her—she'd had a "great season" there in fact—but it still had meant playing far away from home. And Val had learned firsthand the difficulties of overseas basketball: "It's a different culture. You have to learn a different language. . . . You can't tell people your thoughts, and every time you have to tell somebody something, you have to think about it. And every time someone says something to you, they have (to) say it twice or three times." Val was ready for something like the ABL. She wanted a chance to play basketball in the U.S.

Christy Hedgpeth had called Val in Brazil to talk about the ABL. After the tryouts for the last spot on the Olympic team, Val started thinking more and more seriously about the new league. In the end, she officially committed herself to the ABL, signing a two-year contract before the ABL draft. She and Jennifer Azzi would play side by side. They were both assigned to the San Jose Lasers as the team's two premiere players.

Training camp started in September in Fremont, California. "It was fun," Val recalls. "It was kind of a reunion for some people I'd known before and others I'd seen on TV." Val already knew the women from Stanford basketball teams—Jennifer Azzi, Anita Kaplan, Sonja Henning. San Jose had stacked their team deck in favor of Stanford players. The Lasers had the largest collection of former

Stanford stars of any team in the ABL.

The core group of Stanford players, all used to playing under Tara VanDerveer's system, would help the Lasers come together as a team. But starting off, for the team as a whole, everyone was still a new player. "It was kind of like being a freshman again," Val comments.

Among other changes, it was an adjustment for Val to get used to two new coaches. Having played overseas made the adjustment more difficult. "I hadn't really been coached in a long time," she says. "I don't consider overseas coaching being coached," she adds, explaining that her coaches overseas weren't particularly knowledgeable about basketball.

When the season started, probably none of the new ABL teams were really ready. But schedules had been printed, tickets sold. On October 18, 1996, the San Jose Lasers played at home in one of the first three games for the new league. The San Jose Event Center was sold out that night, with 4,550 fans there for opening night. The Atlanta Glory was the visiting team.

The new pro league was history in the making. Val remembers "a lot of excitement, a lot of pregame ceremonies." There were speeches by Steve Hams, Gary Cavalli and Anne Cribbs, and appropriately enough, a laser show before the game. Understandably, after all the pregame happenings Val found it "kind of hard to concentrate on the game."

Probably many players on both teams shared Val's feelings. But the game went forward and the Lasers ended up winning by a score of 78-70. Afterwards there were more festivities. Olympic teammates Jennifer Azzi and Teresa Edwards, now members of opposing teams, spoke to the crowd. A photo in *ABL Courtside* shows Teresa's arm around Jennifer. Teresa's team had lost the game, yet there was a big smile on her face. The start up of the new league was an exciting moment which obviously meant more than just winning or losing a particular game.

The ABL season, of course, didn't remain frozen in time like a moment captured in a photograph. The Lasers played Seattle at home and won again, then went on the road. Throughout the season, Val started almost every game. Being out on the court meant a lot to her because things almost didn't turn out that way. Her whole first season almost didn't happen.

At the beginning of August, she and a friend were driving along

Interstate 95 in Val's home state of Delaware. Val sat in the passenger seat of a Mitsubishi Montero, a four-by-four model that has since been recalled. The song "Brown Sugar" was playing on the radio when suddenly the driver hit a bump. The Mitsubishi swerved, hit a side railing, and turned over.

Val was stunned by the crash. Her right knee was bleeding, cut to the kneecap. Yet Val didn't think about how lucky she was to be alive, or about how fortunate it was that the driver was going no more than the speed limit and that Val herself had a seat belt on. Instead she thought about herself and basketball, and how important the sport was to her. Her gut-level fear was that she'd never be out on a basketball court again.

At the time of the car crash, Val had signed an endorsement deal with Nike. She was supposed to be leaving soon to join the ABL team in San Jose. "My God, they aren't going to want me anymore," she thought. That seemed a very possible scenario. When Val had tried out for the U.S. National Team in 1995, several shoe companies had expressed an interest in her. When she didn't make the team, all of a sudden the companies weren't calling her up any longer.

The medical attention Val received after the accident validated her concerns. This wasn't a band aid type situation. Val's knee needed 40 stitches. Pieces of grass and gravel had to be picked out of her patella tendon and she ended up losing ten percent of the tendon. Her leg in a cast, Val had to stay in bed for ten days. "I couldn't walk, bend my knee, do anything," she told a reporter. "It was very frustrating. I was scared and I didn't know what to think."

Doctors gave Val varying opinions. She couldn't play for eight months. She couldn't jump for about three months. She'd be fine as soon as September. Val went with her own instincts and rushed out to training camp as soon as she possibly could. It was before she was really ready, she thinks looking back on it all. Her knee was only at about 65 or 70 percent during the season. She developed tendinitis and her right knee cap didn't track as straight as it should. Her right quadriceps muscle ended up weaker than the muscle on her uninjured leg.

Val's knee injury was only part of her physical problems. She has a herniated disc in her back that didn't flare up too badly during the season, but it did stiffen her back and caused her to miss two games. Her back didn't typically cause her pain in games but her injured knee did. She blocked out the pain yet couldn't avoid running with a limp.

In spite of everything, Val hung tough during the season, doing her best for her team. With so many games, she doesn't remember each one, but a few stand out for her. In December and then in February, the Lasers played the Columbus Quest, the team with the best record in the ABL. Val describes herself as playing with "a lot of hustle in defensive plays and rebounding." The Lasers won both games, the second in double overtime.

Mid-December was when the first ABL All-Star game was held, and Val hung in for that too. "Not 100 percent" was a TV announcer's comment about Val, just after she had missed a scoop shot in the first quarter. The announcer explained that Val had been sick with the flu and bronchitis before the game.

What the announcer didn't say, and probably didn't know, was that Val had lost something like 15 pounds in the last week, had played three games before she realized she was sick, only sat out one game, then travelled to Colorado with the Lasers where she experienced the one-two punch of playing at altitude plus playing with the flu. What Val wished for was to be at home in Delaware where her mother could take care of her. But instead Val's family was at the All-Star Game and she knew her family and friends, and lots of fans she didn't know, would be watching her and the other players. And then she had the sense of history many ABL players share. This was the first ABL All-Star game after all. "It was a moment in history that I should have been a part of," Val felt.

So Val made the personal sacrifice and played in the game, even though her lack of 100 percent health slowed her down. She missed some shots and sometimes looked as tired as she must have felt. But her basketball savvy and personal pride still kicked in. The 19 foot jump shot she nailed in the second quarter was just one example of how she wasn't giving away anything out on court.

On January 19th, Val returned to action after missing two games due to back spasms. The physical problems she experienced did affect her play. Yet Val still showed her strength as a player—her grit you could call it—and her ability to help her team. There was the nice fake Val made in the second quarter before she took a shot, the move enabling her to draw a foul and get to the line. "She really provides a lot for this team," a TV announcer said about Val, mentioning her strong ability at rebounding. In the second half, Val demonstrated exactly that as she grabbed an offensive rebound, then muscled the ball up to the hoop.

Val doesn't shrink from describing her strengths as a player. She doesn't dissemble or minimize the way many women have been taught to do. "I can post up or I can shoot from outside," she says. "I'm not one dimensional." She can change her game to match her opponents' game, take outside and inside shots, play a physical game or move around opponents and shoot from the perimeter. She can run the court well too, although her injured knee slowed her down her first ABL year. In other words, she's an all around basketball player.

If Val has an achilles heel as a player, she thinks it's mental rather than physical. "My confidence is not always up . . . . " she admits. "I feel like I'm at the point where I can do anything, but there's always something holding me back. I feel it's mentally." She thinks things over after games, maybe more than she should. "I dwell on the past a lot," she says. "I over analyze everything, every shot." The sleep Val loses at night mentally replaying games is a measure of how important her basketball career is to her.

Sometimes Val visualizes herself and her teammates on court, hitting shots and playing tough defense. She mentally sends herself positive messages. It's an approach she didn't use enough of during the first ABL season and one she plans to use more in the future. "No one can stop you, be aggressive," Val tells herself. "Confident and relaxed," is her advice from herself to herself.

Positive messages go along with high expectations for her game. After the first season, Val's self-assessment was that she hadn't yet fulfilled those. No matter that she muscled in for rebounds, blocked shots, made sharp passes to teammates, and took the ball to the basket. Val knows that especially in terms of her scoring and her ability to run the floor, she can do better than she did during her first ABL season.

Val doesn't feel satisfied with how her team, the Lasers, did either. The hardest thing about the season, as Val sees it, was "accepting being mediocre as a team . . . accepting losing."

Before the playoffs, San Jose's record was below 500. The fact that they were in second place in the Western Conference didn't satisfy Val. At Stanford, she'd been used to winning seasons. Like many other ABL players, for most of her basketball career she's gone into a game and known that she and her team would find a way to win. That wasn't always true during her season with the Lasers. "We folded in critical situations," Val says about her team. The ABL play-offs, of course, were the most critical situation of all.

In their first playoff game, the Lasers lost on their home court, in front of the San Jose fans. Val blames herself along with her team-mates for the "embarrassing" defeat. "This game I was moving in slow motion," she describes. "I think we were as a team too. Colum-bus was getting every rebound, every missed ball, . . . hitting every open shot. . . . They just out hustled us totally."

In their second playoff game, which was held in Columbus, the Lasers "started out hot," Val remembers. A little later, she describes, "We started to get blown out and then in the second half, we started coming back." Val's team fought back into the game, with Val doing her share of the fighting. But they eventually lost, 85 to 69.

The Lasers' season was over. Personally, Val felt "disappointed, relieved" and "determined to improve the next season." The sea-son, she says with justification, was a "rocky road" for her person-ally. She was up and down mentally, never felt 100 percent physi-cally, and never felt like her true self, the real Val Whiting. In fact, her description of her year has echoes of Twilight Zone episodes. "In this season, I swear," she says, "that wasn't me out there. I was possessed by somebody else."

Val's first year statistics would seem to contradict the posses-sion theory, or at least to suggest that Val is being too hard on her-self. In the first year, her rebounding was ninth best in the league, her steals eighth best, and her number of blocked shots second best. On her own team, she was tops at rebounding and shot blocking and second in steals and points. But Val's feeling that she can do better isn't surprising.

Val's expectations are high. Like many other ABL players, she's stretching herself, reaching ever higher, trying to be the best athlete she can become. And is medical school still part of her future too? Val affirms that it is, but not just yet. "Right now, Val says, "I'm just trying to reach my potential as a player,"

Linda Godby

Linda Godby was used to experiencing basketball seasons far away from her home state of Indiana. But partway through the ABL season, and much closer to home than she'd often played basket-ball, the rainy Seattle weather got to her. She considered visiting a tanning salon, to absorb some artificial rays of light, even though she knew that wouldn't be the healthiest option for her light complexion. "I was really dragging," she remembers.

It couldn't have been just the rain of course. The constant round of games, practices, and travel wore down all the ABL players to some extent. But for players on the Seattle Reign, a team named with a play on words that Seattle residents instantly understand, the incessant rain was a factor. Rain in Northwest cities like Seattle and Portland often comes down lightly but throughout the fall and winter—throughout the ABL season—many, sometimes most days will have some kind of rain. And even when it isn't actually raining, the sky is overcast. Clear days, the kind with the sun shining down in a blue sky, are a rarity. For Linda Godby, who grew up near Indianapolis and went to college in the south, the Seattle rain and cloudy skies came to feel oppressive.

Then mother nature cooperated. The sun actually made an appearance in the Seattle sky. Robin Moore, the Seattle trainer, told Linda to get outside and stay there until practice started. Linda followed Robin's advice, standing outside for about twenty minutes. Her eyes closed, she stared upward at the sun, just absorbing the warming rays with her lanky, 6'6" frame. That was exactly the medicine she needed as it turned out. She was fine with the Seattle weather after that.

Like many women in the ABL, Linda Godby is accustomed to getting accustomed. Her several seasons of basketball overseas have given her practice in making the adjustment to new places, climates, and time zones. Basketball has taken her far away from Cumberland, Indiana, a suburb of Indianapolis, where she grew up as "your typical tomboy," playing sports with her two older brothers and on school teams, reading a lot, and as a tall girl putting up with the same question over and over. "Do you play basketball?" was a familiar refrain. As if, Linda comments sarcastically, "the only use . . . for being tall is to play sports."

Actually, since Linda's long, lanky build was accompanied by athletic ability, she received her share of recruiting letters from college. She ended up choosing Auburn University, which is located close to Montgomery, Alabama and about a couple of hours' drive from Atlanta, a school which had a "family atmosphere" Linda enjoyed. At Auburn, she led a busy, basketball players' life, the climax of which was the three years her team went to the NCAA Final Four.

After college Linda moved on to very different locales and much more foreign speech. In her junior year at Auburn, she heard about former Auburn basketball players now playing overseas. After her junior year, she began receiving letters from agents and learning more about opportunities in Europe and other countries. At 6'6" tall—she played center for Auburn and plays the same position for the Seattle Reign—she was the kind of player in demand overseas.

Linda had very mixed feelings about combining basketball and foreign travel. Agents told her about possibilities, but was playing in another country something she really wanted to do? "It scared me to death to think of going overseas," Linda remembers. But she still thought seriously about the idea, and in the end she decided to give it a try. If she stayed home in Indianapolis, she decided, she'd always wonder what overseas basketball would have been like.

She ended up playing four seasons overseas—in France, Israel, Sweden, Austria, and Switzerland. France was the first country she travelled to on her basketball journey. Her new home-away-from-home was in a small city in the south of France, Aix-en-Provence. "It was a really beautiful town," Linda remembers. There were mountains to the north of the city, beautiful old churches in the city itself, a fountain in a spacious plaza on the main street.

Linda had gone to Aix-en-Provence with a common stereotype about France. "Oh, the French people, they hate Americans," she remembers thinking. That may be true some places in France—one Portland Power player's situation there justified the stereotype—but it wasn't Linda's experience in Aix-en-Provence.

The loneliness of playing overseas—the separation from family and friends—has typically been a factor for American players. In Linda's case, it helped that a university was located just down the street from where she lived, and she had a kind of connection—she knew the father of one American student there. Although the only other person not from France on her team was from Bulgaria, Linda often socialized with her teammates, who fortunately spoke English.

Another typical problem for American players overseas, as well as for foreign players in general, is that they tend to be blamed for problems on the team. It's difficult for teams to get rid of their local players, but it's comparatively easy to let a foreigner go. As it turned out, Linda's French team wasn't winning enough and so she was released. After only two months, her overseas basketball experience ended abruptly.

She had an opportunity to go to the Canary Islands, but she decided to return to the states instead and finish a last quarter of school at Auburn.

The next year she went to Israel. To Ramat Hasharon, a suburb of Tel Aviv. This time she stayed for seven months, a whole basketball season. She didn't even return home for Christmas, the holiday she'd always celebrated with her family back home in Indiana. It helped that the coach made a party for her and another foreign player, who was Catholic. The coach even got a Christmas tree, a gesture towards Christian customs he'd never made before. The coach's son dressed up as Santa Claus and handed out gifts.

There were no carols at that Israeli-style Christmas, yet the Christmas party helped Linda feel more at home. It helped change the feeling of isolation she had in the first couple of months, which she describes as "really hard" for her. "I can't stay here," she thought at the time. "It was just so hard to be away from family and friends."

Her loneliness had been intensified by the fact that back in the states her brother and his wife had recently had a baby. The baby boy was only three months old when Linda left for Israel, an age when children change so quickly. "I thought I would miss out on his little life," she remembers feeling.

Like many American players, Linda came to enjoy life in Israel. In fact, she labels it as "one of the more fun places that I stayed." She appreciated the large numbers of English speakers there. "I didn't have any problems talking to anybody," she remembers. There were movies and TV programs in English. There were the popular Israeli beaches where she could sunbathe on clean sand and swim in water that stayed warm until the end of October. And there was another benefit for Linda of life in Israel and in other locations overseas. A personal growth benefit, you could call it.

"Every time I go overseas, I ask why am I doing this," Linda comments. "Because it's so far and I feel isolated." But after a while the feeling of isolation always grew less intense. Living overseas, separated from people she already knew, helped her to overcome her shyness. "It helped me to be more outgoing," Linda feels, "because I was forced to talk to people I didn't know."

That experience of going to a new place, adjusting to a new language and culture, meeting new people, continued for Linda for two more basketball seasons. She chose not to return to Israel for a second season because it looked as if she would be able to play in Japan, which offered a shorter season and a higher salary. When the

Japanese team ended up taking a different player, Linda played for Athletes in Action, a Christian group in the states which fields athletic teams. Then Linda's personal basketball road took her overseas again, first to Sweden and then to Austria.

A scarcity of light—which had inspired Linda to think about tanning salons in Seattle—was even more of a factor in Sweden, where Linda stayed in a town called Orebro until after Thanksgiving. Sweden "was even more depressing than Seattle," Linda jokes. "I'm kidding," she adds, but there was some truth to what she said. It would get dark by three or four o'clock in the afternoon and Linda responded by sleeping more than she usually would, going into a kind of basketball expatriate semi-hibernation. Then again, there were things she did like about Sweden, which she describes as "a very pretty country." She liked Stockholm especially. And she liked the old, gray stone buildings in Orebro, and the way the Swedish landscape was transformed after a fresh snowfall, everything covered by a winter wonderland layer of white.

Halfway through the season Linda left Sweden. She wasn't injured; the cultural differences didn't suddenly implode on her; she was forced out. The team was losing, and as had previously happened to her in France, she was blamed for the team's bad fortunes. She went home to Indianapolis and enjoyed a reunion with friends and family. But the push-pull routine of leaving and returning continued when her agent found her a new team, in Oberpullendorf, Austria.

Linda doesn't mince words about Oberpullendorf. "That was the worst place I played," she says simply. The town was three hours away from Vienna, a city Linda would surely have enjoyed. Unlike the other places she'd played, there weren't any men's teams in the area. "There was nothing there," is Linda's non-chamber-of-commerce-style assessment of Oberpullendorf.

Once again she coped by sleeping a lot, piling up sleep credits on her personal time use "ledger." She didn't have many other options for ways to spend time. Her team only practiced three times a week, so team activities didn't keep her busy. The only other foreigner on the team was from Russia. Although she lived in town, she spoke no English and spent most of her time with her husband and little girl. None of Linda's other teammates even lived in the town of Oberpullendorf.

The worst part of Linda's experience in Austria was how the

team manipulated her, the same problem Val Whiting experienced in Italy, and one many other foreign players have dealt with. The team kept stringing her along. "We'll pay you next week. We're having trouble with the bank," they would tell her. By next week there would be some other "problem."

Linda didn't want to think the worst. "I'm a pretty trusting person, up to a point," she says about herself. She didn't want to be "a total ogre about it." She wanted to trust her team. But after a month of living in a hotel and having only promises for her salary, her patience and trust wore thin. She left the team and did finally receive some money, but not all of what was owed her for the effort and sweat she'd put in on the basketball court.

After living out one of the horror stories U.S. women pass along about play overseas, Linda was still willing to give the experience one more try. She travelled to Fribourg, in the French speaking part of Switzerland. Unlike Oberpullendorf in Austria, Fribourg was in a great location, near Geneva, Zurich, and Lausanne. "I'd just get on a train and go all over the place," Linda remembers.

In Switzerland Linda received a visit from her parents, as she had before in France and Israel. In February, her mother, father and older brother visited. "It was a lot of fun," Linda remembers, "We packed in a lot." Her team practiced in the evening, but "we were tourists during the day."

Even with the fun of being a tourist, Linda was rapidly tiring of life overseas. So for a little while she let her life run backwards, back to her roots in the Indianapolis area, where she found a non-basketball playing job. For a year she worked in the office of a sporting goods company, Kessler's Sporting Goods, based in Richmond, Indiana. "I was content to live a normal life for a while," Linda comments, obviously assuming that normalcy didn't include playing basketball far away from family and friends. "I really didn't miss basketball at the time," Linda recalls. "I felt my playing days were over and that was fine."

While Linda was working for the sporting goods company and living her "normal" life, some of her basketball peers, women she'd played with and against were touring the United States and the world with the U.S. National Team, lighting a fire in many people's minds for women's basketball. Perhaps one part of Linda's basketball burnout was due to the fact that like Val Whiting, she had tried and failed to become a member of that select group.

After college, and after Linda's first unsuccessful experience playing overseas, she had tried out for USA basketball, competing against other top players. She made it onto two World University Games teams, going to Sheffield, England with Tara VanDerveer one summer and playing on the same team as Katy Steding. In 1993, she played for another USA team, at the World Championship Qualifying Tournament held in Sao Paulo, Brazil, again with Tara as the coach. Another time, she was a member of a USA Select team which travelled to France and Israel.

In 1995, Linda went to Colorado Springs for the tryouts for the U.S. National Team, which would become the 1996 Olympic team. After all the players sweated through grueling workouts, and sweated the uncertainty of who would make the team, on the last morning the players went one by one into a room where USA Basketball personnel would pass on the news—good or bad.

Just like Val Whiting, Linda was one of the last four cut from the team. Linda took the disappointment somewhat more philosophically than Val, however. "You can't take it personally or you'll think you're a terrible player," Linda says. "I mean, everybody deserves to be there and everybody's a really good player. It's just who the committee wants."

Since the committee hadn't waved its magic selection wand at her, Linda was working for Kessler's Sporting Goods when she first heard about the ABL. Some of her former teammates at Auburn had been getting letters, and Linda was interested enough to call the ABL office in San Jose, which put her through to Christy Hedgpeth, who was by then officially in charge of player recruiting.

All Christy gave Linda was information, not a hard sell for the league. So it was on her own that Linda began to mull over the idea of playing for the ABL, or at least going to the tryouts. Of course, she wasn't at all sure about the idea. "What if I go through getting back in shape and paying the entry fee," she thought, "and don't get drafted?" But "you'll never know unless you try," she told herself, echoing the advice she'd given herself about going overseas.

"Massive" is one of Linda's labels for the ABL tryouts. "Pretty brutal," is another. "Everybody was playing 100 percent, all out, and we were just running up and down the floor, doing sprints while we were playing. It was going so fast, it was wearing me out."

Even with the odds stacked against her numerically, with her international experience and her Olympic team near miss, Linda had a feeling she'd be chosen. She probably was well aware that 6'6" women who are very good at playing center don't exactly grow on trees.

A week before the ABL draft, Linda received a letter from the team in Colorado. On the day of the draft, Linda was expecting to hear that her ABL future was in Denver with the Colorado Xplosion. She'd given the ABL her work number, but hour after hour passed at Kessler's Sporting Goods and still no call had come. She wasn't going to be picked after all, Linda thought. "Okay, I'm gonna be a salesman," she told herself. That was a position she could move into at the sporting goods company if she wasn't headed for a basketball future. She was disappointed, yet knew she had given the ABL try-outs her "best shot."

When she got home after work that day, her future looked different. "You're going to Seattle," her parents told her.

"Seattle?" was Linda's first reaction. It wasn't that she needed a geography lesson, but after the years she'd spent separated from friends and family, she'd been hoping for something closer to home like Atlanta or Columbus. Seattle, on the other hand, was the ABL team farthest away from Indiana. Why did she have to be picked by that team, Linda wondered.

She ended up liking Seattle as it turned out, even though the weather could sometimes get her down. She moved into an apartment near the Pike Street Market, a lively area, and found that Seattle offered many opportunities for having fun. At the beginning of the first ABL season, no longer the shy person she once was, she also liked getting to know her new teammates. Some of them were familiar to her, like Venus Lacy and Tari Philipps. Others, like Christy Hedgpeth and Kate Paye, she'd heard of or talked to but never met. The league and team front office made efforts to encourage team bonding. Together, the new teammates went to welcome receptions, and they went sailing on Lake Washington in a yacht owned by a former president of Bon Marche.

The team policy of rotating roommates in hotel rooms whenever the team travelled helped the women on the Reign get to know each other. Linda has good memories of practical jokes she and her teammates played on the road, like mimicking the movie "Scream" by calling teammates up and trying to scare them. "Do you like scary movies?" they'd ask in voices as sinister and low-pitched as they could make them. Or there was the time on a road trip when the coaches received flowers, didn't want them, and Linda, along with her roomate Christy Hedgpeth, plotted to convince Tari Phillips that the flowers were sent by a romantic admirer.

The college-style jokes helped make life fun on the team. On court for the Reign, fun and games were replaced by a high octane style of basketball which Linda loved. Aside from her experiences with USA Basketball, she had never before played with a higher level of athletes, such as teammates like Venus Lacy, who she describes as "about the most intense player I have ever played with." Venus, Linda recalls, "would make a basket and turn and make this face and shake her fists. . . . So she could really get everyone pumped up."

The Reign started out on the road—a tough way to begin a first-ever season—and lost their first two games, to Colorado and San Jose. Out of their next twelve games, however, only three were losses. The team was definitely coming together and Linda Godby's strong play helped get them there. The time she'd spent overseas had given her an international veteran's savvy. Both as a starter and coming off the bench, whatever role Coach Jacquie Hullah was using her in, Linda made a solid contribution.

Exactly what her role would be was something she was philosophical about. She started from sometime in October until about mid season, then she became a bench player, then a starter once again, and then a bench player at season's end. "it was kind of a yo-yo thing," is Linda's apt description. But she knew basketball well enough to understand that who started and who didn't wasn't as big a deal as some fans, and even some players, think it is. "It's nice to say 'Oh yeah, I'm a starter,'" she comments. "But it's not who starts, it's who finishes and does well in the game."

Linda did indeed play well in many games. In Seattle's home opener, a *Seattle Times* article describes her "floating in a jump shot." On November 21st, when the Reign played another home game, they had the singular honor of becoming the first team to beat the Columbus Quest. It was Linda Godby's twenty-foot shot towards the end of the fourth quarter which gave Seattle a lead which it never again lost.

Linda isn't the kind of player who looks like a bruiser. She has a long build, with muscles lying compactly along her bones. Her long ponytail switching back and forth as if it really were the tail of a pony, Linda runs the court with long, efficient, gazelle-like strides—

if she wasn't so tall she might look as if she belonged on a track team in an endurance event like cross country—but she's quick to find her place in the ever changing defensive and offensive patterns, quick to make a sharp pass or a soft but effective shot.

Linda saw the first ABL season as not unlike an endurance event, in more ways than one. The league, she knew, had to build a fan base and credibility. "I think it's going to take a little bit of time," she told a reporter in late November. "I know in college (Auburn) there were a lot of people who never had seen a women's game, and when they finally saw one they were hooked. It's going to take some word of mouth."

Later in the season, endurance took on another meaning for Linda Godby. She'd been pretty much injury free for much of the year, except for a sprained ankle which she classified as minor, and then on January 17th, in the same home game against Colorado in which Christy Hedgpeth tore her ACL, Linda ran hard into a Colorado player and felt the pain in her hand. It seemed like the kind of minor injury she could just shake off, one of the inevitable bangs and bruises post players especially receive with the often very physical play in the ABL. But the next day that same hand, which was her right and shooting hand, was swollen enough that she got it x-rayed. The verdict was a broken bone on the side of her hand.

"Endurance" was still the operative word to describe Linda's situation. Amazingly enough, even with a bone in her shooting hand broken, she didn't miss any games. Off the court, she wore a silicone cast that went over half of her hand. On court, the cast was too clumsy. Instead, her hand was taped up, stabilized with a combination of pads and white athletic tape which was wrapped around fingers and part way up Linda's forearm.

Playing with a broken finger was taking a risk of course. There was always the chance that the broken bone could take a hit and be damaged further. Yet in Linda's first game after sustaining the fracture, although she didn't spend a huge amount of minutes on court, she played hard when was out there. In the first quarter she made the first shot she took, a close basket. She made other shots as well, went up for rebounds, blocked a shot, and extended her long arms on defense without seeming to favor her injured hand.

The broken bone hadn't fully healed, of course, by the end of January, when the Reign were fighting to make the playoffs and played a home game against San Jose, the Reign's competitors for the second and last playoff spot. With her fingers taped together, Linda had trouble holding on to the ball sometimes. She couldn't follow through on her shot the way she normally would. "I felt like I was kind of shot putting the ball up," she remembers.

But that didn't stop Linda from going hard to the boards. Or from making the shots which tied the game, and then gave Seattle the lead. Linda had to lean a little and lunge a little to make those shots, but they went in and the Reign won the game by two points. "Godby salvaged the night with her two jumpers," is how a reporter for the *Seattle Times* described it. Thanks in part to Linda's efforts, Seattle was still in the running for a playoff spot.

And then there was the final regular-season game, season's end for the Reign, who ended up losing the last playoff position to the Lasers. The Reign won that game at home against New England, perhaps not that huge an accomplishment since the Blizzard had the second-worst record in the league. Yet the victory was a big one for Linda and her teammates. After the "rocky season" the Reign had, both players and coaches wanted to go out with a win.

Even before that final victory, Linda knew that she and her teammates were winners in many people's eyes. All season, Linda had enjoyed the public appearances ABL players were expected to make. At grade schools, boys and girls would come up to Linda. "When did you start playing?" they would ask her. "How did you practice?" Older girls might ask Linda what she had done in high school to increase her chances of getting to play in college.

The boys and girls looked up to her, Linda felt. "Not just because of my height," she jokes. She contrasts the experience of boys and girls now to her own experience growing up, unaware of top women players like Cheryl Miller, unaware until she was a junior or senior in high school that she could go on to play college basketball. When she was their age, Linda would tell the girls and boys, there weren't any women basketball players available to her as role models. There was nothing to compare to "a whole league of women."

After the last game, Seattle Reign players walked around the arena, shaking hands with people and thanking them for their support. When the fans and media people finally left Mercer Arena, and players and coaches left too, suddenly the season was over.

For Linda Godby, just as for other overseas veterans in the ABL, having American fans to express her appreciation to, and receiving the cheers of those same fans, was an important part of coming home

to play in the United States. In Linda's case, that homecoming probably helped make the ABL season seem short.

"My gosh it was over so soon," Linda remembers feeling. "I
couldn't believe that it just went by so quickly."

Two Western Conference Coaches

The coaches in the ABL's first year were also pioneers. They came from colleges all over the United States, from smaller as well as larger, more prestigous schools. Among the ABL coaches in the first year of the league, some coaches, like Lin Dunn of Portland, were old enough to have seen significant changes in women's basketball. Others, like thirty-four year old Cliffa Foster of New England, were not much older than some of their players.

Some first year head coaches and assistant coaches had impressive careers as players. First year Atlanta coach Trish Roberts won a medal at the 1976 Olympics and played for three years in the Women's Professional Basketball League. Denise Curry, first year assistant coach for San Jose, not only was a member of the 1980 Olympic team but also played for eight years in Europe. Denise was named French Player of the Decade in the 1980's, and was recently inducted into the Basketball Hall of Fame. But all the coaches shared one quality—an enthusiasm for women's professional basketball.

All the first year ABL coaches were willing to put their professional lives on the line by taking coaching jobs in a brand new league. All of them faced the challenge of trying to meld individually talented players, almost all of them new to each other, into one unified group. Injuries to players challenged these coaches too, especially with the budget-conscious ABL's limit of only ten players to a team.

But ABL coaches, taken as a group, seem to relish challenges. You could call them a unique breed, the test pilots of the coaching ranks. Two of these pioneering coaches—Jacquie Hullah, head coach of the Seattle Reign, and Lin Dunn, head coach of the Portland Power—led neighboring teams in the Pacific Northwest during the ABL's inaugural season.

Jacquie Hullah

Jacquie Hullah is a woman with a vision. She speaks articulately and passionately about women's basketball and about what the ABL means to her and to others. The ABL "empowers women," Jacquie says. It's a chance to showcase "strong, aggressive, talented, achieving women."

Jacquie emphasizes each of the adjectives as she speaks. She's obviously one of the strong, achieving women she describes. Yet she didn't have the same opportunities that girl and women athletes have today. Only forty years old, Jacquie knows from personal experience how much things have changed in recent years. Her own playing career came to an end after college because of the lack of further opportunities.

That personal experience has given Jacquie a determination that women's sports won't go back to the bad old days. "I don't think there is any question that professional women's basketball is here to stay," Jacquie asserts. "There's just no turning back the clock on this."

When Jacquie turns back the clock on her personal life story, she sees an athletic girl growing up at a time when there were far fewer possibilities for girls and women in sports. Born in 1956, Jacquie grew up on a farm outside Clinton, Wisconsin, a small town near Beloit. The fifth child in a large, active family, all Jacquie's sisters and most of her brothers played sports, but Jacquie was, she remembers, "the most athletic in my family."

She played multiple sports as a child, starting with softball when she was in first or second grade. She was about eight years old when her father put up a basketball hoop. "I fell in love with the game," Jacquie says. She could spend hours outside hitting shots and missing some, running down the ball and then shooting again.

Shooting hoops was fun, but being a female athlete in the late fifties, sixties and early seventies could be tough. As a little girl, Jacquie sat on her mother's lap and cried as she asked her mother why she hadn't been born a boy.

"Honey, why do you want to be a boy?" her mother asked.

Boys "get to do all the fun things," Jacquie's answered, no doubt echoing many other girls' feelings.

She didn't really want to be a boy, Jacquie realized eventually. She just wanted the same chances at sports that they had. She did in fact play football and kickball and other sports with local boys. As elementary school age children, the boys mostly accepted her in their games, but Jacquie still had to deal with disapproving adults.

During cold Midwestern winters, she would often put blue jeans under her dress for the bus ride to school. Jeans kept her warmer and left her freer for schoolyard sports. At school, Jacquie remembers, "the principal would call me down to his office and ask me when I was going to start acting like a little girl."

When Jacquie was in third grade, she once again ran into the athletic double standard. At lunch time that day, the boys were allowed to play basketball in the school gym. The girls, on the other hand, were just told to go outside to play. Jacquie can still see the injustice of that. "I was better than any of the boys in most of the sports," she points out, but "I still got sent outside to do jump-rope-type things."

Jacquie did have the chance to compete on teams in high school. She was a sports do-it-all, playing basketball, field hockey, volleyball, track, and tennis. But the opportunities for girls and boys still weren't the same. In Jacquie's freshman and sophomore years, girl basketball players only played six games each year while the boys had a full season. The number of games were increased to eighteen each year when Jacquie was a junior and senior, but unlike boys, girls couldn't go on to post-season play.

In high school, Jacquie had "a huge crush on the star of the boys' basketball team" so one day she invited him to play a game of horse. "I'm swishing every shot," Jacquie recalls, "and he's bricking every shot." The boy she admired never asked Jacquie out for a date. Disappointed, she learned an important lesson—girls could play sports, but they "weren't supposed to be better than the boys."

Fortunately, Jacquie didn't take that lesson to heart. In spite of all the disappointments and discouragements, she didn't give up sports. After high school, she knew that she wanted to play college basketball. She was talented enough as an athlete that she would have easily won a basketball scholarship a few years down the road. But in 1974, when Jacquie graduated from high school, there were very few athletic scholarships for women. Luckily, Jacquie was able to attend college anyway, playing for Westchester State University in Pennsylvania her first two years. She transferred to Cal State-

Fullerton in her junior year, the same year that her team went to the AIAW national championship tournament.

After college, Jacquie's playing career came to an abrupt halt. There may have been opportunities for her to play in Europe, but if so she didn't know these chances existed. And there weren't any other ways she could have gone on playing. Although Title IX had already been passed by Congress, the big changes in girls' and women's sports hadn't happened yet, and the kind of basketball teams for women that exist now by and large didn't back then. So Jacquie chose what seemed the next best thing. She enrolled in graduate school, with a major in motor learning and sports psychology. Her goal was to go into coaching.

Ironically, after a year of graduate school another playing opportunity came Jacquie's way. The Women's Basketball League had just finished its first year and Jacquie was offered a contract with the St. Louis Streak. She turned down that offer, partly because she was in the middle of her graduate school program, and partly because the style of play in the WBL didn't fit her own style.

The new league wanted its game to be similar to the men's NBA game, with plenty of isolations and one-on-one plays. But Jacquie wasn't a one-on-one player. She was a good passer, defender, and someone who could score behind a screen. She was a team player, someone who fit well into the way women's basketball was usually played.

All the reasons make sense, and yet Jacquie now sees things differently. "I regret that now," she says about turning down a contract with the WBL. Hindsight has given her a fuller vision of the chance she passed up. And she did very much want to go on playing back then. "When my college career ended," Jacquie comments, "I definitely was very frustrated, knowing that I had a whole lot of room to grow and develop and a lot of years left in me to still improve as a player."

Jacquie never had that chance. She never got to see just how far she could have developed her skills. She speaks about that matter of factly yet with an undertone of pain. When she switched to coaching, as a first year graduate assistant at Penn State, at first watching her players compete could be difficult.

There she would be on the sidelines, watching athletic young women, who weren't much younger than she was, running up and down the court, sinking jumpers, setting screens and blocking shots.

"It was hard," Jacquie says, "because I clearly didn't have playing out of my blood." It wasn't easy to "switch over and be on the other side as a coach when you knew that you still wanted to be playing."

Luckily, Jacquie loved coaching from the start. In fact, she'd thought about being a coach ever since she was in the seventh grade. She was also a realist. Coaching, she explains, "was the one avenue that you could take your love and passion for the game and continue to stay with the game in a professional way."

Jacquie coached high school girls' teams for three years. She was an assistant coach at Northwestern before moving on to a head coaching job at Dartmouth. In her nine years there, she turned around the women's basketball program. For five years in a row, her team won Ivy League championships.

When Jacquie moved on to Arizona State, she went to the Pac-10, a strong conference. She also put herself into the kind of tough situation many coaches of women's teams have faced. Jacquie and her team had been treated well at Dartmouth. But at ASU, as has been far more typical for women's sports, money was funneled into the men's sports programs rather than the women's. No TV or radio coverage for women's basketball, and little marketing money, made recruiting difficult, especially when there were schools like Stanford which did support women's programs. At ASU, Jacquie's own survey showed that her team was at the bottom of the Pac-10 in terms of money for recruiting, team travel, marketing, and even with coaches' salaries. The 20-60 record Jacquie's team had in her three seasons there undoubtedly reflected the overall lack of support more than her coaching abilities.

When the ABL began looking for coaches, Jacquie was ready for a change. She'd turned down a contract with the WBL, but no way was she going to pass up the challenge and the possibilities of the ABL. "I think there's a few times that you have the opportunity to get in on the ground level of something that's close to your heart," Jacquie says with conviction. This time around she couldn't say no. This time she was going to jump into a new league, "to be a part of helping to establish professional women's basketball."

After a year in the ABL, Jacquie Hullah is still a believer. "It's been a lot of fun," she says about her first year. She likes coaching an elite level of athletes, certainly the most talented basketball players she's ever worked with. At mid season, as one of two coaches for the West team in the ABL All-Star game, Jacquie had the chance to work with star athletes from all four Western Conference teams. Jacquie also appreciates the fact that in the ABL, players are presented purely and simply as "highly skilled women athletes." There's no expoitive emphasis on sexuality, and no concern about a player's race or sexual orientation or other non-basketball variables.

In spite of all the positives, her first year as head coach of the Reign wasn't always easy. As with all the first year coaches, she had to turn a group of individuals into a team, balancing talents and egos. She had to help some players who starred in the college game to accept limitations on what they could do in this new level of competition. Injuries, of course, were a league-wide wild card, and the Seattle Reign had its share, with the loss of Venus Lacy at the end of November, and Christy Hedgpeth in mid-January having a strong effect on the team composition and undoubtedly leading to some lost games.

The officiating was another area of concern during the league's first year. "These athletes are bigger, stronger, quicker," Jacquie explains, so officiating ABL games was an adjustment for referees. Play in the ABL was sometimes overly physical. In fact, Jacquie characterizes first year play as "way too rough." She gives as an example a Seattle game against Columbus where a player running downcourt got bodychecked and actually knocked out of bounds. No foul was called on that play, even though the incident must have resembled wrestling more than basketball. At one point in the season, coaches were disturbed enough by what they felt was overly loose officiating, something that could put players at higher risk for injuries, that they set up a conference call to discuss the situation with referees.

Still other challenges during the league's first year came precisely from the fact that the league was so new. Because of money problems, at first teams couldn't buy video equipment for taping practices and games. Rather than watching game tapes, coaches and players and other league personnel went out into the community to speak about the league. One week, for example, Jacquie had speaking engagements at two evening meetings and five lunches. All that was in addition to coping with a 40 game schedule during the ABL season, frequent travel, and several games a week.

Jacquie isn't someone who shirks responsibility, but she isn't the stiff-upper-lip type either. She's good with people, someone who laughs easily, who speaks clearly and articulately. At key moments in games, she's intense and focused as she watches from the sidelines or diagrams plays during timeouts. But as Dana Squires describes, Jacquie takes the time to make a positive comment, like "Good D!" or "Nice pass!" to a player coming back to the team bench. Jacquie is focused in team practices too, concentrating on how successfully plays are run or basketball skills are performed, but she can also loosen up and share a joke with the players.

As a coach, Jacquie describes her goal as "a partnership between the athletes and coaches." She doesn't want "a dictatorship style"; she wants "players who think." She wants her players to put into practice the concepts she teaches them so that they "use their talents to the fullest," as well as do what is needed for the good of the team.

In a *Seattle Times* article just before the start of the season, Reign players were quoted speaking positively about Jacquie. "She tries to make practices more fun," Linda Godby said. Christy Hedgpeth referred to Jacquie's style as "very professional," and added that "It's obvious that she's an educator."

Jacquie is also a strong competitor who can push her players hard. Probably all successful coaches have that core of toughness somewhere inside them. The day before an early season game in San Jose, the Reign practiced at the Leeland High School gymnasium. A newspaper account described Jacquie's sense that her team needed to be better conditioned. The practice was a tough one. After a fast break drill, players who missed layups ran suicide sprints. Players ran again at the end of practice.

As the ABL season progressed, injuries to key players forced changes in the Seattle lineup. Players weren't always happy about the positions they played or the amount of playing time they received. Team chemistry wasn't always good, and some players focused at least part of their frustrations on Jacquie.

In the middle of the season, the Reign lost seven games in a row. Then they won four straight games, including a game against Colorado, the west's hottest team. Jacquie knew what an accomplishment winning those games was, and she gave plenty of credit to her team. "I'm just very pleased with the focus the players have now," she told a reporter. "We have been through some tough times to get here."

The reporter referred to "a tenuous agreement" among players and their coach. "Tenuous" was probably an appropriate word. The tough times were far from over yet. In February the Reign lost another six straight games, and losing increased tensions. When the

Reign lost to the Lasers on February 5th, Seattle moved a game and a half behind San Jose in the race for the second and last Western Conference playoff spot. Jacquie was still thinking positively though. She saw this as a chance for the team to step up. "It's time to find out what we're made of," she told a *Seattle Times* reporter. "We need to find out if we're going to rise up to the challenge or make excuses and fold."

Unfortunately, the Reign continued to lose, four more games after the San Jose game. With the level of competition so high even in the ABL's first year, it was easy for teams to play reasonably good basketball and still not come away with wins. However, losing wasn't easy for players used to winning, and a streak of losses didn't help the team's collective mood. An *Oregonian* story mentioned the obvious disharmony between some Seattle players and their coach during Seattle's next-to-last game, played at Portland. The Reign's loss in that game ended their chance of making the playoffs.

After the game, Jacquie stood talking to media people in the narrow corridor outside the visitor's locker room. In the yellowish light, her pale complexion looked paler than usual. Standing against the wall, her shoulders still square, Jacquie seemed to be holding in feelings. She admitted to being disappointed about the outcome of the game and the end of the Reign's playoff hopes. "Losing is tough," she told a reporter a couple of days later. "We all had expectations of being in the playoffs. Despite the obstacles, the injuries, believe me, we all still expected to pull it off."

Like many ABL players, Jacquie Hullah has high expectations for herself. When she spoke to the reporter about the Reign's season overall, she made no excuses." Really, the buck stops with me," she said. "We didn't perform well during the second half of the season, and a lot of the responsibility lies with me." She was "too flexible" at times she added. She needed to set "higher standards" for her players.

But Jacquie has enough inner strength to hang tough through disappointments and team problems. They haven't changed her feelings about coaching in the league. In fact when she speaks about what the league means to her and to many others, she has a pioneer's enthusiasm.

To illustrate her dream for women's basketball, Jacquie retells a story which Cindy Fester, the media director for the Reign, told to her. After a game at the University of Washington, two little boys went out on the court and one boy picked up a ball. "I'm going to be Rhonda Smith," one of the boys said, and "you're going to be Tara Davis."

Rhonda and Tara are former University of Washington stars who both played for the Seattle Reign during the ABL's first year. Boys as well as girls, Jacquie thinks, are getting exactly the message the league founders intended. Top female basketball players, the founders saw, would make "great role models for their children, boys and girls."

Jacquie Hullah's basketball vision includes the past as well as the future, and she knows she's had some good role models herself. "I'm really grateful for the women who came before me," she says, "who gave me the opportunities that did exist" to play in college and to coach.

Coaching in the ABL is her "way of giving back," Jacquie explains. "I want to ... continue to do things," she adds, "to give the next generation of women more opportunities."

Lin Dunn

ABL coaches are definitely not wimpy people. Lin Dunn, the head coach of the Portland Power, is the kind of person whose presence is felt. During games, she often stands on the sidelines, shouting instructions to players and reactions to referees, talking with players as they come in and out of the game. In practices Lin can be sharp tongued with her comments, or she can switch to a humorous mode and leave her players laughing.

At 49, Lin may have been the oldest coach during the league's first year. She is, as she says, "one of the few coaches who allows the true color of their hair to shine through." Along with her gray hair, Lin has a personal history which reflects the dramatic turnaround in women's basketball.

Lin grew up in the south—she still has a strong Tennessee accent—playing basketball when girls and women were restricted to the half court game. She played at a time when female basketball players were often not allowed to compete against players from other schools. She started her coaching career in an era when women coaches, like girls' and women's sports, were not valued.

Sports are simply part of Lin Dunn's world. She describes herself as coming from "a sports family. A very competitive family." Lin's father had run track at Vanderbilt; her mother had played basketball in high school. Not surprisingly, both parents encouraged their children in sports. Lin's mother is "to this day a great sports fan."

Lin was the oldest of four children, but she and her brother Harry, nicknamed Bud, were especially close. "Every afternoon my brother and I were out in the backyard competing in something," Lin recalls. They played baseball, football. They threw balls hard and tackled each other. They even had their very own pole vaulting pit in the backyard.

Lin's father worked for Ralston Purina as a salesman, so the family moved around, but from Lin's third to tenth grade years, they lived in Florence, Alabama. In junior high, Lin was lucky enough—luckier than many other girls her age at the time—to encounter a good sports program. She competed on the swim team, diving team, and in gymnastics.

In basketball, girls didn't compete against other school's teams, but they still played the game. Even with the restrictive rules then used, basketball still found its place in Lin Dunn's heart. "I think that's where my love for basketball developed," Lin says now, "probably in those junior high days."

Most of Lin's high school years were spent in Dresden, a small town in west Tennessee. With a population of only about 5,000, Dresden is small enough that even today it has no stop lights, no fast food places, and not even any place to buy the nationwide newspaper, *USA Today*. But Lin has strong family roots there. Her grandparents grew up in Dresden, her mother lives there now, and Lin still considers it her "primary home."

Lin moved to Dresden and lived with her grandparents because there she'd have a chance to play high school basketball. In Alabama, high school basketball for girls was illegal at the time! In Tennessee, girls' basketball was a half court game, three on three. Roving guards and forwards hadn't come in yet. And basketball was the only sport for girls there. "It was not a time when you had a lot of sports opportunities," Lin says succinctly.

But Lin made the most of the chances she did have. "I was good, real good," Lin told a reporter about herself as a high school basketball player. "I'd never pass the ball . . . . I was a shooter. I wasn't selfish. I was just good." Her team's record backs up Lin's claim. Her team went All State. And in one high school basketball game, Lin remembers, as her team won 56-42, Lin put in 52 of those points.

Lin's sports options expanded a little at the University of Tennessee at Martin, where she studied health, physical education, recreation, and English. As a member of the volleyball, tennis, and badminton teams, Lin enjoyed competing against teams from other colleges. But basketball was a different story. There weren't any basketball teams for the women, only intramural play.

Lin remembers herself as "extremely frustrated" by the restriction on play. Even years later, an edge of the frustration comes through in her voice. Speaking of her encounters with college teachers and administrators, Lin recalls that "I probably drove those people crazy. I just couldn't understand why we couldn't have a team."

As a young woman in college, Lin's inner toughness undoubtedly came through as she made her case for competitive basketball, as she argued with teachers and administrators again and again. But like many other young women must have at the time, Lin ran into the brick wall that narrow definitions of females and sports had built.

The response Lin received was the party line for many, perhaps most, physical educators at the time. Basketball competition wasn't suitable for women. It simply wasn't acceptable. Whether spelled out or not, the message was clear. Competitive basketball crossed the line of gender boundaries; it was too unfeminine a sport for women.

Lin didn't win that battle during her four years as an undergraduate. She received her bachelors degree in 1969, her masters in physical education in 1970. In the fall of 1970, she began her first head coaching job at Austin Peay State University in Clarksville, Tennessee.

By then roving forwards and guards were being used in women's basketball. Two women on each team could actually run the whole length of the court. A year or so later, the game changed to a five on five, full court game. Just as important, women college basketball players could now compete against players from other schools. All these changes were good, but they weren't nearly enough. Women's basketball, and women's sports in general, were still in the dark ages in those pre-Title IX days.

Lin Dunn's job description reflected that. At Austin Peay, she was a busy woman. She was the head coach for women's basketball, tennis, and volleyball. She also taught eight classes in the PE Department and coached the cheerleading squad. Her salary, however, didn't reflect her impressively large list of responsibilities. Lin was paid to teach and to coach the cheerleaders, but for coaching the three women's teams she received no compensation at all. Essentially she was treated like the volunteer coach for a Little League team.

"It was a mentality of coaching a women's sport has no value," Lin summarizes. "It was also the thought that women competing in sports has no value." Lin doesn't mince words. She's been there, done that. She knows that's exactly the way things were.

A few years down the road, Lin Dunn took her stand. "Either you pay me to coach these teams," she said, "or I'm not going to do it."

The college's response was predictable. "Fine, don't do it," administrators simply said. If Lin had an attitude, that was no problem. The women's teams were turned over to a graduate assistant. After all, women's sports didn't really matter anyway.

But they mattered a lot to Lin. She moved on to a head coaching job at the University of Mississippi. There she was hired to coach only, not to teach. She coached volleyball, tennis, and basketball. From the University of Mississippi, Lin went on to the head coaching job at the University of Miami. In 1976 and 1977, the university gave its first scholarships to women basketball players.

Things gradually improved for women's basketball, but making change for the better, Lin remembers, was always a struggle. Golf, tennis, and swimming, the more "acceptable" sports, received scholarships before basketball. For women's basketball, on the other hand, Lin's experience was that "there was no budget, there was no support, there was no nothing. You were strictly on your own to figure out a way to have a team."

Lin Dunn

There was no money for basics like uniforms. Lin remembers her players using warmups that were hand me downs from the men's team. For road trips, she piled large numbers of players into her car. They scrunched long legs and large bodies together as ten or twelve people went down the road together in "one old car." On these trips, players had to use their own money and Lin chipped in money too. To save on expenses, players and coaches took bedrolls and slept on the floor in gyms.

Times were tough for women athletes and their coaches. But for a coach like Lin Dunn, there was one bright spot—the players. "They played because they loved the game," Lin recalls. "They were the joy of being a part of coaching in that era."

That joy, and her own competitive spirit, helped Lin persevere during a difficult era for women athletes. By 1987, when Lin moved on to Purdue, Title IX had had some impact. Equity for women's sports, of course, had not been achieved—not by a long shot. But things were definitely better.

In her nine seasons at Purdue, Lin built the women's program into a powerhouse for women's basketball. When she started coaching there, the Boilermakers were fifth in their conference. Under Lin's coaching, they went from fifth to first. She recruited top players and built a very successful program. They won three Big Ten championships and went to the NCAA Final Four in 1994, an event Lin commemorated as she'd promised her players, by getting a tattoo. It was a basketball-focused tattoo with a simple message: "Final Four."

Lin's success at Purdue was rewarded with more money for her program. But she still had to fight for fair treatment for herself and her program. "The battles never stopped," she remembers. "To get more money, to get more support, to get more travel money. It was always a battle."

Depending on your point of view, you could say that Lin Dunn won or lost her final battle at Purdue. Purdue didn't renew her contract at the end of the '95-96 season, with the conflict between Lin and the university basically about pay equity. Lin states her own position unequivocally: "You can only go so long with knowing that you're one of the most successful coaches in the conference and yet you're paid in the bottom."

Lin left Purdue in April of '96. She was temporarily unemployed, and back living in Dresden, Tennessee with her mother, when the first ABL season began. She'd heard about the league even before then. Steve Hams had called many top college coaches to get their input. Coaches had received press releases about the league. From Dresden, Lin contacted Steve again but their conversation was brief at that point. The ABL already had first season coaches in mind.

In some ways, that was fine with Lin. After twenty five years of Division One coaching, she was ready for a break. A time to think, to consider her options. Time moved more slowly in Dresden. Lin's family roots were there. Meanwhile, the ABL knew that she was interested in a coaching position if the league expanded in the second year or made any coaching changes.

Change did happen. After several months of conflicts with players, Greg Bruce, head coach for the Portland Power, resigned. Lin wasn't surprised to get a call from the league. On January second, she took over as head coach of the Power.

Greg Bruce, Lin's predecessor, came from a Division II program at Portland State University, where he'd been a highly successful coach for the women's team. But as a new ABL coach, Lin had several advantages over Greg. The most obvious one was that she was a woman. In spite of Brian Agler's success with the Columbus Quest, some people saw it as a point of pride that ABL teams have women coaches.

Aside from the gender issue, and probably much more important, Lin came from a nationally recognized Division One program at Purdue. She'd been the assistant coach for the 1992 women's Olympic basketball team. Over a twelve-year period the teams she'd helped coach included a world championship team and a team which competed at the Pan Am games. Both from the college game and through USA Basketball, Lin was already familiar with many of the ABL players. She had credibility with the players, an intangible but important asset that some first-year ABL coaches have lacked.

Even with all these positives, coming in mid-season was hardly an ideal situation. True, players and fans were supportive. But Lin knew that the welcome she received wasn't without strings attached. Everyone hoped that the Portland Power, who were last in the league, would start to win more games. Lin wanted that too of course. However, time to put in her own offensive and defensive system was a luxury that she simply didn't have. "You can't stop the season," she comments dryly, "and say, hey, I need three weeks to practice."

Tough situations, though, have never intimidated Lin Dunn. She simply isn't the type to back down from a challenge. "Give up" may not be a phrase in her active vocabulary. When she took hold of the coaching reins of the Portland Power, Lin provided strong leadership right away.

The first and most important change she made was to get all the Power players behind their new coach. She inspired laughter in her players during their first team meeting. Players worked hard at their first practice with Lin, even though it was on a game day and just a shootaround would have been more typical. After practice, players who spoke to a reporter quoted Lin as saying things like "we can't be throwing the ball away like a bunch of rabbits." And for her post players, Lin offered equally memorable advice: hold your position "like there's people buried there."

When Lin Dunn was introduced as head coach of the Power, TV cameras and spotlights were focused on her. Fans at Memorial Coliseum cheered, clapped, and actually came to their feet to express their enthusiasm for the new coach. "I'll always remember that first game," Lin comments, "because it was such a high emotion."

The Power players hit the floor with what seemed like a surge of fresh energy. They played like inspired women and they won their new coach's first game against Richmond, 79-63. More wins followed, although not every game went the way Lin would have liked.

Lin brought her own intensity to team practices. "Great play!" or "Nice shot!" she would shout to players. She was quick to point out the negatives too, and ordered players who messed up in practice to do five pushups before they continued with whatever offensive or defensive patterns were being run.

In games as well as practices, Lin tinkered with the Power lineup and strategy, as much as she could during the fast-paced ABL season. She played two fast guards, Falisha Wright and Coquese Washington, at the point guard position. She took the bold step—in a city where Katy Steding, the recent Olympian, was one of the team heroines—of changing Katy from a starter to a bench player. More and more, Lin managed to get the Power, a team which had suffered through chemistry problems, to play together.

Lin remembers a game against Seattle when Mercer Arena was packed with fans. The Power won that game by one point in overtime, and the win meant a lot to Lin. It showed something important about her team. "It was an indication that we had become mentally tougher," she comments, "because we had every opportunity to give up or lose that game and we really showed a tremendous amount of tenacity." You might say that the Power players were mirroring their coach's attitude.

Lin's goal had been to have a winning record from when she started as coach and to see her team go to the playoffs. Even though she didn't quite reach that goal, Lin describes the last game of the season as another high point for herself and her team. The Power was already eliminated from contention for the playoffs. "Yet we were still playing like there was hope," Lin recalls. "We were still playing to get better." The Power played focused, team-oriented basketball and won the last game of their first ABL season.

Lin Dunn plans to coach many more ABL games. "Good lord willing, the creek don't rise, I'll be here."

The uncertainties of life for ABL coaches don't seem to bother Lin. About coaching changes, she simply states that winning coaches will stay and losing coaches go. "You just never know. Always keep your resume ready," she says, a hint of irony in her voice.

But Lin is obviously not busy revising her own resume. She's got some important business on her coaching agenda, drafting the best players she can get to help build up her team. New players, of course, mean some first year players will not return. Lin sees that as simply part of the reality of pro sports. Lin certainly knows how competitive the American Basketball League is and will continue to be. Yet her goal for her team's second year is an ambitious one—"to go from last to first."

Lin Dunn's office for much of the Portland Power's first year is small and windowless. It can easily seem constricting, too small a starting place for Lin's big dreams. But the cramped quarters which are all a start up league can afford don't seem to deter Lin Dunn. She speaks glowingly about the challenge of coaching elite athletes in the game she loves.

"Basketball," Lin describes, "is like a game of chess and Monopoly and Trivial Pursuit all wrapped up into one."

A quick smile crosses Lin's face. "Throw in a little Jeopardy."

Home at Last

The life stories of so many ABL players have included playing in foreign places that the experience seems almost defining for a woman professional basketball player.

Although the two new women's leagues would seem to be changing that, many of the greatest players of the game have been shaped by their experiences in faraway places. Stacey Ford, of the Power, and Adrienne Goodson, of the Rage, are two of the numerous players who have come home at last.

Stacey Ford

Stacey Ford grew up in Anderson, South Carolina, a mid-sized town near the border of South Carolina and Georgia, but basketball gave her a chance to travel, to move beyond her home town. It all started with the basketball camps she went to in high school and continued through her years after college. After playing collegiate basketball at the University of Georgia, she made a personal study, you could say, of the pluses and minuses of basketball overseas. Through it all, she's never lost her South Carolina accent, the strong religious faith she was raised with, and her sense that at heart she's a southern girl.

Stacey is a tall woman—6'2", a post player's height—with long graceful hands that help emphasize her point when she speaks, skin colored a rich, deep brown, and a friendly, straightforward manner. She's someone with a lot to say about the many places basketball has taken her.

In Anderson, South Carolina, where Stacey Ford began her basketball journey, college recruiters were practically beating down her door. All the attention early in Stacey's high school years was fun at first. But the fun changed to something she describes succinctly as a "nightmare." What was so unpleasant about her experience with recruiters? Practically everything, it sounds like. "The lies, the deceit, the phone calls," Stacey recalls. "It was horrible."

Recruiters would come to Stacey's high school games, which she didn't mind, but they also appeared at her school during the day. They would talk to influential people in Stacey's home town or friends and acquaintances who would then call up Stacey to pass on messages from recruiters. The recruiters also called Stacey at home. The phone calls alone became so bothersome that when a college or a recruiter called, Stacey would whisper to her mother. "I'm not here. I don't want to talk to anybody." But Stacey knew her mother would never lie, so Stacey began to adopt another strategy. "When the phone would ring, I would just dash out the door," Stacey recalls. That way her mother could truthfully say that her daughter wasn't home.

Stacey's mother has been a strong influence on her daughter. Among other things, Stacey describes her mother as someone who is a "no holds barred . . . all or nothing person" about the religious convictions which mother and daughter share. She and her mother are fairly close, even though basketball has often separated them geographically. Stacey obviously respects her mother's strength, and the way she's made the most of fairly limited opportunities. Her mother grew up in the south, working in the fields and often missing school to do so. She was intelligent enough to come back to school and make all A's after a month away, but because her father kept her away from high school so much of the time, she wasn't able to graduate.

While Stacey and her siblings were growing up, her mother worked in a factory, then became a nurse's aide, a job she had to return to school to train for. She later received her G.E.D., an accomplishment of which both Stacey and her mother are proud. She tells her mother, "If you had the opportunities to go to school, . . . then you could have been a doctor." Stacey has a clear sense of how limited her mother's chances in life were. "I just hated that," Stacey says emphatically. "The way her life went, and the things that didn't happen, and the opportunities that weren't there for her."

Basketball gave Stacey far more opportunities. After all the hassles with recruiting, Stacey picked the University of Georgia, a college with a strong basketball program which Stacey describes as "close to home and . . . far enough away from home." Playing for the Lady Bulldogs, Stacey adjusted to play in the strong Southeastern Conference and to the "all out screaming" style of coach, Andy Landers, who sometimes got on Stacey's case extra hard because he saw her potential as a player. In 1991, the Lady Bulldogs won the SEC Championship and went to the NCAA Final Eight, and Stacey herself picked up plenty of individual honors, including being named as a Kodak honorable mention All-American and the All-Southeastern Conference player.

After college, Stacey began a basketball journey that would take her to five different countries. Her first stop on this basketball tour was Japan, where she lived and played in Kawasaki City, which was 25 minutes by train from Tokyo. Fujitsu, the company which owned the team, had seen both Stacey and another University of Georgia basketball alumna play and recruited both of them for the team. The two women shared an apartment in Japan, which helped them cope with the loneliness they felt overseas. The company paid for them both to take private Japanese lessons from an older woman who took her students on excursions to see Buddhist statues and explained the history and culture of Japan as part of her language instruction.

Stacey's Japanese teammates were another good part of Japan for her. "They were so helpful," she remembers. "Anything you asked they would do in a heartbeat." One time she mentioned that she liked a certain kind of food. The very next day a teammate was knocking on her apartment door, offering to cook the dish for her. If she tried to take off her sweats in the middle of practice, someone would be sure to help her pull them off.

Japanese coaches have the reputation for being abusive, for punching or kicking or slapping players, and Stacey did witness players being kicked or spit on while she was in Japan. But although her own coach was "extremely tough," he wasn't abusive. He did demand a lot from all the players, though, and the practices were routinely three hours long. Additionally, there was always the pressure on a foreign player to be the go-to person for the team.

There was also the pressure of getting used to a different culture, and in Japan part of that was the expectation that co-workers would socialize and drink together. Fujitsu would make a party, for example, and it was expected that players and coach would sit together and drink—whiskey, beer or other alcoholic beverages. "Come on, come on, drink with us," her teammates and her coach would urge Stacey. It was an eye opener to her that young women would do such heavy drinking.

Initially, Stacey had seen the fact that Fujitsu required her to work in their office as a benefit too. "When you stop playing," Fujitsu had told Stacey, "We'll give you a job in one of our locations in the states." That was a big part of why she had decided to try basketball in Japan, seeing it as a job training opportunity for herself. In fact, however, the company didn't provide her enough meaningful work. Sometimes Stacey could perform small tasks like checking the English on company brochures. On many other occasions, she would sit around the office with nothing special to do.

"You're paying me to play basketball," Stacey protested to the company. "If I was doing something more important in this office, I would have no problem with it. I can't just sit here and not do much of anything." The company wouldn't change its policy, however, and so Stacey opted not to return to Japan the following year.

The next season an agent found Stacey a spot on a team in Bourges, a small town in France about two and a half hours from Paris. It proved to be a tumultous year which Stacey sums up as a "negative experience." The team had money, and salaries were good. But there was hardly anything to do in the town. Stacey and another American woman on the team were extremely homesick, a situation which was exacerbated by the fact that the assistant coach hated Americans. "You Americans," he'd complain. Americans "didn't know anything," the coach would say. All Americans "eat at McDonald's" and "have no culture." American women, he told strong, beautiful, fit athletes like Stacey and her American teammate, are fat and definitely not beautiful.

That season in France was Stacey's worst experience overseas. "Sometimes we would come to practice and just cry," Stacey recalls about herself and the other American woman. "We wanted to go home so bad."

Although she did want to return home and stay in the United States, Stacey wanted to play basketball even more strongly. She returned to Europe the next season, travelling to Sodrtalje, Sweden, which is located only twenty minutes from Stockholm. Luckily, Stacey's experience was much more positive there. "I had too much fun," Stacey says, laughing, to describe her Swedish experience.

When her Swedish team decided to let go of their foreign player, Stacey moved on to Viterbo, Italy, which she also referred to as Viterrible because there was so little to do in the town. However, since Stacey had a car, she was able to spend quite a bit of time in Rome, which she describes as the "most beautiful city in the world."

Since her Italian team moved down to a lower division, Stacey made one more geographical move, going to Israel for her last season of basketball overseas. As has been true for many other American players, Stacey loved Israel. She appreciated the fact that so many people spoke English, that there were English movies available, and many other Americans playing there, including some American men who had become Israeli citizens.

While Stacey was in Israel, she experienced a life-changing event of the non-basketball variety, although there was a kind of basketball connection to that event. Stacey's father, who had left her mother when Stacey was an infant, had heard about his daughter's basketball career, called the University of Georgia to inquire about her, and later contacted Stacey's mother. It was in Israel that Stacey received the phone call from her mother, letting Stacey know that her father wanted to speak to her. Her mother gave Stacey her father's telephone number and simply said that it was up to Stacey whether or not she wanted to make contact with her father.

Stacey had to think things over. Growing up, she had resented the fact that her father wasn't there for her, sometimes wished for his presence even though she'd never known him. She'd had difficulties in her relationship with her stepfather, blaming him for the fact that he wasn't her real father. But she was 27 years old now, grown past those childhood times.

She called her father from Israel. He was apologetic; she was forgiving. "We just forgot the past," is how Stacey sums up the relationship she and her father created. When she was back in the states, she went to see her father, and met his wife and her father's two children, her half brothers and sisters. Stacey's small degree of fame as a basketball player had enlarged her family circle.

Basketball had already enlarged Stacey's world in many other ways. By now an experienced foreign traveler, she felt comfortable enough in Israel that she was ready to play another season there. But her plans began to change when two other former players from the University of Georgia, women who were playing professionally in Israel, told her about the ABL.

Stacey was interested but unsure what to do. She called her agent, who gave her the contact number for the ABL, and she called the league office in Palo Alto. By then it was close to the deadline for getting applications in for the tryouts. But Christy Hedgpeth, who had already helped out many other women, helped Stacey as well. "I know you," Christy said to Stacey. "I played against you my freshman year at Stanford. You're a good player." Instead of the old boys' club, it was the young woman's network in action. Christy faxed and Federal Expressed the relevant forms and information out to Stacey so she could get her application in on time.

Not surprisingly, Stacey's agent was far less encouraging than Christy Hedgpeth. Stacey's agent basically took a hands off attitude to the ABL tryouts. "If you want to do it, fine," he said. "If you've got two hundred dollars to bounce around and you're not going to miss it." He wasn't optimistic about the new league. Regarding the ABL tryouts, Stacey's agent left her with one piece of advice: "Just don't sign anything when you get there."

Stacey did go to the tryouts and felt she did well there. That good performance landed her in the draft pool, and Portland drafted her in the sixth round. Stacey was pleased, but still unsure about signing on with the ABL. "I was iffy," she recalls. Before she committed herself to the ABL, she again contacted her agent. "What kind of offers do you have for me right now?" she asked him. If he had something good lined up for her, maybe she'd go with that instead of the ABL. Her agent had previously told her he could find her overseas positions with very good money, but this time he didn't mention any overseas options.

Stacey knew that many players shared her fears about the ABL. A friend of hers, LeJuana "Lady" Hardmon, who had also been drafted by Portland, decided not to sign with the Power. "It's not going to work," was the most often expressed sentiment by the doubting players, who opted instead to go back overseas and wait for the WNBA. Stacey wasn't sure about the ABL either, yet an emotion many other American basketball expatriates have felt tilted her personal balance towards the new league. "It has to work," she told herself about the ABL. "I don't want to go back overseas."

Stacey still had some reservations though. When she talked to Portland head coach Greg Bruce, she complained about the ABL not providing moving expenses. After all, she had to move herself and her possessions all the way across the country, from South Carolina to Oregon. And even beyond the moving expenses, she wanted to be sure that if she joined the ABL, and the new league folded, she wouldn't end up holding the bag for at least part of her salary, as many American players have ended up doing overseas. "You guys have got to reassure me that the money's going to be there," she told Greg Bruce. She was a professional basketball player after all. Basketball wasn't just a hobby; it was how she made her living.

Greg suggested that she talk to Steve Hams. When she did just that, Steve convinced her that the ABL wasn't going to treat its players shabbily. "We have the money for this year," Steve reassured her. Even if the league didn't continue after the first year, Stacey would definitely get her salary. At that point Stacey was sold. The ABL offered her a two-year contract and she probably would have agreed to it except for the advice of her agent. "Take it one year at a time," her agent said, so Stacey signed on for a year with the ABL.

Keeping the mental escape clause of playing in the WNBA afterwards if the ABL folded, Stacey headed for the Portland Power training camp. In spite of her reservations about the league, Stacey quickly felt glad to be in camp. Getting used to new teammates was no problem for her after all the different places basketball had taken her to. "I was used to getting used to," she comments. Being coached by Americans felt good after being in Europe so long. And joining a team where all the players were talented, instead of being one of two foreign players on a European team who were basically expected to do it all, was something that Stacey really appreciated. In fact, the whole experience was a kind of homecoming for her. "It was exciting," she says, "because I was going to play with Americans now."

Of course, playing in the ABL was more of a challenging than a relaxing homecoming. Stacey had to get used to some new roles on court, such as playing the high post position and getting the ball to teammate Natalie Williams in the low post. At first Stacey felt uncomfortable in her new role; then she began to really enjoy playing with a teammate she describes in glowing terms as "a strong player, a tremendous player."

Her new teammates were equally appreciative of Stacey. "You have great moves," teammates said to her. But Stacey herself sometimes felt disappointed with her play. In the season opener, she came out too slow, she felt, was too nervous and didn't get into the game quickly enough. It helped that her coach told her she had done well when it counted, such as by making some three-point plays at the end of the game.

"I put too much pressure on myself," Stacey comments. "Hey, great game!" her teammates might say to her. But Stacey's self-evaluation was more critical. "I sit and I would think about everything that I should have done better," Stacey comments. There were shots she could have made. Defensive positions she could have improved on. Did her teammates have enough confidence in her, she would sometimes wonder. As one of the veteran players on the team, she felt a special obligation to do well.

Perhaps most ABL players went through that kind of thinking at times, especially because the level of talent and competition in the league was so high. For Stacey and her teammates, the losing streak they endured made for some especially challenging times. "I think we got to a point where we just went out there to play," Stacey recalls. "We didn't play to win. We played to lose because we were so used to losing." Yet the Portland fans stayed supportive, which helped the players' mood, and the players still stuck together as a team on and off the court. "We weren't like the Brady Bunch," Stacey comments, "but we got along pretty good."

Sticking together helped players cope with the extensive travelling which was one of the challenges of the season, and which could leave players drained both physically and emotionally. This wasn't the NBA after all. There weren't any luxurious private jets and travelling schedules planned for the players' convenience. "It seemed like we always had to get up early for the next flight," Stacey remembers. But she and her teammates coped, giving themselves pep talks to keep going. "You're okay. You're not tired. It's all in the head," players would say to themselves.

Something that wasn't in players' heads, according to Stacey, was any racial tensions. Race, she thinks, is "irrelevant" to players' relationships with each other. In her view, that's been true throughout her basketball career. "One of my best friends in college, she's a white girl," Stacey jokes, laughing at the reversal of the usual statement.

The players' example, their role modeling of a mini-society where individual differences like race and sexual orientation and ethnic backgrounds by and large didn't matter, is one especially appealing aspect of the life in the league. For many other reasons as well, Stacey and other ABL players made a lot of friends during the first season. With individual players like Stacey Ford trying so hard to do their best, with their best being so good, and with players demonstrating team play and mutual support, instead of the self-serving actions some male athletes get into, it's not surprising that many people look up to the women of the ABL and want more contact with them than just sitting and watching from the stands during a game.

Like most ABL players, Stacey cooperated by doing her share of public appearances, in schools and other locations. That made for one more responsibility in an already full schedule, yet the public appearances were something she was glad to do, especially speaking to children. She tried to be honest with them, telling them about mistakes she's made as well as successes she's had. She feels a sense of her responsibility to the children. "You have to be positive with these kids," she says. "Not fake it, but be a good role model, because you are a role model."

Stacey Ford

The ABL has brought many American players home to their own country, and in Portland, Oregon, where the Power have drawn sizeable crowds to home games, people sometimes recognize Stacey around town. They say hello to her or ask her for her autograph. Stacey is willing to oblige and finds being recognized "a good feeling," yet it still takes her somewhat by surprise. Sometimes she wonders why people even want her autograph.

Like many other ABL players, Stacey is light years away from having a superstar complex. In spite of all her basketball accomplishments, she remains an approachable, non-egotistical person. Even after all the places basketball has taken her, the way she sees herself is still simple: "I'm just Stacey Ford," she says. "From Anderson, South Carolina."

Adrienne Goodson

For Adrienne Goodson, her first year of the ABL was one long homecoming. "It felt good," she says. "Just the opportunity to be home and playing in front of so many friends and family that didn't have the opportunity to watch me play because I was playing down in Brazil for five years."

There were times when that renewed closeness, with family for example, could rub a little. Adrienne describes herself as "very, very close" with her mother, but Adrienne did have some reservations about her mother and stepfather's plans to just drop in at Adrienne's apartment in Richmond. "You could give me the key," her mother would say. Adrienne's response was to remind her mother about her sometimes crazy ABL schedule. "Ma, I'm going to come in on the red eye late at night," Adrienne pointed out. "The first thing I want to see is my bed. It's not you and Dad and the dog."

But playing basketball in the United States felt wonderful. And part of Adrienne's good feeling was the change she saw in women's basketball. In 1991, the year she left for Brazil, women's basketball didn't draw nearly as much attention in the United States. After five seasons of basketball in Brazil, Adrienne found the change in women's basketball back home to be "phenomenal." "People had actually started to take women's basketball seriously and consider it a sport."

Actually, why anyone would doubt that women's basketball is worth taking seriously is something to wonder about. Especially when there are exciting players like Adrienne Goodson to watch. Adrienne is a versatile, very athletic player who can drive to the basket, grab more than her fair share of rebounds, fire off a pass to a teammate, and put both jumpers and close shots in the hoop. Her expressive face reflects the ups and downs of a basketball game. A youthful-looking grin often spreads across her face if she makes a tough shot or earns a trip to the free throw line. Adrienne plays with an intensity, a competitive fire, that coupled with her natural athletic gifts and the hard work she's put into her sport, have made her one of the top players in the ABL.

Adrienne's years of preparation for the role she's playing now started when she was growing up in Bayonne, New Jersey. She was in seventh grade, and moping around the house after being grounded by her mother, when her mother told her to go watch basketball on TV. That was when Adrienne saw her first women's basketball game on television, the championship game between Old Dominion and the University of Tennessee. That was the first time she had a chance to watch stars of the women's game like Nancy Lieberman. And it was in fact the first nationally televised collegiate women's championship game.

Unfortunately, the chance to watch top women players wasn't a typical experience either for Adrienne or for many other girls at the time. As Adrienne told a reporter from the *Richmond Times-Dispatch*, she didn't grow up with female athletes as role models. "Basically I had to pave my own road," Adrienne said. "You never heard about women's basketball then, which meant I had no female role models—no one I could look up to. The players I liked were all male."

Adrienne persisted, though, in spite of plenty of negative feedback and comments on the order of girls don't belong on a basketball court; girls can't play basketball. For all those skeptics, Adrienne had a snappy comeback. "If it's impossible, how come I'm doing it already?"

The pavement Adrienne pounded, the blacktop or cement basketball courts found in parks and playgrounds, has shaped her into the kind of player she is today. She shares a city style with other players from the New York-New Jersey area, Adrienne feels. "We all like to make the nice move and take it all the way to the basket," Adrienne commented to the *Richmond Times-Dispatch* reporter. "That's what you learn when you grow up playing pick-up games with the guys on the playgrounds. That's the mark of a city player."

Adrienne played sports in a more organized fashion as well on girls' teams in the Police Athletic League. From age of seven or eight, she competed on basketball, softball, and volleyball teams, and also ran track. Her high-scoring and high-rebounding ways at Bayonne High School led to her recognition as an All-American and a *USA Today* "Top 50" player, among other honors. Adrienne's high school even retired her jersey, making her the first girl they'd honored in that fashion.

Adrienne's collegiate basketball career was similarly stellar. In her freshman year at Old Dominion, the college she'd watched on television as a girl, her team won a national championship. It was an experience she'll never forget. "I was a baby. I was 17 years old, "Adrienne describes, "and we won the championship, we were the best in the country. We got to meet the President of the United States."

Adrienne characterizes winning the championship as a "highlight and a turning point in my life." She is quick to describe as well the way in which her coach at Old Dominion, Marianne Stanley, has shaped her as a player. "My whole personality and my whole attitude on the court is Marianne Stanley," Adrienne feels. Her college coach taught her to strive for excellence, to work hard in the off season, to practice hard and to concentrate on building her game.

Throughout her college career, Adrienne showed that she was taking her coach's advice to heart. The individual honors she earned, such as her recognition as the Sun Belt Conference Player of the Year in 1987-88, and her selection as a Kodak All-American in 1988, only confirmed her basketball achievements. After completing her four years of eligibility for college basketball, and before finishing her marketing degree in 1989, she received a small preview of basketball overseas by playing briefly in Germany. But she didn't like the climate or what she perceived as the coldness of the German people, so after playing for most of a season there, she left Germany. Adrienne returned to Old Dominion to finish her degree, then took a job as Assistant Manager for a Walmart in Arizona.

It's hard to imagine such a talented young athlete holding down an ordinary job where her strong, flashy, take-it-to-the-hoop moves meant nothing. Luckily, Adrienne's former coach at Old Dominion, Marianne Stanley, who had moved on to the University of Southern California, helped liberate Adrienne from a non-basketball-oriented future. Adrienne told Marianne that she wanted to play more basketball and Marianne, in her capacity as assistant coach for the USA Basketball World Championship Team which travelled to Brazil in 1990, made friends with the coach of the Brazilian National Team. The Brazilian coach needed a player for a team back in Brazil, Marianne called Adrienne, and Adrienne was on her way to Brazil.

During her five seasons there, Adrienne played in several cities in the state of Sao Paulo—for teams in Piracicaba, and Aracatuba, and Campinas, and Paulinia. The exotic sounding names became familiar to Adrienne, just as the Portugese language did. She taught herself to read, write, and speak the language fluently using Berlitz language tapes. Just as Portugese began to flow easily from her tongue, Brazil itself began to flow for her, to seem more like a second home than a foreign country.

Every summer Adrienne would leave for Brazil and every February she would return to the U.S. Not only did Adrienne always receive her pay, which wasn't necessarily true for American players in Europe, but the basketball competition in Brazil was excellent. Adrienne played with and against some world renowned players, including most of the members of the Brazilian National Team. She played on the South American Championship team in 1992, and the Inter South American championship team in 1993. And she kept busy. During each six month period, Adrienne and her Brazilian teammates would play something like 75 games, which made for a very full schedule. But Adrienne loved the competition and felt she was growing as a player.

Aside from basketball, Adrienne simply enjoyed being in Brazil. She loved the food, for one thing. A type of beef called picanha, she remembers, "was the best beef I ever ate in my life." The vegetables, prepared without preservatives, were fresh tasting. In Piracicaba, the city where she spent her first year, Adrienne would go out to dinner with teammates, or sit at one of the outdoor cafes or bars by a river, such as the barbeque places called churrascaria's where skewers of cooked chicken, beef, fish, and pork would be brought by the tables. Or she and friends would go shopping at The Center, an outdoors market where vendors sold leatherwork, bracelets, and other goods.

The Brazilian people, Adrienne found, were warm and accepting of foreigners. "They basically rolled out the red carpet for me when I was down there," she says. "I met a lot of good friends. I still have a lot of people that I keep in contact with as of today."

Part of that red carpet was written into Adrienne's contracts. She wanted to live the way she would in the United States, she told the teams she played for. In Brazil, she lived in furnished apartments with a television, a VCR, and she received a generous food allotment.

Even with all the good aspects of life in Brazil, living there could be alienating at times. Adrienne missed her family, and as has been typical for American players overseas, she racked up high phone bills. Everyone in her family, she remembers, had signed up for an international plan with their telephone service. Aside from the separation from family members, there were other things that told Adrienne she was far from home. There was the fact that she was the best American player in Brazil, yet the teams typically promoted their Brazilian players rather than her. Shoe companies like Nike and Reebok used the same approach, primarily marketing Brazilian athletes. But overall, Brazil was a positive experience for Adrienne. And even if it hadn't been, Brazil or some other foreign country was Adrienne's only choice if she wanted to keep on playing basketball. "That was my career," she says. "That was what I chose to do and what I wanted to continue to do."

Then Adrienne's choices expanded. During her last season in Brazil, when she played in Paulinia, an American player named Val Whiting joined Adrienne's team. It was through Val that Adrienne heard about the ABL. Val gave Adrienne a packet of information about the league—a financial summary, a projection of the number of ABL teams, etc. Adrienne was interested, but the information about the ABL stayed in her closet while she was in Brazil. It didn't seem as if she could do anything about that while she was so far away.

When Adrienne left Paulinia at the end of the season, her team wanted her to return to Brazil in May, but Adrienne wasn't sure she wanted to do that. Instead, she called the ABL number given in her information packet and reached Christy Hedgpeth. "I know it's late," Adrienne said to Christy. The deadline for submitting applications for the ABL tryouts was already a week past. "But I would really like to come and try out."

Christy was her usual helpful self. Her friendly, flexible approach surely smoothed the way for many women interested in the league and probably encouraged many women to think positively about the ABL. "Great. Come on, try out," Christy encouraged Adrienne.

The ABL immediately recognized what an excellent player Adrienne Goodson was. The Richmond Rage had two premiere players already assigned to them, the 1996 Olympians Dawn Staley and Lisa Leslie. But Adrienne was the first player the team picked after that in the ABL draft, and unlike Lisa Leslie, who ended up not signing with the league, Adrienne went ahead and signed her contract. It was partly that a lawyer she hired to look over her contract thought it was an okay deal, that she would at least get paid for the first year. But the main reason Adrienne decided to go for the league had nothing to do with financial security.

"I just wanted to stay home," she says simply. "I had been gone from the United States for a long time, and for a long time I've known that I've been one of the best players in the United States, but it was like, nobody knew that about me."

It's a statement that reflects the hard choices American women basketball players have faced. They could compete overseas, and be recognized there as professional players, but they would be mostly forgotten at home. Now those veterans of international basketball were coming home. The ABL reunited Adrienne with American women she'd played with or against in college, or for USA Basketball, or overseas. Aside from Val Whiting, Adrienne had played with Edna Campbell in Brazil. Tonya Edwards had competed against Old Dominion when she played for the University of Tennessee. Taj McWilliams, Adrienne's teammate in Richmond, had previously been on a U.S. National team with Adrienne. And there were many other women as well.

Adrienne was also reunited with Marta Sobral, a Brazilian player and member of the 1996 Brazilian Olympic team whom Adrienne had recruited to come play in the ABL. Adrienne was glad to have Marta as a teammate on the Rage, yet that situation also forced Adrienne into a dual role on the team. She couldn't just play basketball. She had to function as a translator for Marta as well. In timeouts, Adrienne would listen to the flow of English and then translate to Portugese for Marta. Out on the floor, Adrienne would often shout instructions to Marta in Portugese, which left Adrienne as a kind of on-the-court coach for Marta as well, because Adrienne had to stay aware of whether Marta was doing whatever the team wanted her to. It was a situation which took away some of Adrienne's concentration on her own game.

Making the change to professional basketball in the United States presented other difficulties. For one thing, there were some differences in the way the game was played. In Brazil, for example, referees wouldn't touch the ball as much so the game moved more quickly. And Adrienne also found it difficult to get used to being around all the different personalities on her team. Somehow, the fact that she was back within her own culture made the team togetherness feel more intense. With all those changes, it took Adrienne a while to really get into the flow of her game. It was the second part of the season she feels when she played her best basketball.

That may have been true of a number of players in the ABL. In fact, during the league's first year, Adrienne thinks, everyone experienced an extra high amount of stress. Players wanted to be successful personally. Players, coaches, and other league personnel all wanted the league to make it. "Everybody was just kind of like really tense there for a minute," Adrienne recalls.

Adrienne's performance on the basketball court, however, showed that she didn't let all the varied pressures interfere with her play. Game accounts from the *Richmond Times-Dispatch* confirm how important Adrienne was to her team. In a mid-November game against the New England Blizzard, Adrienne had a starring role in the nail-biter ending. With only a second remaining in the game, and no time to get her feet set under her, Adrienne took a shot from the foul line and made the winning basket. Another article, about a game on November 22nd, describes the way Adrienne "scored 18 points and created one big play after another in the fourth period." The similar headlines of other articles reinforce the theme of Adrienne's strong play: "Goodson leads Rage over San Jose 83-69" and "Goodson leads Rage past Glory." The last headline referred to a game against Atlanta in which Adrienne scored 24 points and grabbed 10 rebounds.

The stories in the *Times-Dispatch* include an account which shows Adrienne's toughness and heart. At the end of November, in a game against New England, Adrienne played 26 minutes, a more limited number than usual but still a substantial amount of time on court. She put in 19 points, an impressive number considering the fact that she was playing while sick. In the fourth quarter, the article describes, Adrienne "became dizzy and dehydrated," and had to sit out the rest of the game, a rest which was well deserved. Even though she was sick, Adrienne had sucked it up, as basketball players say. She'd stayed in the game and done the best she could.

The statistics sportswriters keep don't reveal that kind of commitment, the inner drive that keeps a player going, yet Adrienne's stats certainly testify to her strong play. During the regular season, she ended up averaging 17.3 points, the fifth highest in the ABL, and 8 rebounds per game. In the playoffs her averages went up further. Her shooting percentage was an impressive 51.6 percent, as she put in an average of 18.7 points, grabbed 9.9 rebounds, and handed out 3.3 assists.

Adrienne's excellent play landed her on the All-ABL first team late in the season. At mid-season she received another honor, this one more than purely symbolic. Not surprisingly, she was one of the Richmond players named to the All-Star team. It was an experience which Adrienne thoroughly enjoyed. Aside from the game, the league had social events for players; Reebok made a party and provided a room where players could hang out; the Women's Sports Foundation was there. Adrienne enjoyed the chance to get to know other top players and "celebrate being an All Star."

For the game itself, of course, players didn't really know each others' moves; teams had only had two days to prepare. Yet Adrienne still appreciated having "all of that talent on the floor. We actually needed ten balls or eleven balls," she comments, "because everybody was really wanting to play."

The same number of balls could have been on the floor during the ABL playoffs, which were the highest point of Adrienne's season. As the Rage competed against first the Lasers then the Quest, Adrienne entered what sounds like an altered state of consciousness. She characterizes the playoffs as "a lot of adrenalin pumping. Just thinking basketball 24 hours a day." It was basketball taken to the highest power, a normally intense game intensified further. "Throughout the season you have the ability to kind of separate your life from basketball a little bit," Adrienne comments, "but during the playoff there is no separation. It consumes you. It's your life in everything that you do."

That intense focus showed during Adrienne's playoff performances. In the first finals game, for example, almost at the end of the first quarter, Adrienne ran the length of the court with the ball and made an off-balance shot which found its way into the basket. Later in the second quarter, Adrienne ran the court with her usual fast, slashing style, then passed the ball to Dawn Staley, who made a layup. On the halftime highlight video shown on TV, Adrienne soared for a layup with her long arms reaching towards the basket. She raced down court, then made a slick, behind-the-back pass to a teammate.

Adrienne continued to play a strong game. In the third quarter she hit the first basket after a timeout, giving her team a one-point lead. Later she put in a close shot and then made her free throw. In the fourth quarter, she hit a three-pointer, demonstrating both her shooting range and the versatility of her game. In spite of her efforts, though, her team didn't come up with a win.

The second game of the finals was a turnaround game, one which might have led to Richmond's winning the ABL championship. The lead paragraph of a *USA Today* article describes the "Richmond forward combination of Adrienne Goodson and Taj McWilliams" as "too much for the Columbus Quest." The significant rebound edge the Rage had over the Quest, 49-32, was partly due to the 12 rebounds Adrienne pulled down. Among other accomplishments, she scored the first two points of the game, slicing to the basket to put in a close shot. Almost at the end of the first quarter, she made a long two-point shot at the buzzer. Adrienne smiled after she put in a two-point jumper in the second quarter. A TV announcer described her as "on fire."

The second half featured more strong play from Adrienne. She drove hard to the basket. She put in a one-handed, very athletic shot. After missing a close shot, she grabbed her own rebound and was fouled, no doubt showing the tough, scrappy style of play she learned growing up in New Jersey. Later she made a nice reverse layup from the baseline. She missed some shots too, but she remained on the court for long minutes, and showed her steadiness at the line by hitting three of four free throws at the end of the game. She even grabbed the very last rebound of the game.

For Adrienne and her teammates, it was disappointing to lose the fifth and deciding playoff game. Yet Adrienne could look back on a season where she was able to show that she could play at a level only a few players ever reach. "I know that I'm one of the best players," she comments, "and I needed to prove that to myself more than anybody." Her selection to the All-ABL First Team, her fifth-highest scoring among league players and sixth-highest number of rebounds, provided tangible evidence of Adrienne's achievements.

Adrienne is solid about the future for pro basketball in the United States. She likes being able to play at home, and she sees that as something which will undoubtedly continue to happen both for herself and for other players. "It's going to take some time to wake some people up," Adrienne says, "but we're all dedicated to that, those of us who are in the league. We're dedicated to . . . bringing the fans to us and making women's basketball as something that is here to stay, not here today, gone tomorrow."

Two Different Seasons

Every player lived through her own version of the American Basketball League's first season.Kirsten Cummings, of the Richmond now Philadelphia Rage, and Trisha Stafford, who played for the San Jose Lasers and now is a member of the Long Beach StingRays, had very different first years in the league. The fact that a preseason injury kept Kirsten on the sidelines, while Trisha was able to keep on playing in spite of her own injury, is only one aspect of these women's distinctly different first seasons.

Kirsten Cummings

Kirsten Cummings was 33 years old during the ABL's first year, which makes her one of the league's oldest players. Like many other women she played overseas but not for just a few years. Kirsten spent eleven years away from the United States, competing on teams in Italy, France, Japan, Israel and Germany, and receiving MVP awards in three different countries. She was an international basketball player by the time she came home to play in the United States.

Like all the ABL women, Kirsten is a gifted athlete. But there's something else remarkable about her. She's someone who has achieved athletic excellence in spite of a physical limitation that many people might think would keep her from playing top level basketball. Kirsten Cummings is 85 percent deaf.

Kirsten can read lips, and does fine when "listening" to one or two other people. She wears hearing aids in both ears to maximize the hearing she does have. Her speech is easy to understand, in spite of being pitched differently, sounding a little slurry. But out on the basketball court, Kirsten can't hear the shouts of the fans. If someone on her own team shouted something to her from across the court, Kirsten couldn't hear it.

Basketball has shaped Kirsten's life, yet her hearing impairment, she feels, has been even more central. "I am who I am because of my deafness," Kirsten says. It's strengthened her other senses and given her "a much more intuitive way of looking at people." She picks up visual messages much more than many other people do. And she can be like a human weather vane with her ability to sense atmospheres, to pick up on moods of individuals and groups. She can often sense what teams need to develop good chemistry. One of her goals as a player is to do what she can to help her teammates come together. At times, when Kirsten talks about her experiences with various teams, she sounds like a basketball therapist.

Actually, therapy isn't a foreign concept to Kirsten. She spent eleven years in speech therapy to develop her skills with English. Eleven years imitating sounds as well as she could, feeling for the correct position of her lips and her tongue, learning the hard way speech patterns which come naturally to children without hearing loss. All that hard work also taught her the value of persistence towards a goal. It was a lesson that would serve her well during her sports career.

Growing up in Pasadena, California, the land of year-round sunshine and palm trees, Kirsten's first vision of women's professional sports came early. She was only nine when she went to see a women's professional softball team called the Queen and her Maids who travelled around the west coast. Rosie Debeer, the queen, was the team pitcher and the other players were her "maids."

As Kirsten watched women hitting line drives, women winding up for pitches, women running the bases, she could see herself out there too. She'd already been playing on softball teams after all. "I saw them play," she recalls, "and I knew then I wanted to be an athlete." And not just someone who plays on weekends. "I wanted to be a professional athlete," Kirsten emphasizes.

In the media guide for the Richmond Rage, each player's photo is accompanied by a quote. What Kirsten has to say fits with her early experience. "There's nothing truer than what comes from your heart. Find it, then follow it and then share it." From an early age, Kirsten did her best to follow her heart in sports.

Along that road, the chance to watch the women's softball team was a lucky break for her. Like other girls growing up in the sixties and seventies, if Kirsten wanted sports heroes, she had to look almost exclusively to male athletes. Kirsten watched Mickey Mantle and the New York Yankees and thought about playing baseball. She watched Pele playing soccer and tried to picture herself out on the field. The media did cover women playing professional tennis and golf, but Kirsten always preferred the camaraderie of team sports.

Kirsten may not have had many female athletes as role models, but she did have the strong support of her father. Her dad, Kirsten recalls, "recorded my stats and talked to my coaches and made sure I got the best coaches." He pushed her to do her best in sports. He "drove me," Kirsten describes. He often acted like a coach to her as well as a father.

Kirsten didn't start basketball until she was 15 years old and already in high school. But it was a natural fit for her, and she developed quickly as a player. In her senior year, her personal basketball statistics included impressive averages of 36 points and 16 rebounds per game. When Kirsten played for Long Beach State College, from 1981-1985, her team went to the NCAA tournament all four years. By the end of the 1996 season, years after Kirsten had graduated, her personal statistics—for scoring, rebounds, and blocked shots— were still among the best for all Long Beach women basketball players.

After college, Kirsten went overseas to play basketball. That was where the best American women had to go if they wanted a basketball future, and Kirsten knew that she did. She was still following her heart, and it led her to teams in Italy, France, Japan, Israel and Germany. Over the years Kirsten has accumulated languages the way some people collect travel decals. She can speak fluent French, knows Italian fairly well, and has a survival vocabulary in Hebrew, Japanese, and German.

Playing overseas wasn't easy. Kirsten was homesick, especially early on. She missed the little things, the things people often take for granted. "I missed the wide roads," she remembers. "I missed the conveniences of getting food any time of day." She missed her family too, including her sisters Romney and Katelyn.

For many young women, homesickness and loneliness have been so strong that they simply couldn't or wouldn't continue playing basketball in other countries. But Kirsten wasn't among that group, even though her hearing impairment made learning new languages more difficult and could make her feel isolated as well.

She went to Italy first and played there for three years. She dealt with the stereotypical scene of Italian men staring at her, trying to hustle her, making "romantic" comments as she walked by, her 6'3" body an obvious target. Kirsten's deafness, rather than being a handicap, was actually something of an advantage in Italy. What the men said didn't bother her; she couldn't hear them.

France was next on her international basketball itinerary. She played there for four years with a team called Orchies, located in the north of France close to Belgium. Off court, she went through more speech therapy so she could learn to pronounce the unfamiliar French sounds. On court, she helped her team move from the second to the first division. Her ability to make a good team better and her reputation as "basketball therapist" was taking off.

Kirsten's international basketball journey continued with teams in Germany, Japan and Israel. Over the years, her average points, which started at around 25-30 points per game, decreased a little as her assists went up and as she worked even harder at involving other players, at helping to build up her whole team.

From 1991-1993, Kirsten played in Urawa, a town near Tokyo. The money was good there. Pay in Japan, Kirsten recalls, was the highest of any country. The four hours a day Japanese teams practiced could seem long sometimes, but it wasn't a big deal. "The Japanese players have such good attitudes. They never complained," Kirsten recalls.

Kirsten herself isn't the complaining type, yet the years overseas did add up. She actually contemplated retirement after a bad experience in Israel, where she tried to help her team win and felt that the rest of the team wasn't doing enough of their part. "I left with kind of a bitter taste in my mouth," she says. "Okay," she thought, "I'm done. . . . I'm tired of giving so much."

A friend of hers, who was also her personal coach, thought differently. He looked at her strong, athletic frame, and her competitive spirit, and her big heart. "You're not ready to retire."

As it turned out, he was right. Kirsten went on to play a year with a team in Osnabruck, Germany. It was a good year for her, a year she describes as her "best year ever." Her averages of 23 points, 5 assists, and 10 rebounds certainly didn't suggest any need for retirement. When she heard about the ABL, she knew she wanted to continue in the game— but at home and in front of American fans.

After years overseas, being back in the states is a change for Kirsten. She gets homesick for Europe sometimes, for the rich mix of languages and cultures. But she has no regrets about her decision to play in the league. Even though things didn't go the way she had planned.

The game Kirsten won't ever forget took place in October, just 72 hours before the regular season started. Kirsten's team played an exhibition game in Philadelphia against the New England Blizzard. While a New England player attempted a layup, Kirsten went up to block the shot. That leap into the air with long arms raised, that attempt to intercept the rising path of the basketball, was something that she had done innumerable times. But the team had been training hard in the preseason and Kirsten was a little tired.

She landed wrong: off balance, with too much weight on the back of her left knee. She twisted at the same time that she landed incorrectly. In an instant, in one quick snapshot of time, her ACL snapped.

Kirsten screamed when she felt the pain. According to a reporter, Kirsten's scream was loud enough to be heard in the parking lot outside. It was loud enough that Kirsten herself could hear it. Yet because of her deafness, at first she didn't realize that she was the one who had screamed.

Kirsten didn't cry out because of the physical pain. That wasn't the worst thing for her. What she was afraid of was that this was it for her. That her basketball career was finished.

Shortly after the injury, she did some hard thinking. In all her years overseas, she hadn't ever had a major injury. Now she faced surgery and an extensive rehabilitation process. "I'm 33 years old," she considered. "Maybe it's time to go on. . . I've had a great career in Europe and all that." Maybe she could find something else to do now. It only took a couple of days before she changed her thinking. She wanted to come back from her injury—all the way back. She wanted to go on playing.

The ACL tear did end Kirsten's season though. After her surgery, the main work she had to do was to rehab her knee. For an extroverted, team-oriented person, someone who gets much of her inspiration from being around other players, the mostly solitary process of rehabbing a knee was difficult. "It was very very challenging for me," Kirsten recalls. "To go into the room, into the training room and work on my knees day in, day out, by myself, that was tough."

"Tough" was one adjective that fit. "Painful" was another. Surgery, especially with an ACL tear, leaves the knee stiff. Kirsten had to bend her knee, twist her leg in place, stretch the knee. The whole process involved, as she puts it, "excruciating pain" which she had to endure on a daily basis.

She got depressed sometimes, but she never threw in the towel, never said, okay, I'll rehab the knee just enough for ordinary activity. Watching her team play inspired Kirsten. She wanted to be out there with them again. The new league couldn't afford to pay travel money for an injured player, so Kirsten usually couldn't travel with the team to games on the road. But she was always there at home games, sitting on the bench, cheering on her team.

Watching her teammates instead of playing was difficult as well as inspirational. "Very, very tough," Kirsten says. Above and beyond her personal disappointment, she knew that her experience would have been valuable for her team. That her maturity, her ability to empathize with feelings, and her basketball savvy would have positively affected the team performance and chemistry.

"Experience at this level is hard to find," Kirsten told a reporter for the *Richmond Times-Dispatch*. "You work so hard for so long to develop it. And now I can't put it to use. I want to be out there so badly. We've lost so many close games. I know I could have helped us win some of those games."

While Kirsten struggled with her role on the sidelines, her teammates and coaches were always supportive. "How are you doing?" they would ask Kirsten, their concern letting her know that they still considered her a member of the team. Kirsten felt connected too, in spite of her injury, yet her deafness created obstacles as well. Her ability to read lips didn't help her when the team sat together at a table to eat a pregame meal. Typically, everybody talked at once, making points, telling jokes. Dawn Staley might be saying something, and then Lisa Boyer, the coach, might chime in. Across the table, Taj McWilliams might crack a joke. Everyone on the team could follow what was being said, except for Kirsten. She could sense the mood of the team, yet not understanding their words could make her feel isolated, a lonely deaf athlete in a hearing world.

Off the court, Kirsten would often make the effort to reach out to a teammate, invite her to a one-on-one talk where Kirsten could read the other woman's lips. Moments like those strengthened Kirsten's ties with her teammates. And those connections with teammates will continue. Kirsten's initial contract was for one year, but shortly after the season ended she signed a contract for another two years. Kirsten appreciated the vote of confidence from her team, especially considering the fact that during the regular season and postseason play, she couldn't play a single game with the Rage.

At the end of that last season, as the Rage went all the way to the ABL finals, they wanted to pour champagne to celebrate a league championship. As it turned out, another team did the pouring, but Kirsten is still ready to pour champagne for the league overall. All those years she was overseas, she says, the best players were usually Americans. Foreign players and fans alike didn't understand why there wasn't a professional league in the United States. Players and fans need to cherish the ABL, Kirsten feels. She adds a note of caution. "We need to take it slowly," she says, "we have to play for the love of basketball for now." Rather than demand more money right away, "we should just all hang in there until we start getting a little more fans and more marketing exposure, media exposure."

Kirsten is definitely going to hang in there. Out on court for the Philadelphia Rage, she'll be playing a somewhat different game—a more silent game—than that of her teammates. She'll feel the sharp, springy release of a pass or the slap of hands against the basketball as she blocks a shot. She'll watch the perfect arc as a basketball skies toward the net. She'll watch the body language of teamamtes, the ever changing pattern of moves on court, and feel for the right team chemistry.

Kirsten won't hear the fans cheer for her. But she'll know that she belongs among that select group of top women players who are following their hearts onto basketball courts across the country.

Trisha Stafford

Trisha Stafford is an outgoing woman with a warm smile who isn't afraid to speak her mind. She'll tell the truth about her relationship to the ABL. Initially, the league hadn't been the place where she saw her basketball future.

Trisha grew up in Los Angeles, not too far from the Great Western Forum which is the Lakers' home turf. "I grew up a Laker fan," she says. Like many other girls and women, she had dreamed of playing in the NBA, even though it didn't seem as if that dream could ever become reality. When Trisha heard about the WNBA, her reaction was instantaneous. "That's what I've always wanted to do," she felt. There was no doubt in her mind. "My heart was in the WNBA from the very beginning," she says.

But Trisha didn't end up following her heart into the WNBA. Three days before she was scheduled to return to Brazil to play with a team there, she committed herself to joining an ABL team, the San Jose Lasers. She had already talked to the front office staff with the WNBA team, the Los Angeles Sparks, yet Trisha decided that staying in the United States to play with the ABL made sense for her. It was "the better business decision for me monetarily," she says frankly. Also, playing for the ABL, as opposed to playing another season in Brazil, would give her more exposure as an athlete in the U.S., and thus more chance of being picked up by a WNBA team.

Trisha Stafford

After one season in the ABL, Trisha is still a big fan of the WNBA. She likes its catchy slogans like "We got next." She appreciates the fact that the WNBA has the money and marketing clout of the NBA behind it and the television contracts to prove it. "I like the exposure, I like the television, I like the hype," she says. The idea of a summer league doesn't bother her too much. Basketball fans, she thinks, will watch basketball whenever it's on. And for herself personally, if she can make about as much money in three months with the WNBA as in eight months with the ABL, that seems like a pretty good deal.

Yet a year in the American Basketball League has given Trisha an appreciation for what the ABL is all about. "The talent is overwhelming," she says about ABL players. She doesn't like it one bit when people refer to the ABL as the "other league." Or when people she knows seem surprised that she'll be playing in the "other league."

Trisha's first year in that league was an intense one, engendering strong loyalties between her and her teammates, creating frustrations in her when she sat on the bench at times, and causing or worsening a knee injury which she somehow managed to play with until the end of the season. It's a basketball year she's glad she took part in. And yet Trisha' s first ABL season was often a rocky one.

Trisha's a sunny, people person who often seems to have a positive outlook on things. But Trisha had a problem with her coach, Jan Lowrey. Jan, Trisha feels, was "not capable of coaching the talent and the level of play" in the league. As Trisha sees it, Jan lacked rapport with her players, lacked the ability to motivate the team, and lacked sufficient knowledge of the "X's and O's" of basketball.

Probably coaches on teams generate more strong feelings among players than any other figure. Coaches can inspire to-die-for loyalties and quite the opposite reactions. Jan Lowrey, the head coach for the San Jose Lasers during the first season, is an approachable, intelligent woman who comes across as someone who really cares about women's basketball. She inspired positive reactions from other first year coaches such as Lisa Boyer, and from her assistant coach Denise Curry, who was quoted in the Lasers' media guide as saying that "Working with Jan Lowrey is going to be exciting. We are on the same page with regards to our philosophies and approaches to the game."

There is no doubt that the loss of a key player, Jennifer Azzi, early in the season helped neither Jan nor the team as a whole. Although Jan came from a Division Two college, as did some other first year ABL coaches, she may have been perfectly capable of coaching an ABL team. However, Trisha reports that almost all her teammates had problems with Jan Lowrey. "I would say 90 percent of our team complained," she states.

The conflict between Trisha and her coach, which had a strong effect on Trisha's first season, was perhaps rooted in a personality conflict between the two women. Trisha is an expressive woman who willingly shares her feelings and experiences. She's a large woman, six feet one inch tall with a stocky build, who has a solid physical presence. She's neither physically nor temperamentally the type of person to fade away into a corner or passively accept how things are going. Her own assessment of her personality is that "I'm the type of person who would never be disrespectful, but I don't have a problem expressing myself."

When Trisha expressed herself to Jan, the interaction between the two women often didn't go very well. Trisha would ask her coach questions, such as "Do you want us to play man to man (defense) even if this person on another team . . . is killing us?" In response to Trisha's questions about various basketball possibilities, Jan's reactions would be something like "We're just going to do it," or "Just do it because I said do it." From Trisha's perspective, Jan didn't have enough confidence as a coach. "It's like she was intimidated by my personality, it's like she always felt like I was trying to do something to make her look stupid," Trisha describes.

The disagreements with their coach, Trisha feels, helped the players become closer. "We had great chemistry," Trisha says about herself and her teammates. "Each of us had respect for one another. . . . We were closer than an average team would be because we felt as if we were sharing the same type of troubles." By and large the players on the Lasers became their own cheering section for each other. The feedback and support players gave each other seemed to function as the main glue for the team.

Trisha was one of the key ingredients in that glue. "Since I was a kid," she recalls, "teachers would write on my report card, 'she's a natural leader.'" Trisha's leadership had an impact on her team. "I could say something and I'd get the attention of the team," she comments. She doesn't mean to be "boastful" by saying that. It's simply the truth.

Trisha would encourage her teammates to do their best. "You can score easily. You can score when you want to. Take your time," she'd say to teammate Sheri Sam. Or "Sheri, keep your head in the game. Don't worry about the referee." Or to teammate Val Whiting, "Val, they're double teaming you, so look out."

When she discusses the way she talks to her teammates, Trisha sounds very aware of interpersonal dynamics. "I think you always say things in a positive way. Then people don't have a problem when you critique them. If you're always coming down on them, they never want to listen to you."

Trisha's teammates reciprocated her support as she went through many changes regarding her role on the team. For about half of the 40 regular season games, Trisha was a starter. Other times she metamorphosized into a bench warmer, a transformation she wasn't thrilled about. "I thought it sucked," she says honestly. She's willing to be out front about a reaction some other players might have yet keep to themselves. More thoughtfully, Trisha comments, "I really felt that when I was on the bench, I really shouldn't be there." It didn't help matters that Trisha felt she received very mixed messages from Jan. "You're the most versatile player on our team," Jan would tell Trisha sometimes, referring to Trisha's ability to play several positions. Yet on many occasions Trisha still sat on the bench.

Trisha's teammates encouraged her. "Trish, hang in there. You should be playing," women on the team would say. "We need you. Our team needs you. We need you to play," another teammate told Trisha. "Forget about the coach," the teammate added, "because we need you to win."

Trisha tried to keep the positive mood going by showing her feelings about her own performance on court, something which can help to inspire teammates. If Trisha scored a basket, she felt pumped and she showed it. She might raise a fist into the air or flash a bright smile. If she got fouled, she'd exchange high fives with teammates. "You have got to have attitude on the court," Trisha affirms.

Confidence—another intangible element that seems essential for top performance in almost any field—is something Trisha Stafford learned early in life. She had strong family support to help inculcate that attitude. Her parents basically encouraged her in whatever she was interested in. "I felt if I wanted to do it," Trisha comments, "my parents were always there for me to say, 'go ahead, baby, do it.'"

Both the church and the extended family Trisha was raised in have always been important parts of her life. Her father is a pastor of a church in Los Angeles, her older brother ministers to a church in Detroit, and Trisha sings soprano in her church choir. Growing up, she hung out with a close knit extended family. And she also played sports, lots of sports, at school and with her brother and friends in the backyard. She was, she considers, "a tomboy," a self-assessment many ABL players share. At Westchester High School, Trisha lettered in basketball, softball and volleyball. She excelled at all of them, but basketball was the sport she gave her heart to.

Named the Los Angeles City Player of the Year in high school, Trisha had numerous colleges offering her athletic scholarships. She decided on the University of California because of "the academic and athletic balance" and because the campus wasn't too far from her home in Los Angeles.

Trisha had a good four years at Berkeley. The only really negative aspect of her college experience was when she tore the ACL on her right knee in her freshman year and had to have the knee reconstructed. It must have been hard at the time, but Trisha is enough of a positive thinker to see an upside to her injury.

"It helped me put a lot of things in perspective," she says. "Basketball is not first . . . God is first." As well as reaffirming her religious faith and personal priorities, while Trisha couldn't play basketball, she developed better study skills. And sitting on the sidelines watching basketball games, she believes, helped her to understand more about the sport and ultimately to become a better player.

During Trisha's senior year, the 1991-92 season, she averaged over 20 points, a scoring level only one other Cal player has reached. Her junior and senior years in college, she was recognized as a member of the All-Pac-10 Team. In 1992, she also received a Kodak All-American Honorable Mention.

Throughout her college years, Trisha's individual basketball achievements included international competition as well. At the U.S. Olympic Festival in 1990, Trisha's team earned a silver medal, and in the same year she was a member of the U.S. Junior National Team. In the summer of 1991, Trisha played on the Pac-10 All-Star Team which went to Taiwan to compete for the Jones Cup. For USA Basketball, she was a starting forward in the 1991 World University Games.

Initially, Trisha hadn't planned on playing basketball overseas, but when she graduated from college, as a highly successful post player with USA Basketball experience, the opportunities were there for her. She ended up playing four seasons for teams in Spain, Italy, Israel, and Brazil. Unlike some American players, Trisha describes her overseas basketball experiences as mostly positive. "You as a foreigner are always treated as a queen," she says. "The fans think of you as a celebrity."

Trisha had studied Spanish in high school, so communicating in Spain was reasonably easy for her. In Israel, she found Hebrew difficult but appreciated the fact that so many people there spoke English. In Italy, she learned a survival vocabulary and her lack of fluency in Italian—she was only able to hold simple conversations—could be an advantage at times. Like Kirsten Cummings, Trisha wasn't able to understand what Italian men said to her on the street, so she took their comments as compliments.

Brazil, where Trisha played for the 1995-1996 basketball season, was her favorite of the four countries. One advantage was the short season there, but she also enjoyed the good food, entertainment options, and warm atmosphere. "Everything seemed to flow," Trisha says about Brazil. Among other advantages, movie theatres and television offered some English programming; there were lovely clean beaches with warm water, and many places to go on sightseeing excursions.

Overall, Trisha found that being in other countries was both "enlightening and a great experience." But it was also lonely being so far away from family and friends. "I'm a homebody," Trisha says about herself. She missed family, friends, and even though her mother and her brother visited her sometimes, and Trisha practiced the sometimes forgotten art of letter writing, she still racked up "horrendous" phone bills.

Trisha's overseas experiences also inspired patriotism in her. "You realize how great of a country we are, once you go away," she says. Although she's perfectly aware of poverty in the United States, the easily visible poverty in a third world country like Brazil still struck her. Near Sao Paulo, she saw people living in shacks with no electricity or other amenities. Slum areas were in plain view for anyone to see just driving around the city.

When Trisha ended up in the United States, playing in the ABL instead of on her way to Brazil again, she appreciated many things about her new basketball location. "The season was fun," she says simply. She loved playing with such talented teammates and going up against the talented players on other teams. She enjoyed seeing other cities for the first time, checking out the different arenas, the size and kind of the crowd different teams would draw. She enjoyed the travelling, unlike some ABL players who found it wearing.

"It was cool," Trisha says about being on the road with her team. She liked the ABL policy of changing roomates each time on the road so everyone on the team had a chance to room with everyone else, and she has no complaints about the hotel accomodations. Even when the team had to wait at an airport for transportation—which was the responsibility of the host team—Trisha saw a positive side. She and her teammates would joke around, saying "Well we're going to do this to them when they come."

It was true that flying coach on commercial airlines could present special difficulties to players like Trisha who were over six feet tall. On Southwest Airlines, where seats aren't assigned, Trisha remembers teammates fighting with each other to get the seats with more leg room. In spite of such minor irritations, and in spite of the much more significant loss of key player Jennifer Azzi, the team hung together throughout the season. When Shelley Sandie from Australia came in to replace Jennifer, the team welcomed Shelley. In San Jose and throughout the league, teammates formed into a kind of family for each other as they shared the ups and downs of a season. Individual differences, like a teammate coming from another country, were simply accepted as part of the "family."

Race of course was one of those differences. And in women's basketball overall, Trisha sometimes feels that the opportunities available aren't completely equal. "A lot of times I do feel like more opportunities are granted to the Caucasian women of basketball," Trisha says. But about the relationship between teammates on ABL teams, Trisha has a different view. Here race doesn't matter. "We had respect for one another and . . . for one another's talent," she says emphatically. "If we don't like you, it's because we don't like you as a person, and not because you're black or white."

Players hung out off court, hung closer together in practices, based on individual personalities rather than on race. The players were comfortable enough about racial differences that they would tell black/white jokes like about "white people not being able to dance" and about "not being able to see black people in the dark." The jokes may seem hokey, perhaps even in poor taste. But they reflect one of the achievements of many sports. To the women on ABL teams, race was simply no big deal.

Basketball rather than skin color mattered to Trisha and her teammates. And for Trisha, the final basketball frustration of a difficult season came during the first round of the playoffs, when San Jose played Columbus and lost in two straight games. Her team seemed overmatched in those two games, Trisha recalls.

Leading up to the playoffs, Trisha had been starting many games and felt that she was making a solid contribution to her team. Then at the start of the playoffs, coach Jan Lowrey changed the team lineup. Trisha found herself sitting on the bench for long minutes. That was "frustrating," she says. She could have made a contribution to her team, she felt. "I know that no one can stop me off the dribble, penetrating and passing," is Trisha's honest self-assessment.

She might have been remembering regular season games like the one in late January, when the Lasers went up against the Reign on the road. The Lasers had ended the first half behind 23 points, and they ended up losing the game, but Trisha did her best to make things happen for her team. She played assertively. She played with attitude.

Early in the third quarter, she drove to the basket, made the shot, then nailed her free throw. Twice after that she made a strong move to the basket, got to the line, and made more free throws. After a short breather on the bench, she made a three-point basket, then drove between opposing players and got to the line, then penetrated to the hoop and passed the ball to a teammate at just the right moment. In the fourth quarter, Trisha completed her personal highlight tape performance by stealing the ball and later by hitting a three-point shot.

"My teammates, they really look to me for energy," Trisha says. Her performance against Seattle is a good example of the energy she can provide. Yet in San Jose's last playoff game, Trisha remembers playing only nine minutes.

Trisha's personal end to a somewhat rocky season was rocky as well. First there was her interview with Christine Forter, general manager for the Lasers. All the players received evaluations at the end of the season, and Christine let Trisha know that the team didn't want her back next year. "They felt like I would be better off somewhere else," is what Trisha remembers Christine saying to her.

Trisha of course wanted to know the reasons for the team's decision. "You're a great person. You've proven that you can be great in this league. But you need to be somewhere else," was the basic message.

"Why would you give away a piece of gold?" Trisha asked Christine, once again expressing herself honestly. "If you feel that I'm so valuable," Trisha said, "and my qualities, my personality and all these things are so great, why would you give it away? I don't understand."

Christine didn't give Trisha an answer which satisfied her. "Basically I was left with no explanation," Trisha comments. At season's end, her ABL future was uncertain. She might have simply gone into the ABL draft pool as one more unassigned player.

The other tough part about Trisha's end to the season was that like Kirsten Cummings, she went through knee surgery. The Lasers' last playoff game against Columbus was February 25th. Just two days later, on February 27th, Trisha had her surgery.

She hadn't had one dramatic injury during the season, unlike Kirsten and some other players, but the wear and tear of the season and no doubt of other basketball seasons before that had damaged her knee. She had managed to keep on playing, even though sometimes during the season Trisha's knee would lock up in a partially bent position and she couldn't straighten it. The doctors knew Trisha had a torn meniscus but when they performed surgery on her, they found that Trisha's ACL was torn as well. How her knee had held together as well as it did surprised the doctors.

Surgery to repair an ACL is vastly different from the minor sort of arthroscopic repairs basketball players routinely undergo. But post-surgery, Trisha's attitude is positive. Her rehabilitation is coming along and she can ride a bike, swim, jump, and do other sorts of exercises. She's getting herself in shape for the next ABL season. And she's excited about where she'll be next season. The league assigned her to the expansion team in Long Beach, California.

During the first ABL season, Trisha's parents flew up to some games in San Jose, but overall it was hard for her friends and family to follow her games. Now members of the church where her father is the pastor, which has a congregation of more than 5,000 people, keep coming up to Trisha, eager anticipation in their voices. "I can't wait. I'm getting my tickets at Long Beach," people tell Trisha.

Trisha is upbeat as well. "To be able to work minutes from my home, where I grew up, I'm excited about it" she says. For the moment, at least, she doesn't talk about playing for the Los Angeles Sparks, the WNBA team which plays even closer to her home. In spite of the ups and downs of her first season, she seems to have given a lot of her heart to the American Basketball League.

Back to Basketball

The chance to play professional basketball has been like a magnetic field, attracting women away from other life choices, drawing women together from places far removed from basketball courts. In the first year of the American Basketball League, those players included Shanda Berry of the New England Blizzard, who took a leave of absence from her other job as a police officer; Vonda Ward of the Colorado Xplosion, who had been a volunteer firefighter and plans to return to firefighting after her basketball career is over; Dena Evans of the Richmond Rage, who went from teaching high school algebra to living out the X's and O's of basketball; and Sonja Henning of the San Jose Lasers, who left a career in labor law. All these women love basketball enough that they couldn't pass up the opportunity to return to the sport and to help start up a women's professional basketball league.

Three of these basketball "career changers," Falisha Wright, Coquese Washington, and Lisa Harrison were teammates on the Portland Power during the 1996-97 season. Falisha had worked for the San Diego County Water Authority while Lisa held a job with an athletic company and did TV and radio commentary. Coquese was a law student before donning her Power uniform and somehow managed to fit in law classes during the first part of the ABL season. Coquese has a promising future as an attorney, but basketball courts pulled her away from courts of law.

Coquese Washington

After the last game of the season, fans at Memorial Coliseum waited in line for autographs from players. "You can only get two autographs," fans were told. "We need to keep the lines moving."

"I'm gonna get the one with the orange hair," one girl of about eight years old said.

Coquese Washington wasn't sitting close enough to hear that comment. But if she had, she surely would have smiled or laughed. Short cropped, slightly orange tinted hair and all, Coquese might have had the sunniest personality of any player during the Power's first year. Coquese is someone who always seems easygoing and friendly, glad to take a moment to talk.

On the basketball court, Coquese's enthusiastic temperament translated into an energetic commitment to the game. Playing two positions, point guard and shooting guard, she used her speed to run downcourt, to play pressure defense on an opponent. With her quick hands, she could steal the ball or make a sharp pass to a teammate.

Coquese has always had high levels of energy and enthusiasm. Basketball was only one of the sports she grew up playing in her hometown of Flint, Michigan. "I think I was always athletic. I was always running around," she recalls. Coquese has two sisters and two brothers, but she and her brother Kenyatta, who is about a year younger, were especially close. He was her "best friend" and they did "boy things" together like wrestling and climbing trees.

Playing with her brother helped fire up Coquese's competitive spirit. Her brother didn't want to lose to her because she was a girl, but she didn't want him to beat her because he was her younger brother. "I hated losing just in general," Coquese recalls, "but I hated losing to my brother more than anything in the world."

Coquese and Kenyatta invented all kinds of competitive games. At home, she remembers, the two of them would balance books on their heads, probably doing wonders for their posture as they challenged each other to walk through the living room, up the stairs, touch the bathroom door, and come all the way back down again. Outside in their neighborhood, Coquese and Kenyatta hung out with the other children, mostly boys, who were around their age. Together they played all kinds of informal games—football, baseball, basketball, tag.

"I just enjoyed playing," Coquese remembers. She speaks with assurance. "If they were going to get a game of something, Coquese was going to be in the middle of it, somehow, someway."

When Coquese was in the fourth grade she began organized sports on school teams. Definitely not a one-sport athlete, she participated in soccer, basketball, kickball, and hockey. In junior high, Coquese played on her school's soccer, softball, volleyball, and basketball teams. All that, plus schoolwork and friends, would be plenty for most teenage girls. But Coquese somehow found the time to play percussion instruments in her school's marching band, trombone and baritone in the concert band, and the violin and viola in the orchestra.

"My mom liked us to be busy so we'd stay out of trouble," Coquese explains. She admits with a smile that her own childhood was "pretty uneventful" in terms of any significant misbehavior.

Both of Coquese's parents worked in the auto plants—General Motors is one of the largest employers in Flint—and they were decently paid but "basically slave labor," as Coquese describes it. Even though Coquese's mother and father divorced when Coquese was five, her family remained close and supportive. Her mother and father encouraged all their children to set their sets high, not to follow in their parents' footsteps in the auto plants. "Get an education," Coquese's parents stressed to their children. Coquese took their advice to heart.

Both Coquese's family and her community encouraged her in sports. There was only one occasion when that wasn't true. When Coquese was around eleven or twelve, her father told her she couldn't play football anymore. "Girls don't do that," he said firmly. But aside from that one incident, Coquese never got any messages that girls shouldn't play sports.

Growing up, Coquese's basketball hero was Isiah Thomas, the point guard for the Detroit Pistons. But sports inspiration was closer to home as well. "We had a strong legacy of women's basketball players in Flint," Coquese recalls. A fair number of local girls starred in high school and college and some went on to play overseas.

These women, such as Tonya Edwards, who now plays for the Columbus Quest, would come back to Flint, sometimes referee games, and often encourage younger players. "Hey Coquese, you're working hard," a young woman would say. Verbal pats on the back like these meant a lot to Coquese and other budding athletes.

"I have the same obligation to kids coming up after me," Coquese feels. As an article in the *Willamette Week* described, Coquese returns the favor by helping out children in her old neighborhood in Flint. When children meet their scholastic goals—such as by achieving a 3.0 GPA—she might take them shopping for "shoes or sweatpants or whatever they want." She wants the children to learn "the value of working hard, of setting goals and doing the things to achieve those goals."

In Coquese's own case, the support of family and community, plus her own natural ability, helped her become a star athlete in high school. Once again she played multiple sports, but basketball was by far her favorite. It was "head and shoulders above the rest."

In high school Coquese set records at her school for assists, steals, number of field goals, and for three-point shooting. Her high school team wasn't always high on the basketball hill. In her freshman year, "we stunk up the joint," Coquese admits candidly. But when she was a sophomore and junior, her team had two especially good years, both years losing in the regional finals to the eventual state champions.

College was always in the picture for Coquese. Her family had stressed it all along, and Coquese's mother had a rule about "eighteen and out." When each of her children turned eighteen, she told them many times, she expected them to become independent adults. "You can go to the rescue mission, you can go to the military, or you can go to college," Coquese's mother warned, "but you're not staying here."

Coquese took her mother seriously. "All the time growing up," she recalls, "I used to be so scared of turning eighteen. I thought I'm going to be homeless." Coquese's father's stories about serving in the army during the Vietnam war had left her certain the military wasn't for her. An honor student in high school, for Coquese college was the logical option.

Coquese was recruited by over 80 colleges. Eventually she chose Notre Dame, partly for its academics and its national reputation. "I wanted to go to a school," she says, "where I knew when I got my degree, the degree would carry a lot of weight."

The other reason Coquese decided on Notre Dame was quite different, more similar to her reasons for signing with the ABL. She didn't want to join a basketball program which was already solidly established. "It was really important for me to go where I could help start something," Coquese explains.

Helping to start something was exactly what Coquese and her teammates did. During Coquese's four years at Notre Dame, her team gained their first national ranking and went to the NCAA tournament for the first time. As the starting point guard all four years, Coquese topped the list for numbers of steals, and in her sophomore through senior years, she led in numbers of assists. Off the court, she received high grades and with typical energy finished her regular college classes in three years so she could spend her fourth year taking graduate classes in history and law.

That energy never failed her. She was injury free except for knee surgery her junior year. And even then, her personal strength amazed her doctors. Coquese laughs when she tells the story. "I tore my anterior cruciate ligament in high school. But I didn't know it and I just played and I never had any problems with it."

When the doctors at Notre Dame finally examined her knee, according to Coquese, "Their jaws were on the floor." They were amazed that she hadn't had problems from such a serious injury. Since in fact she seemed to be doing okay, they let her go on playing until the knee finally acted up in her junior year.

Coquese had the necessary surgery, then worked hard to rehabilitate her knee. "There was never a moment when I didn't believe I'd be back," she says. She made a full recovery after surgery and was back on the basketball court.

College basketball both challenged and rewarded Coquese. The "friendships and the comraderie" with her teammates has always been one of the most important parts of basketball for Coquese, and at Notre Dame she made friends with women from all over the United States and from many different backgrounds. The strong relationship Coquese had with her college coach, Muffet McGraw, was another important part of her basketball life. The two of them had a "mutual respect." Her coach "got on my nerves sometimes and I'm sure I gave her many gray hairs," Coquese adds. But Coquese would be the first to acknowledge the valuable lessons she learned from Muffet McGraw.

Self control was perhaps one of the hardest lessons to learn. The style of game Coquese likes best is a fast, open court, up and down game which allows her to use her natural speed, but she learned to play a slower, half court style if that worked best in a particular situation. "Keeping things in perspective" was another important lesson. Muffet McGraw taught Coquese to accept her own mistakes, yet not to focus on them so much that it could negatively affect her play. But the most important lesson of all, Coquese explains simply, was "about being competitive with myself." In games or practices, Muffet urged, "you've got to challenge yourself."

Coquese did that challenging both on and off the basketball court. In her fourth year of college, after one semester of graduate history classes, Coquese decided that a career as a college professor wasn't for her. Instead she set her sights on law school, which she saw as her next new challenge. Always a positive thinker, she had already mentally prepared herself for the end of her basketball career. She didn't want to go overseas to play and there weren't really any other options.

Before law school Coquese did something uncharacteristic of her. She took a break. In spite of her typically high energy level and ambitious goals, Coquese realized she was tired. "Mentally exhausted" is the way Coquese describes her post-college state. She wasn't ready to plunge into the demanding life of a first year law student. Instead she travelled around the states, visiting her sisters in North Carolina, then moving on to California where she volunteered on a TV show. She went to Washington, D.C. next, helped with a movie a friend was making, then headed for Savannah, Georgia where she spent time with her mother.

Five months later, when Coquese's money ran out, she returned to Flint and took a job teaching history and social studies to special education students at an inner city high school. Her students presented her with plenty of challenges, their mix of needs going far beyond a conventional education. Coquese remembers one girl saying, "I can't come to class, I got to take my baby to the doctor."

Coquese hung in there with her students, challenging herself and challenging them as best she could. The experience left her with a permanent respect for the job teachers do, but she didn't want it to be her own job. At the start of the next school year, she enrolled as a first year law student at Notre Dame.

Coquese loved her law classes and did well at them. Law seemed to be a natural field for her. "I'm an argumentative person," she says about herself. "I like to think and talk and argue and figure things out." A promising law career seemed to be just ahead for Coquese. But after almost two years of law school, Coquese's plans suddenly changed. A professional basketball league for women, right here in the United States, was becoming a reality.

When Coquese first heard about the American Basketball League, she didn't think it was an option for her. "I'm in law school," she told herself. "I haven't played in three years."

But the friends at law school she played pick up basketball games with had a different opinion. "Coquese, you gotta go try out," they urged her.

Coquese's family and other friends said basically the same thing. She would always regret it, they told her, if she didn't at least give the league a try.

Coquese mulled over her choices and decided that her friends and family were right. If she didn't go to the tryouts, she would always wonder if she could have made an ABL team. "I wanted the competition," she explains. "I wanted to see if I could stack up with the best women basketball players in the country."

Her bags packed mentally and physically, Coquese travelled to Atlanta for the ABL trials. Part of her baggage was a good attitude. She would do her best but not feel that she absolutely had to make a roster spot. She would keep things in perspective, just as Muffet McGraw had taught her.

The odds were very much against her. "Slim to nil," Coquese thought. There were close to 600 women trying out for 40 spots in the ABL. Eighty players total would play in the league but about 40 players, such as many of the 1996 Olympians, had already been signed.

Her positive attitude helped Coquese. She was loose physically and mentally and played well. After every roster cut, Coquese remembers, "I'd look and see my number and my name up on the wall and I'd think 'I can't believe I didn't get cut.'"

Greg Bruce, the original coach for the Portland Power, and Linda Weston, the Power General Manager, were impressed with Coquese's play. She was drafted as the first alternate for the team, but when a player ahead of her didn't sign, Coquese was offered the roster spot. She initially said "no"—she'd go on with law school—but the Power persuaded her to sign.

Chances are, it didn't take all that much persuading. Even though she'd been offered a job with a Michigan law firm, Coquese's risk-taking, pioneering spirit was on the side of the Portland Power front office. "Ultimately, I decided this was an opportunity to make history," Coquese decided, "to be the first at something. When I looked at it like that, I couldn't turn it down."

Coquese has no regrets about joining the ABL. "It's just been a lot of fun to play basketball again," is her main feeling. But she freely admits that her first year in the ABL involved plenty of challenges.

Number one was the stretch on her time. Playing in the ABL is not like being in the NBA. The new league puts far greater demands on its players. One important part of their responsibilities is to be representatives of the league, to help publicize professional women's basketball by speaking to school groups and to numerous other organizations. An articulate, outgoing person, Coquese did her part on the public appearance front. About the time team practices began, she also started the first semester of her last year of law school. Notre Dame permitted Coquese to take one semester's credits at Lewis and Clark Law School in Portland.

Aside from her law school classes, and aside from her off-court responsibilities for the league, Coquese practiced hard along with her teammates. Then she injured her knee, in the team's first exhibition game, which was against Simon Frasier University.

Injuries to players—and women basketball players have a higher rate of certain injuries than men—are a part of the game. Players know that and accept the risk. But that didn't make it easy for Coquese to sit out five or six weeks after having arthroscopic surgery for her torn cartilage. For game after game she sat with her teammates, her street clothes contrasting with their blue and white warmups and uniforms.

Coquese didn't get back to playing until the season was well underway. She had expected to be the starting point guard but another player, Michelle Marciniak, had assumed that role.

The long losing streak the Portland Power suffered through was another challenge for Coquese, as it was for all her teammates. Shortly after Coquese returned to the active roster, one of the team's strongest players, Natalie Williams, went out with an injury. The players were also having problems with their coach, feeling that he wasn't a strong enough leader. Coquese felt that he didn't experiment enough with the lineup, that he didn't give enough minutes to bench players like herself who might have come in and helped the team.

Coquese sometimes felt frustrated with her own performance too. "I felt that I should have been doing a lot better leading the team as a point guard," she says. She did have some good games, such as the time in late November when she came off the bench to score seven points, hand out three assists, and pull down three rebounds in only 18 minutes. But overall, she wasn't happy.

When Greg Bruce resigned as coach and Lin Dunn took over the job, Coquese was relieved. Even though she didn't play much at first, she felt that the team was working harder in practice and that she herself was improving. She took extra time on her own to work in the gym. "I felt that if I ever got an opportunity," she says, "I would be ready."

An opportunity came soon. It wasn't long before Coquese was spending far more time on court during Power games, either as a point guard or in a less familiar role, as the shooting guard.

Coquese thrived under the new coach's system. Lin Dunn "demands excellence from you," Coquese says. Sometimes in a game, Lin would call Coquese over to the sidelines. "Coquese, think!" the coach would say emphatically, tapping her head as if to model the behavior. In practice as well the coach made her points forcefully. "Goddawgit Coquese," she might say, "that was a stupid pass!" But then she'd explain how Coquese could do it differently. All of that was just fine with Coquese. "I want to be better. I want to do what's right," she says with emphasis.

In the last game of the season, when Portland played Colorado, Coquese hit a jump shot early in the game with only one second left on the shot clock. At the end of the game time was once again running out. This time there was less than a second left on the game clock. A Colorado player made a quick cross court pass. Coquese caught the pass and stood there smiling as the game ended.

Coquese isn't all smiles when she considers the future for the ABL. She wonders about the competition offered by the WNBA and what that means for the ABL. "We don't know how long this league is gonna last," Coquese feels. "Whether it'll be around five years from now, ten years from now."

But none of that makes Coquese sorry about her decision to be part of the first year of the league. It doesn't dim the sparkle in her eyes when she talks about playing professional basketball.

"I feel so fortunate," Coquese says, "to be doing something that I would do for free, that I would do anyway, just because I love the game."

Falisha Wright

Falisha Wright loves the game too, which helps explain why during the first season she literally played for free some of the time. If there's a best candidate for a Cinderella story in the ABL's first year,

Falisha Wright is surely it.

At 5'5," Falisha is short by basketball standards. Her close cut hair frames an often serious face. Not even drafted by an ABL team, Falisha spent a good chunk of the first season as an unpaid practice player and minimally paid replacement player. Then in the second part of the season, she became the starting point guard for the Portland Power. Her explosive speed and tenacious defense helped the team to some late-season wins.

When the season began for Portland, Falisha didn't even have a name on her uniform. Coquese Washington had been injured, and Falisha was signed to a temporary contract to replace her. Many fans had no idea who Falisha was.

It was a tough way to start her season, but Falisha is used to tough times. Her mother died when Falisha and her twin sister Lakeysha were only twelve years old. "We had to grow up at an early age," Falisha says about herself and her sister.

Aside from her sister, her mother was the only person in her family Falisha would talk with. "It's just tough losing your mom," Falisha describes. "When you have to grow up without one for the rest of your life, it's kind of unsteady."

While Falisha's mother was still alive, she had done her best to prepare the girls to stand on their own two feet. She'd taught them to cook and to clean. She'd stressed good performance in school. "If you don't get good grades, you won't be playing basketball anyplace," she would say to her daughters.

The death of a parent at an early age can shape a son or daughter's entire life. As an adult woman, Falisha is a quiet person. "Steady" is another good word to describe her. Somehow she's found that steadiness she lost for a while when her mother died. While playing point guard, she commits few turnovers. On and off the court, Falisha isn't someone who wears her feelings on her sleeve. "I'm a person that really doesn't show how happy or how excited I am," Falisha says about herself.

After her mother's death, Falisha had to find some of the steadiness she needed inside herself. She and her sister weren't close with their father—Falisha didn't get along well with him—so the girls also looked for support from what Falisha calls "surrogate mothers"—high school teachers, coaches on AAU teams. Towards the end of high school, Falisha moved in with one of her high school teachers.

Even before her mother died, though, Falisha was a tough kid who hung in there with what she loved best—playing sports. She was a "sports fanatic," Falisha says, as she grew up in Paterson, New Jersey. One sport she played was football, touch and tackle, with mostly boys in her neighborhood. "I was a tough little thing when I was younger," Falisha recalls. "I wanted to let the guys know that I could play whatever they (played), I could do whatever they do."

There might be snow on the ground, but Falisha was still up for a football game. Sometimes boys called her a "tomboy" or other names, teased her for being a girl playing football, said she should be doing something more girl-like. But when teams were picked, Falisha was usually the first one selected.

Boxing was another "unladylike" sport Falisha took up. She boxed with her older brother Victor and with her sister Lakeysha. She went with her father sometimes to the boxing ring, following him to the gym.

Her father had built a definitely nonregulation basketball hoop in front of their house. He made it out of plywood, a pole, and a rim from an old tire. Falisha and Lakeysha shot baskets there, and the sisters also played in a recreational league, introducing a foreign element—girls—into a previously all boys basketball team. Falisha played basketball in neighborhood gyms and playgrounds too. "It was all a challenge for me because I was going up against guys," she remembers. And sometimes the "guys," including her own brother, weren't all that welcoming.

"I'm going to play basketball," Falisha's brother might say, in an act of family theatre that often repeated itself.

"Can I go with you?" Falisha would ask.

"No," was the the usual plain-and-simple answer. But Falisha would complicate the plot by waiting a minute or two, and then following her brother. If he spotted her, he would throw rocks at her. Or he would yell at her. "Why are you following me? Go home. You shouldn't be down here with the guys." Her brother, Falisha thinks, wanted a sister who did what most girls did, like talking on the phone or hanging out in front of someone's house. Eventually, however, Falisha's brother changed his attitude. He began to bring his little sister with him to basketball games.

At John F. Kennedy High School, Falisha and Lakeysha helped their basketball team to an impressive record. During their four high school years, their team had 114 wins, only five losses, and won three state championships. Falisha set a Passaic County record for the over 2,000 points she scored. In one game alone, she hit 11 three pointers and put in a grand total of 57 points. She also played softball and tennis in high school. Tennis wasn't her best sport but she liked the challenge. The only thing she didn't like was "the little tennis skirts."

After high school, Falisha and Lakeysha were recruited "by a lot of big time programs," Falisha recalls. She and her sister ended up choosing San Diego State. With all those opportunities, why did they choose a school which wasn't nationally ranked? "Everyone asks me that question," is Falisha's first response.

Beth Burns, the new head coach at San Diego, had initially recruited Falisha for North Carolina State. When Beth took the job of head coach at San Diego State, her mission was to build up the program. Falisha had to make a decision. Did she want to "be a part of a program that's rebuilding and try to put that program on the map?" Or did she want to "go to a program that's already established," already big time, like Virginia or Tennessee or Old Dominion.

The go-for-it attitude that helped Falisha make a place for herself in the ABL revealed itself in the decision she made about college. She'd choose the rebuilding program at San Diego and do her best to help make that a strong basketball team. "It was the right decision for me at the time," Falisha says. Beth Burns was "a great coach" and a "good teacher of the game." She helped Falisha become a better player.

Falisha's twin sister Lakeysha also played on the basketball team at San Diego State. When her sister was on court, Falisha switched to the two or shooting guard. At five feet five inches, Falisha is an inch taller than her twin sister. If Lakeysha wasn't on court, Falisha would play the point.

Some people might find it strange to be playing with, and sometimes competing against, a sister, but Falisha thrived on all that. "We're very competitive," she describes, "I mean we beat each other up in practice. . . . She makes me play harder because we both want to win."

The competition with her sister must have helped Falisha to excel, as did the pointers she received from Beth Burns. While Falisha was at San Diego State, she was her team's choice for the All-Conference First Team for three years. She became the top three-point shooter for the college and took second place in the college's history for number of points scored. She received national recognition as a Kodak Honorable Mention All-American. Her heads up play was a big part of why San Diego State went to the NCAA tournament Falisha's sophomore, junior, and senior years.

Falisha still remembers that last NCAA tournament game she played in. She'd sprained her ankle badly the last week of regular season play, but she couldn't stand to sit on the bench during the tournament game. "I had to play, hurt or not," she felt at the time. But with the sprained ankle, she couldn't play her best. San Diego State ended up losing on their home court to a team Falisha felt they should have overcome. It was a tough loss for her. "Pretty devastating" is the way she describes it. "If I was 100 percent it would have been a different outcome of the game," Falisha asserts.

The way her last college season ended is a bitter memory, yet basketball at San Diego was a good experience for Falisha. The downside came only afterwards. San Diego State is part of the Western Athletic Conference, a conference which doesn't have as much prestige as some others. When players are chosen for USA Basketball teams, or when players were drafted for the ABL, women like Falisha who came from colleges which aren't big names are often overlooked. So Falisha didn't play on any USA Basketball teams. She didn't go overseas either. Instead she switched fields. She made a radical switch in fact, just as Coquese Washington did.

Her degree was in public administration, and after receiving it, she began an internship with the San Diego County Water Authority, the water company for the area. Her position was in the Emerging Business Enterprise Department, which did outreach to the community, with the goal of involving minority organizations as contractors.

Falisha is not an outgoing, extroverted type of person. She's not somebody who bubbles over with conversation, someone who would be a natural for a job which involves plenty of public contact. "I only talk when I have to," is something she says about herself. But Falisha has a quiet confidence about her. By her own account, she liked her public sector job just fine. She met various influential people in the San Diego area and got "hands on experience" in a responsible job.

If the ABL hadn't come along, she might never have found her way back to basketball. But when Falisha heard about a pro basketball league, she wanted a piece of the action. She went to the ABL draft as part of the second or B group of players, players from Division One colleges who didn't win championships or play internationally. She wasn't unrealistic about her chances. "I knew going in that it was going to be . . . very hard to make a team," she says. Still, Falisha felt she had a chance. "I had a pretty good tryout, and I was excited about that," she recalls.

She survived a number of cuts. Her speed and toughness made her stand out in hour and a half sessions where coaches and general managers had to make quick judgments about players. In spite of the odds, Falisha nearly made it. And then almost at the end of the tryouts, she learned that she was cut. Ironically, it was the next to the last cut before she would have made it into the ABL draft pool. "I was pretty devastated," she remembers, "because I felt that I could play with these girls and I could play in this league."

The ABL tryouts had quickened Falisha's basketball pulse. They'd given her a taste of what pro basketball would be like. She still wanted in to the league and she wanted to do whatever she could to help make that happen. So she wrote letters to all the ABL teams. "If you need a practice player, I'm willing to do that," she offered. As a practice player, she wouldn't be paid for her efforts. But she would be there, available, in case there was a need for a player on a team.

The letters may or may not have helped. The Old-and-Young-Girls Basketball Network definitely did. Debbie Gollnick, the assistant coach for the Power, had played basketball for the University of San Diego. When Coquese Washington was injured and the Power needed a guard as a temporary replacement, Beth Burns, the San Diego coach, gave Falisha's name to Debbie. Before long, Falisha was signed to a temporary contract with the Power. For much of the season, she was sometimes on the roster, sometimes not.

As a temporary player, Falisha would be paid, but not very much. Whenever she was officially on the Power roster, she would earn $500 for a week of practices and games, playing time and bench warming, whatever came her way. "I thank God I was on the roster at least once a month," Falisha told an *Oregonian* reporter. "But I didn't worry about the money. I just wanted to play." She lived for free with a host family in Portland, and she lived with the uncertainty of being sometimes on and sometimes off the roster.

At opening night for the Power, Falisha appeared on court as a temporary player, without a name on her uniform. She sat on the bench most of the game—only playing about five minutes and hitting one basket—but that didn't matter to her. "Just to be a part of that night was just the highlight of my year," she comments. "It was the first game of the inaugural season and that's like a dream come true. It's part of history. It'll go down in history books and I played in that game."

For about three weeks afterwards, Falisha stayed on the Power roster, until Coquese Washington returned to action. A little later, when Jennifer Jacoby was sick, Falisha was again transformed into a Power player. "It was kind of on and off the whole year until the last eight weeks of the season," Falisha remembers.

Whenever Falisha wasn't playing with the Power, she played with her other basketball team, an AAU team called the Portland Saints. Although Falisha must have been by far the best player on the team, she describes playing with the Saints as a good experience. It gave her a chance to to find her confidence as a player after doing so much bench warming for the Power.

After another Power guard, Tonya Sampson, tore an ACL on January 9th and was out for the season, Falisha's replacement player contract was extended through the last game of the regular season. She still wasn't making big bucks, but at least she was definitely on the team.

Then suddenly she was more than a bench player. The new Power coach, Lin Dunn, saw Falisha's potential. Falisha had several qualities—speed and steadiness and unselfish play—which could help her team. On January 23, Falisha not only played, she started. And she did her best to prove to the coach, her teammates, and fans that she deserved to play pro basketball. In early February she put in 11 points, a season high for her, against San Jose. On February 9, when Portland beat Seattle in overtime, Falisha had another season high of 18 points. Five of those points came during the pressure-filled overtime period. Instead of wilting under pressure, Falisha sank a three-pointer. Then with only seconds left in a basketball cliffhanger, she hit a two-point basket, giving Portland a narrow one-point victory.

Her teammates hugged Falisha. "Falisha grew up as a point guard tonight," coach Lin Dunn told a reporter. "At times she took control of the game."

Falisha might argue that the league has helped her grow up. The ABL provides the best basketball competition she's ever had. The play is fast and physical, hard and explosive. As players cut to the basket, pass the ball through a maze of opponents, dive to the floor for balls and play pressure defense, Falisha is right there in the thick of things. "You're going up against the best players in the country," she describes. "I mean you're going up against Olympians. I'm going up against people I've idolized since I was a kid like Teresa Edwards."

"Teresa in my eyes," Falisha explains, "is like a Michael Jordan in everybody else's eyes." Of course Michael is far more famous than Teresa, and that frustrates Falisha. "A lot of kids don't really know about Teresa Edwards," Falisha comments. Maybe they didn't see her on TV when she played in college or in the Olympics. They couldn't, of course, watch her during all the years she played overseas.

Like Teresa Edwards, Falisha remains a down to earth person. Unlike some male athletes, she doesn't act as if she's better than anyone else. She isn't someone who would refuse to sign autographs for a little girl or mouth off to a referee. The ABL founders wanted the players to be role models on and off the court. In her quiet way, Falisha fulfills this ideal. "Hi, how're you doing," she'll greet people. If a newspaper reporter or radio host has questions for her, she'll patiently answer them.

In an *Oregonian* article profiling Falisha, her teammate Michelle Marciniak told a story that reveals a lot about the kind of person Falisha is. The Power were returning from a game in San Jose in which Michelle had hurt her hip when she took a hard fall. As Michelle limped through the airport terminal, Falisha took Michelle's bag from her. It didn't matter to Falisha that she already carried three other bags. She still did what she could to help out a teammate. "She wanted to make sure I was OK," Michelle said. "She is very quiet, but she lets you know that she cares about you in her own way."

Falisha is the kind of player whom coaches put their faith in, whom coaches like to see succeed. After one Portland home game, where Falisha played and did well, her Portland Saints coaches, John Phillips and Jeff Gamble, gave her big hugs. Power coach Lin Dunn speaks glowingly about Falisha's speed. "There's not many people in this league that have a fifth gear like Falisha," Lin told a reporter.

As Falisha sees it, there's plenty of room for improvement in her game. "I showed flashes of what I can do," she says about her play in the first year. "I mean, I'm a better player than what I've showed." Earning a regular spot on an ABL team should help her continue to grow as a player.

Towards the end of the first season, Falisha Wright and Coquese Washington were often on court at the same time, usually with Falisha playing the point and Coquese the shooting guard. They could read each other well, guess each other's moves. They were both making good use of the second chance at their sport which the ABL gave them. Together, they made a dynamite combination.

Lisa Harrison

Lisa Harrison, Coquese and Falisha's teammate, spent three years away from basketball. After majoring in broadcasting at the University of Tennessee, and playing for the legendary coach Pat Summitt on the women's basketball team there, she made a foot-in-the-door entrance to the world of television and radio. As a part-timer, she did color commentary on women's basketball games for Sports South Network and radio commentary on Lady Ball Network, the radio station for the University of Tennessee. Meanwhile, her day job was as an employee of Bike Athletic Company.

At Bike Athletic, Lisa started out as a summer intern, travelling around the United States representing the company at a series of basketball tournaments for children and adults called Hoop It Up. Every weekend, Lisa travelled to a different city. . Eventually, in her full time position for Bike Athletic, Lisa was involved with in house sales and international accounts, travelling to Germany and Holland as part of her job.

Lisa's experience at Bike Athletic, and her television and radio gigs, could all have translated into a bright future for her in the corporate world. She has the photogenic features and bright smile of someone who could be a model, and with her background on one of the best teams in women's collegiate basketball, it's possible to imagine her becoming successful as a TV sports commentator. Yet she describes her non-basketball jobs as "a great experience but not what I wanted to do." When she heard about the ABL, she was interested right away.

Christy Hedgpeth, who spoke with so many players about the league, was Lisa's point of contact as well. Christy encouraged Lisa to come to a meeting Steve Hams had previously arranged with two other women. At that meeting Steve offered Lisa the chance to sign an agreement to play in the league prior to the ABL tryouts. She would still have to go to Atlanta and try out, but she would be guaranteed a place in the ABL. Lisa accepted the offer. In January, she quit her job, moved back home to Louisville, Kentucky, and began preparing herself for the tryouts.

After not playing basketball for three years, Lisa had to work hard to get in shape. She trained on her own, but had a hard time finding what she needed most of all—people to play the game with her. It was the middle of basketball season, and women on college teams were busy with their games and practices. As she struggled to get into basketball shape, she had a mental radio broadcast, her own personal color commentary, running in her head. "Is this really worth it?" she wondered. "I can't believe I'm doing this. I have no job. What's going to happen?"

Lisa Harrison

After the tryouts, Lisa was pretty sure she'd be drafted by Seattle. Jacquie Hullah had called her and asked her numerous questions. When Portland drafted her instead, Lisa was surprised rather than pleased. She had originally hoped to play for Atlanta, a city where she has family, and when she looked at the map to locate Portland, it seemed so far away.

Lisa made the long trip out to Portland with her new teammate Sheila Frost, caravan-style. Sheila was driving out from Virginia, and was going to pass through Louisville. The two women followed each other all the way to Portland, sharing hotel and motel rooms along the way, and the part-time companionship made the trip more enjoyable. Even though Lisa hadn't been thrilled about coming to Oregon, she was struck by the beauty of the Columbia Gorge, the steep, green cliffs and sculptured rock formations, as she passed through it on Interstate 84. Her introduction to Oregon was also helped by the fact that the rainy season hadn't yet begun.

The Power arranged for Lisa, Sheila, and other women on the team to stay for a week at a Shilo Inn while the women were finding apartments. On the second day Lisa was there, Roman Jones, a Power staffer, came to the hotel and told the women to get their shoes. They were going to play some basketball. But Lisa didn't even have any basketball shoes; she had thrown out her old ones because she was planning to get new ones in Portland. So she ended up playing in running shoes for the first week and risking injury, because running shoes don't give the side-to-side stability needed for basketball. Having to do that inspired Lisa to have some second thoughts about the league.

In spite of Lisa's somewhat shaky beginning, her college and high school basketball experiences gave her the kind of high-achieving basketball background which fitted her well for the ABL. In high school, she'd been recognized as the Naismith High School Player of the Year, a national honor. While Lisa was at the University of Tennessee, her basketball accomplishments could hardly be described as shabby. She helped her team win a national championship in 1991, and by the time she graduated in 1993, she'd piled up individual honors, including being recognized as a Kodak All-American and a Naismith Award finalist, and being selected by her teammates as the Most Valuable Player on the team during her senior year.

Lisa's three years away from basketball had given her a desire to return to the sport—she looked forward to sharing games, and travelling, and whatever else with her new teammates, to having the kind of companionship she'd missed during the years she hadn't played. But those years also lowered her expectations. At the start of the ABL season, Lisa remembers, "I came in with the attitude, I didn't really think I was going to play that much because I hadn't played in three years. So I was just going to use the first year to get back in shape and just try and get back into basketball."

Lisa's expectations made sense, considering that the Power had only drafted her in the seventh of ten rounds. In spite of her strong collegiate record, she'd been away from basketball for quite a while. "I was a has-been," Lisa joked to a reporter just before the start of the season. Lisa also knew Katy Steding was also going to be on the Power, and they both played the same position, the three, or small forward. "Oh great," Lisa thought, "Katy Steding, we play the same position. She's on the Olympic team. I'm never going to get to play."

In practices, though, Lisa held her own against her new teammates. And as it turned out the Power coach, Greg Bruce, named her as one of the starters for the team, not at Katy Steding's position but at the two or shooting guard spot. That was something Lisa had to get used to. In college she had played as a three or small forward. "I was totally out of position," she comments. She'd never even shot a three-pointer until her first year in the ABL.

Even so, Lisa was ready to play and excited about being a part of the new league's first year. In the opening game, she remembers walking out onto the arena floor and taking in the large crowd. "Wow, this is it, the ABL, it's really happening," she thought. "Look at all these people."

Running through the pyrotechnic displays, which flared up whenever a Power player was introduced, was a little scary. Lisa had goosebumps anyway, was anxious and "too pumped up" for the game. When the game finally began, she felt excited to be out there, excited to have the assignment of guarding four-time Olympian Teresa Edwards. Even though defense hadn't been her specialty in college, she felt proud to receive such a tough defensive assignment. She can still remember blocking a Teresa Edwards shot.

As the ABL season continued, Lisa settled into her new role. One thing that helped was that unlike many of her teammates, Lisa got along well with coach Greg Bruce. "I think I was one of the few players who had a good relationship with him," she recalls. "I felt bad for him that he had to take the blame for everything that went down which wasn't totally his fault."

For the Power, one of the things that went down was their league-longest losing streak. On December 5th, when the Power finally added a victory to their previous 13 and 2 record, Lisa showed just how valuable she was to her team.

"In a zone," cliched though it may be, is the most accurate way to describe Lisa's performance in that game. Throughout the game, Lisa shot the ball as if some sort of outside power was guiding its path to the basket. And she wasn't just shooting from a foot or two away. Perimeter shot after perimeter shot of hers, with only an occasional miss, found its way to the hoop.

In the first quarter, Lisa's mid-range jump shot was one of the first two baskets for the Power. Soon afterwards, she made another outside shot that gave Portland a ten-point lead. With a smooth, seamless shooting motion, Lisa released the ball smoothly from her fingertips and let it arc towards the net. She looked poised, focused, and somehow calm as she ran back down court after the basket.

Her game continued in the same fashion. Towards the end of the first quarter, she nailed another jumper, giving her six of her team's twelve points. "Lisa Harrison is in a nice groove," the TV announcer commented, with what would come to seem considerable understatement. And shooting wasn't Lisa's only contribution. She was active on defense, windmilling her arms to distract an opposing player. She stole the ball six times during the game for a career best. She grabbed rebounds and fought hard to keep them.

In the second quarter, Lisa made more outside shots, often finding nothing but net. Her expression remained calm as she nailed the shots and added point after point, far exceeding her usual scoring average of eight points per game. She had twelve points at the end of the half and was the only player on either team to score in double figures. Then in the second half it was more of the same. "Lisa Harrison continues to have the hot hand," a TV announcer commented. Again, that seemed like understatement, especially while watching Lisa hit another jumper, then soon afterwards streak down court and make a layup.

It was a game that Lisa Harrison would surely long remember, and not just because her team had finally won a game. She had put in a career high 24 points, making an impressive 65 percent of her shots. And most important, she had played her very best, played as if there were no barrier between her vision of shots falling and the reality, no interference in the connection between her mind and body, nothing to get in the way of an almost perfect performance.

After Lisa Harrison's three years away from basketball, she was back.

The Australia Connection

All the U.S. women who had played overseas made up only one part of the ABL's international flavor during the league's first year. There were also several players from other nations, including Marta de Souza Sobral, a tall, long limbed Brazilian woman who had played on the Brazilian Olympic Team which won a silver medal at Atlanta. And then there was the Australia connection, a basketball link between the land down under and the United States.

Among the ABL players, there were two U.S. women who had competed in Australian leagues. One of them, Rehema Stephens, had played for the Toowoomba Eagles in Queensland for one season. The second player, Debbie Black, was less of a basketball tourist and more of a settler. During the seven years she starred for the Tasmanian Islanders, she applied for citizenship, ending up as a citizen of both the U.S. and Australia. Shelley Sandie, the third member of the trio, was a native of Australia and a member of the Australian Olympic Team which won a bronze medal in 1996.

Shelley Sandie

Shelley Sandie seems like a quintessential Australian. She's friendly, unpretentious, willing to chat with people she meets and not filled with self-importance about her considerable basketball accomplishments. Yet she projects strength and self-confidence. It's easy to see her as a descendant of the Australian settlers who were shaped into strong, self-sufficient personalities by the size of the land and the pioneering it demanded.

It seems only fitting that Shelley Sandie is part of a group of modern pioneers, the women of the American Basketball League. She didn't arrive in time for the start of the first season—she was a mid-season replacement for injured San Jose player Jennifer Azzi— but Shelley finished up the year with the Lasers, her new team, and plans on a future with the ABL.

"It's the best league that I've ever played in," Shelley says about the ABL. "That's a pretty big statement," she adds, because she's played in Australia, in Germany, in the European Champions Cup. The ABL teams, she finds, are simply stronger, the level of talent much deeper.

Shelley is 28 years old. Born in 1969, she grew up in Melbourne, where she began playing basketball when she was nine years old. A true basketball veteran, she competed for Australian leagues and national teams from the age of 15, and recently she spent four seasons playing in Germany as well.

In Melbourne, where Shelley was born and raised, her mother worked in a post office and her father worked on building sites. Growing up, Shelley describes herself as "just interested in all sports." She played tennis, netball, basketball, swam, and was involved in what Australians refer to as "athletics" and Americans call track. When Shelley was a girl, some people tried to discourage her from spending such a large amount of time with sports. "Oh you're spending too much time with basketball," they said to her. If her basketball team was going to travel to an away game, some of her teachers were far from encouraging. "You should be . . . concentrating on your schoolwork," a teacher might say. "You'll never make any money out of basketball."

That was "a fair enough comment back then" is Shelley's attitude now, since when she was growing up, it was hard for people to imagine that she would eventually be making her living by playing basketball. When Shelley was a child, however, she basically just ignored the negative feedback. Her friends played sports; her parents were strongly supportive of Shelley and her athletic brother; and Shelley simply went on with basketball and other sports.

When Shelley was 15 years old, however, she narrowed her sports focus. After being selected for a spot on the Australian Junior Team, she was told that she had to make a decision. Did she want to commit herself seriously to basketball? Shelley decided that she did— basketball was the sport she was best at—and she moved ahead with what was to became her career.

Without seeming at all boastful, Shelley can describe what she's good at as a basketball player. She's a hard worker, a determined player, with an "all around game." She can catch a pass and shoot from the perimeter and play strong defense. The club system of Australian basketball was where Shelley developed all those skills. "Basketball has really grown in Australia and they have a well structured system," Shelley describes. "Anyone can play at any age. You can start playing at five years old and if you want to, you can play five times a week at 70 years old." Perhaps the main drawback was that the Australian club system didn't provide Shelley the chance to play collegiate basketball which other ABL players have received.

The Australian Junior Team, which Shelley joined at 15, is a national team and competes in a junior world championship. When Shelley was 18, she moved up to the senior team. She also played for 12 years in an Australian semi-professional league called the Australian Women's National Basketball League (AWNBL) which has teams all over Australia. Three of the ten teams in the league are from Melbourne, which was where Shelley played initially, but she switched to Sydney for her last four Australian seasons. As a member of the Sydney Flames, she was honored as the team's Most Valuable Player for three years, and in 1994 she was the highest scorer for the entire league.

But Shelley didn't limit herself to Australian competition. For four years, she did basketball double duty. She travelled to Germany and played a full season there, then returned to Australia for another basketball season. It was a basketball endurance contest she describes as "really tough, just both mentally and physically."

Shelley's first German season was spent in Cologne, and her next three seasons in Wuppertal, a city located between Cologne and Dusseldorf. While in Germany she also had the opportunity to play in the European Champions Cup, a round robin competition where the best team from each country plays and in which many top players participate.

Shelley's husband Hugh—a former professional basketball player turned agent—was with her in Germany, and the two made some good German friends who would drive them on trips to different parts of Europe. Another woman from Australia, one of Shelley's best friends, was on one of her German teams. Even so, Shelley sometimes felt isolated and lonely. "The hardest thing," she says, is "being away from your friends and your family." And the time of year the European basketball season ran didn't help an Australian used to more sunny climes. "It's the winter over there," Shelley describes, "it's really cold. . . . You got a lot of time on your hands over there. . . . you sit there and you think about what everyone else is doing and how much fun they're having at home."

That fun at home could include sunbathing on the warm Australian beaches, or spending sunny weekends with friends and family. Over in Germany in the European winter, Shelley was missing out on the Australian summer. Her internal weather calendar was reversed, you could say. And yet there were compensations. Basketball meant a lot to Shelley. "You think about what you're doing there," she says about her basketball experiences in Germany, "and you know you're achieving something pretty special."

"Something pretty special" is a good label for another place basketball has taken Shelley: the Olympics. In addition to competing in several world championships, she was a member of the 1988 Australian Olympic Team, a year when Australia finished fourth. Australia didn't qualify for the Olympics in 1992, but Shelley was among the group of women who gave it their best try. Then in 1996, Australia's Olympic team did make the cut. Shelley was a member of that group of elite basketball players.

The players on the Australian National Team were already competing in the Australian National Women's Basketball League, but every three weeks or so they got together for a kind of mini training camp. They packed a lot of basketball into four-day periods, playing six hours a day in two three-hour sessions. Two weeks before the Olympics, they came to the United States and competed in two tournaments. "I think that we were pretty well prepared," is Shelley's assessment.

Going up against the U.S. women's Olympic team was a "great experience," Shelley describes. They "just dominated every other team." But the Australian team forced the U.S. women to respect them. "We were probably the team that pushed them the hardest," Shelley comments. She and her teammates played a style of basketball she describes as "aggressive, really defensively oriented" and "a fast break transition game offensively," the same type of game the American women often liked to play.

As Olympic basketball got underway, the United States women first competed against the Australians on a Saturday night. Both teams were up for the game, especially after a record of close games between the two opponents during the American women's visit to Australia a number of months before. "I'm scared of Australia," Teresa Edwards commented, author Sara Corbett reports in *Venus to the Hoop*. "Some teams, you can break their backs, but not Australia. You can't tell them anything. They're the fighting type. They'll fist fight you. They're never going to quit."

In the first Olympic match between the U.S. and Australian women, a game attended by a record number of 33,000 fans, the lead went back and forth before the U.S. finally came up with the victory. Australia and the United States met again in the semi-final game. Now the stakes were even higher. The winner of that game would compete for the gold medal. The loser could only receive a bronze. And the Australian women were ready to play. In their previous game they'd overcome the Russian women, the former gold medalists, in an overtime victory.

Shelley Sandie

The U.S. women, Shelley believes, knew that one of the Australian's strengths was their fast breaking style of play. The well-coached U.S. team managed to force the Australians into a more of a half-court game while once again a large number of fans watched and cheered their respective teams.

After a hard-fought game, the U.S. women defeated Australia 93-71. Sara Corbett describes the exuberant celebration of the Americans, which was in sharp contrast to the way some of the Australian women sat on their team bench, hid their faces with their hands, and cried. Defeat when the stakes are so high is always hard. Yet what Shelley remembers most vividly about the Olympics is not that painful moment.

When all the games were finally over, and the U.S. women had won the gold medal and Brazil the silver, the Australian women also had an achievement to be proud of. Previously, neither an Australian men's or women's basketball team had ever won a medal in either an Olympic or a world championship competition. Shelley had been the second highest scorer on her team in the '96 Olympics. Now she stood on the podium, along with her teammates, and received her bronze medal.

Over 30,000 fans were watching, including team supporters who had travelled from Australia for the Olympics. Shelley's husband Hugh and her mother was there. It was an emotional moment for Shelley, a moment that repaid her and her teammates for all their hard work. "It was just special and was just a really proud moment," is the way Shelley sums up that experience.

After the Olympics, Shelley could have joined an ABL team in September, the way many of the U.S. Olympians did. She'd already been in contact with the team in San Jose, but she hesitated to sign a contract which committed her for twelve months and didn't allow her to play for any other professional league during that time. "It was just too restricting," Shelley felt. So she headed back home to Australia to play, and afterwards was planning to travel to Austria to play professionally when she heard that Jennifer Azzi of the Lasers was injured.

San Jose invited Shelley to join their team, and Shelley decided to accept the invitation. "I'd already spent four seasons over in Germany and Europe anyway," she comments, "and I felt like I'd been there and I'd done that." By contrast, an ABL team represented "a whole new challenge" for her. She thought that the standard of play would be higher than that in Austria, and her experience in the ABL proved her to be correct. "It's been such a huge challenge and there's so many great athletes and great players here," Shelley says.

Shelley arrived in San Jose on December 23rd. Her first game with the Lasers was on December 27th, only four days later, not even enough time to fully recover from the international travelers' heavy-duty version of jet lag. Because of the Christmas holiday, Shelley only had one practice session with her team before the December 27th game.

It was a tough first act for Shelley. The game was at home in San Jose, but it was against the Columbus Quest, who had the best record in the ABL. Shelley was handicapped by lack of familiarity with both her own teammates and the players she would face from the Quest. Actually, she did know Quest players Andrea Lloyd from

European basketball, and Nikki McCray from the 1996 Olympics. But most of Shelley's first or almost first impressions of players had to be made in the heat of game action.

"I was really nervous," Shelley remembers. "Usually I'm really well prepared for games and when you're not, . . . it was difficult." But the supportive fans in San Jose helped a lot. "We had a huge crowd there and they were all going crazy," she remembers. "Just the whole atmosphere of the night was, it was a real buzz." When San Jose beat Columbus, fans and players alike celebrated.

As Shelley settled into her new life with the Lasers, she had help from her husband Hugh Sandie. Hugh, now working as a players' agent, was with Shelley to support her career, something she says that more and more men are doing for wives and girlfriends. That support means a lot to Shelley. When she first began playing in Germany, she and Hugh were apart for a while, a situation she found "really tough." In Germany, Shelley says, "I know I played my best basketball when he was there with me and supporting me," and the same was true for her in the U.S.

The toughest thing for Shelley about her first ABL season, or really part of a season, remained the most obvious challenge. "Coming in, you know, half way through the season," she comments, "the team was established and I had to try and fit in and learn the offenses really quickly." She had to "read" the moves of her teammates, of players on opposing teams, and of course it took time for her new teammates to learn about Shelley's own game, such as where she preferred to receive the ball. It was far from an ideal situation, of course. "I felt like I didn't get comfortable with the offense till right near the end," Shelley says.

She had to adjust to a differently paced schedule too. A typical Australian basketball season involves eighteen games over a span of four months. Australian players typically practice all week for one game, or if they're lucky, play two games over a weekend. "It's just great having a forty game schedule," Shelley says about the ABL setup. "This is a lot more fun playing so many games." On the other hand, the travel and frequent games could be tiring; with muscles and joints sore from the pounding they took on court, players still had to embark on road trips or simply get ready for another game. Perhaps that's why for Shelley, many of the ABL games she played have blurred in her memory, places and players and final outcomes all running together.

One game that does stand out for her was during an eight game road trip in late January. At the Hartford Civic Center, the New England Blizzard's home court, nearly 12,000 fans filled the stands, shouting noisily in support of their team. The Lasers were 16 points down during the game, but they fought their way back into the game and ended up winning it.

Five days before that New England game, the Lasers played another road game, this time against the Seattle Reign. It was only the third time Shelley had started for the Lasers and she didn't always look comfortable out on court. TV announcers commented that she'd had to adjust to the faster, more physical game in the ABL. Yet Shelley played long minutes, doing her adjusting on court in front of fans and TV cameras, and demonstrating that she was a quick study.

There was the three-pointer she drilled in the first quarter. And the way she drove to the basket in the second quarter, made a close shot, then shortly afterwards pulled up and hit another three-pointer. At the half, Shelley had nine points, making her the leading scorer for San Jose.

"She's starting to be a spark for them," a TV announcer said about Shelley. That "spark" involved more than just the baskets Shelley had made. She was an energetic presence on court, hustling for rebounds and working hard on defense. She might hesitate when dribbling, allowing the ball to be taken away from her, yet she could also double pump the ball in a savvy, veteran-smart way before going up to make a basket.

In spite of Shelley and her teammates' efforts, the Lasers lost that game against Seattle. But they won enough other games to make it to the semi-finals of the ABL playoffs. Columbus, the Lasers' opponent, was, Shelley describes, "a great team" and "a really well coached team" who "play so well together." Knowing that didn't soften the blow when the Quest swept the Lasers in the playoff semi-finals, with the second game taking place in front of the Lasers' own fans.

"It hurts," Shelley says, "ending your season like that with two losses." Personally, she didn't play at her best, she feels. Looking back on that season ending game, however, she's able to be somewhat philosophical. She has the resilient personality that Australian settlers must have needed, and that many of the modern pioneers in the ABL seem to possess. "That's the sport and that's the way it goes," Shelley says, "and you're depressed for a bit, but you then, obviously, got to get over it."

Getting over it, for Shelley, will involve future seasons with the ABL—she signed what is essentially a two-year contract. She'll have a chance to return to Australia first, for the U.S. spring and part of the summer. Her ABL contract restricts her from competing in the Australian league, but she's going to train and practice with her club team in Sydney, and then do some playing with the Australian National Team.

For the ABL overall, Shelley sees fan support increasing. The league, she thinks, will "keep growing and getting stronger." Part of that growth, Shelley hopes, will involve other players from Australia. They could come over to the U.S., play in the ABL, and learn more about the American style of play.

When the Australian National Team competes at the Sydney Olympics in the millenial year of 2,000, Shelley hopes to be on the team. Michele Timms, her teammate from the 1996 Australian Olympic Team, played for the WNBA in its first season. Perhaps by the time the next Olympics comes around, a number of other women from the land down under will be playing their game for American fans.

Debbie Black

Debbie Black, the ABL's Defensive Player of the Year for the 1996-97 season, is also the shortest player in the league. At 5'3", she's the Spud Webb of the ABL, someone who can zip past taller players.

Debbie doesn't think short though. "When I'm out on the court I really do not feel that little," she says. On the basketball court she feels as tall as the other players. Only off court, such as when she's watching a game video, she might notice the height discrepancy. "Geez, I'm little out there," she sometimes thinks. But on court, she says, "my mentality is like, I'm as big as anyone. . . I can do anything that anyone else can do out here."

Debbie's performance at games bears out her words. She's lightning fast, tenacious on defense, a good penetrator with quick hands who can steal the ball from opposing players. Her teammates' and opposing players' nicknames for her include the "Tasmanian Devil" and the "Little Termite." The Tasmania part recognizes Debbie's overseas experience. For seven years, she was a star player for the Tasmania Islanders in Australia. And all Debbie's nicknames, although they may not sound that way, are actually names given out of respect, names that recognize just how good Debbie Black is as a basketball player.

With her outgoing personality, Debbie comes across as 'just folks,' without a trace of a star complex. She smiles and laughs a lot, and seems to enjoy meeting people. Perhaps growing up the youngest child of four siblings gave Debbie her people-oriented personality and encouraged her not to consider herself as better than anyone else. In Lancaster, the suburb of Philadelphia where she grew up, Debbie's two older brothers and one older sister were her first sports competitors. Playing sports with them, she thinks, is what gave her her toughness. Debbie, her brothers, and her sister competed against each other in backyard games, playing basketball in a little court they had in their yard, and playing football as well. Debbie laughs at the suggestion that it was touch football. They played the real thing—tackle football—minus amenities like helmets and pads.

"If you guys are going to play, you're going to play," Debbie's brothers said to her and her sister. "If not, if you're going to cry, you're going to go home." Crying wasn't allowed, even for girls. Debbie's brothers and the other neighborhood boys who joined in the games treated her and her sister not like girls but simply like players. If they were tough enough to cut it, they could join in the games.

The rough support Debbie received from her brothers didn't reflect her father's attitude. Although her father later became a strong and proud supporter of Debbie's sports accomplishments, her father's ideas about sports when Debbie was a child were more traditional. Her father was "very much a male chauvinist when I was growing up," Debbie remembers. He had been an athlete himself, lettering in football, basketball, and baseball, and he strongly encouraged his sons in sports, but he didn't see sports as important for girls.

When Debbie was a girl, her father was the president of a Community Youth Organization (CYO) league. In fact, he was the one who organized the league. But when someone asked her father about starting a girls' league, his response was simple. "No way." Her father, Debbie says, shared the common attitude that "girls shouldn't be playing sports. They should be at home . . . doing something like sewing or cooking." She doesn't do those things especially well, Debbie says with a laugh.

Debbie did and does do sports well, and she went into sports in a big way at school, playing on girls' basketball, soccer, softball, and field hockey teams. She loved soccer, and had the perfect build for it, but since she was before the curve for the soccer boom, her high school only had a club team in that sport. At Archbishop Wood High School, however, Debbie and her teammates won a basketball championship and three field hockey championships in the Catholic League. By that time, Debbie's father's attitude was changing—he eventually became supportive not just of Debbie but of girls' and women's sports overall—and he began to give Debbie and her sister some informal coaching.

Because her high school played in a smaller league, and probably because of her height as well, Debbie wasn't heavily recruited by colleges. She accepted a full ride athletic scholarship to St. Joseph's University in Philadelphia, a fairly small school which would allow Debbie to letter in three sports, field hockey, basketball and softball. Debbie and her sister are still the only athletes, male or female, to graduate from St. Joseph's with twelve letters.

Debbie learned a great deal about basketball fundamentals at college. "Basketball isn't just about running around," she comments wryly. In college she worked on dribbling—through her legs, behind her back—and on staying with better players than she'd had the chance to compete against in high school. Sports were her priority. Debbie admits that she didn't put all the effort she could have into her academic studies. She did work hard enough to graduate with a 3.0 average and a marketing degree, which she thought could help her find some sort of career in business.

She ended up using her marketing degree, but not close to home the way she might have imagined. After college, she was recruited by the Tasmanian Islanders, a basketball team in Tasmania, an island in the south of Australia. How that happened makes up a comedy-of-errors episode, or comedy-of-error actually.

There were plenty of good reasons for a team to recruit Debbie. While she played point guard for St. Joseph's University, the school went to the NCAA tournament four years in a row. They were a small school, but in her junior year, they even went as far as the NCAA Sweet 16. The name opposing players in the tournament gave the St. Joseph's team seems appropriate. "We were always considered the Giant Killers," Debbie remembers. "We knocked off some great teams."

Debbie herself received individual honors, such as being named the Philadelphia Big Five MVP, and posted especially strong numbers in steals and assists. But when her senior season had ended, Debbie was up in the air about her future. "What am I going to do?" she asked Jim Foster, the college coach who was a kind of father figure to her and other athletes.

"Well, you can go overseas," her coach said.

"Gosh, that sounds a little scary," Debbie thought. Even though she was fearless on court, she wasn't at all sure about a basketball future far from home.

An odd kind of "fate" had a hand in her decision. When Debbie was named to the All-Atlantic-10 team after her senior year by *Street and Smith* magazine, the magazine made a mistake that may have been crucial to Debbie's future. It listed her height erroneously as 6'3" rather than 5'3".

No doubt impressed by such a tall point guard, someone from a team located in Tasmania called. "We're interested in your point guard," the caller told Jim Foster. Because of the kind of basketball statistics Debbie had, the Australian team had already guessed that Debbie probably wasn't quite as tall as listed, but of course they didn't yet know her actual much more diminutive height.

Jim Foster told the Australians that Debbie was really quite short, 5'3" in fact, but he encouraged the team to send a ticket so Debbie could come try out. He plugged all of Debbie's strong points as a player. "Just give her a shot," he told the Tasmanian Islanders. "You'll see whether you like her."

Debbie didn't go over to Australia convinced she was going to become a female John Stockton or Isaiah Thomas. And the location of the Australian team, Tasmania, didn't set off bells and whistles in her mental map of the world. "Oh God, where is this place," she questioned. But she figured she might as well make the trip. "If nothing else," she thought, "I get a free trip to Australia. I can hang around the beaches if I don't make it."

In 1989, Debbie travelled to Tasmania, made the team, and essentially never looked back. Tasmania, she found, was "a little bit behind the mainland of Australia, but in a nice way." Hobart, her new home, was the biggest city in Tasmania, with a population of 280,000, and was situated by the ocean with snow-covered Mt. Wellington in the background adding to the picture-postcard ambiance. All in all, Debbie found, Tasmania was a great place to live—relaxing, safe, and friendly to Americans.

On court, however, the Australian style was anything but relaxing. Debbie definitely doesn't agree with Shelley Sandie that the ABL is more physical than Australian play. "The Australian competition is very, very tough, very physical, very demanding," Debbie says. "The guard play was rough, rough, rough. I mean, I got away with a lot over there." She laughs about that now.

As the point guard for players who might be in their thirties, Debbie had to assert herself, be a strong floor leader. The Australian players might not be as athletic as some U.S. women but they were strong competitors. "I love their attitudes," Debbie says about them, "They fight hard every night." It was a style of playing that she fit in well with, and a style that shaped her into the player she is today.

Debbie's life in Australia was a good one. Aside from games, her team practiced twice a week at night, and she earned only about $20,000 a year for playing basketball. But she supplemented that with her day job working for an energy management company. The marketing degree she'd received had come in handy. She eventually became a permanent resident and then, in her last year there, a citizen of Australia.

Debbie was well known in Australia. She describes herself as "a big fish in a small pond," obviously not referring to her height. Her team was recognized as well. They won the Australian National Championship in 1991, the first time any women's teams from Tasmania had won it. Tasmanians celebrated with a huge parade. "That was one of the biggest thrills I've had when we won in 1991," Debbie remembers. When her team won the Southern and National Championship in 1995, that was icing on the cake.

Of course, Debbie couldn't share that cake with members of her family. Australia is a long ways away from Philadelphia, and being separated from the family she has always felt very close with was difficult for Debbie, although her sister, who is a teacher, was able to come out for a year. The Australian basketball season ran from February to August, and Debbie would go home to Philadelphia in December, then return to Australia in January. She thought sometimes about being back in the United States, but didn't have any plans to return there, at least not while she could still play basketball in Australia. A women's professional basketball league would start eventually in the states, Debbie thought. But she figured she'd be too old to play by the time a league got started.

Looking back on it all, Debbie thinks that there was a purpose to her personal sequence of events. She was in Australia "for a reason," Debbie feels. "Maybe it was so I could come back and play in the ABL." Playing in Australia kept her basketball game strong, kept her a conditioned athlete. If she hadn't kept on playing, she's convinced, she never could have found a place on an ABL team at the age of thirty.

Her oldest brother was the one who told Debbie about the ABL. He sent her a three-page fax about the ABL which included an application. Debbie wasn't sure if it was worth the trouble to apply. "I don't know," she thought, "I've been away so long." But she argued with herself about those negative thoughts. "If I don't do this, I'll regret it," she told herself.

A couple of weeks later she received a letter from the ABL. She was one of the almost 600 women whom coaches would consider at the ABL trials. "This is a joke," Debbie thought. She figured that the $200 application fee had just been a scam. But what if it wasn't? "God, if I don't do this," she told herself, "I could be blowing an opportunity." She could be losing out on the chance to come home.

The tryouts at Atlanta in late May and early June were right in the middle of the Australian basketball season, but Debbie's team gave her permission to go. She flew out to Atlanta and found that she was in the B group, which meant that she entered the tryouts on the second day. That was a step up from the A group, the players who started on the very first day and whom the ABL assumed were least likely to make it into the league. But it was below the C group, considered the best players. Since Debbie had been playing in Australia for years, no one really knew who she was.

It was hot and humid in Atlanta, much warmer than in Tasmania. After her years away, Debbie was something of a foreigner. She had forgotten what the summer humidity was like. However, it was cool in the gym, a relief from the enveloping heat outside, and there Debbie could "speak" the international language of basketball.

Every day Debbie looked on a door where players' numbers were posted. If someone's number was still there, that player was a survivor and could go on to another round. Debbie's number was two, always high up on the list, so she could spot it quickly and see if she was still in the running. Every day her number was still posted on the door. By Friday of the weeklong tryouts, when the C group came in, Debbie was feeling much more confident. "I'm as good as anybody out here," she told herself. When she made it all the way into the 120 player draft pool, she was up for playing in the league, but she still didn't know if that would happen. She hoped that someone would draft her, hoped that her shortness wouldn't count too much against her. "Someone's got to like me," she told herself, "just got to pray that one person likes me."

The Colorado Xplosion was the team that answered Debbie's prayer. They drafted her in the sixth round of the first ABL draft. After she was drafted, and her future was set, Debbie finished her season in Australia at the end of August, then came out to Colorado in September.

When training camp began, Debbie wasn't sure what to expect. She wasn't intimidated—her experience at the ABL tryouts had shown her that her game was on the level of the league—but she was a little nervous. "It was a little bit unnerving," she remembers. She was going to be on court with great players, she knew, but she herself was pretty much of an unknown. "I really felt like I needed to go out there," she remembers, "to show these people that I could play."

She also wanted to get to know her teammates, to become friends with them, and with her outgoing personality that can't have been hard. In fact, all season one of the Xplosion's strengths was the friendships the players felt for each other. "We all get along so well," Debbie comments, "and there's nothing but respect for each other."

The opening game for the Colorado Xplosion was at home in Denver, with the Xplosion playing the Seattle Reign in front of about 4,500 fans. As Debbie stood together with her new teammates and heard the national anthem playing, she got "a goosebumpy feeling." Tears filled her eyes. All the years away she'd listened to the Australian national anthem and wondered what it would be like to hear the Star Spangled Banner instead. "I just never thought I'd be back home in front of my home crowd and in the United States," she comments. Doing exactly that was "an incredible feeling."

At the start of the game, all the Colorado players were nervous. Everyone had the sense that they were a part of "history in the making." It was a good but also unsettling feeling. "It was such an important game for a lot of reasons," Debbie comments. "You didn't want to blow it."

Debbie herself was "extremely, extremely nervous," more so than she ever remembers being for any other basketball game. She had a knot in her stomach before the game. She almost felt as if she could throw up. When the game started, at first she felt too tentative, not quite sure how to move. "Geez, I've never felt this way before," she remembers thinking. It took about five minutes before she settled down, forgot about all the fans there to watch something new, forgot about the new league itself, and just concentrated on playing basketball.

When the season started, Debbie and her teammates hadn't come together the way they would a little later on. They won their first game, but soon had put together an unimpressive four wins and nine losses record. Then they took off. They became one of the ABL's hottest teams.

How did it happen? What brings a team together is partly magic, it seems. Or just one of those things, you could say, that's impossible to fully define or to recreate at will. "All of a sudden the chemistry just hit," Debbie remembers. With Debbie as the starting point guard, the Xplosion team won ten games in a row. Their confidence grew. They became very difficult to stop.

For Debbie, playing in the ABL was a chance to develop as a player. She had learned a great deal while playing in Australia, but there were some drawbacks. The coaching was just okay rather than really good, the team only practiced twice a week, and the quality of the players wasn't as high. In the ABL, Debbie continually went up against other talented point guards like Dawn Staley. That was "very, very challenging," Debbie says, but it's the kind of challenge she loves. She'd heard about players like Dawn Staley and Teresa Edwards when she was overseas. She'd always wondered how she would stack up against them. Now she had the chance to find out.

Of course, going up against the best wasn't easy. And Debbie isn't the sort of player to hold back. "I see a loose ball, I'm gonna dive. If I have any opportunity to get anything, I'm gonna go on the ground," is how Debbie describes her personal style. She knows that extra level of effort is what makes her successful as a player. Even when she plays pickup games, she always has to play "flat out, as hard as I go." Out on a basketball court, even in a pickup game, Debbie is always revved up to her fifth gear.

Debbie's a resilient player and person, someone with a big heart in a small body. The ABL players are all gutsy—they couldn't make it in the league if they weren't—but Debbie takes more risks with her body than some other players.

"The way that I play, you know, I tend to throw myself around a little bit," is Debbie's understated description of her anything but wimpy style on the basketball court. With minor injuries, she says, "you're going to have some pain. . . but you overcome that. . . . You just don't worry about it until the next morning." Debbie laughs. "That's when it hurts."

Watching Debbie accumulate floor burns, or zip down the floor and end up crashing into the padded posts supporting the basket, a spectator might wonder just how long she could stay healthy. "I would probably have the most falls in the league if there was a statistic on that," Debbie laughs. But she seems to have an innate sense of how to fall. She's been "really lucky," she says, and hasn't ever received a major injury playing basketball. She makes light of the injuries she sees as minor which came her way during the first ABL season.

When Colorado lost to the Richmond Rage on Friday, November 1st, in an exhausting triple-overtime game, Debbie emerged with battle scars. Molly Goodenbour, a guard for Richmond, drove to the basket with Debbie Black as her no-surrender defender. The two players crashed into each other, fell to the floor, and Debbie ended up on the bottom of the pile. She came up for air with bruises on several ribs, a concussion, and a hairline fracture.

After the collision, Debbie told the Colorado trainer that she didn't have any feeling in her legs. She was carried off the court on a stretcher. On Saturday, though, doctors let Debbie leave the hospital, and just a day later, on Sunday, she was playing again. Debbie's coach, Sheryl Estes, wanted Debbie to play more cautiously in that game, but didn't have high hopes that Debbie would follow her advice. "I told Debbie, 'Don't take a charge.' I knew she wouldn't pay attention," Sheryl Estes told a reporter from the *Rocky Mountain News*.

On December 3rd, Debbie put on a basketball show, ending up with 18 points, 8 steals, nine assists, and 8 rebounds, leading a *Rocky Mountain News* reporter to describe it as a "red-letter performance," and "one of the finest performances to date in the infant American Basketball league, which has yet to see its first triple-double."

The reporter may have had some sort of precognition going. Soon afterwards, on Sunday, December 8th in a game at home against Atlanta, Debbie simultaneously made history for the ABL and did something she'd never done before in her entire basketball career— scored a quadruple double. She posted double figures in points scored, assists, steals, and rebounds. A rare achievement in both men's and women's basketball.

Debbie's fast hands and tenacious defense led to the steals. Her acute court vision and unselfish play helped her get the assists. She didn't have a height advantage with rebounds, but her quickness as well as willingness to dive to the floor or insert her body into a crowd helped her to capture loose balls.

At halftime, it looked as if Debbie might end up with a triple double without having scored any points. But although her main mission as a point guard isn't to score, she can shoot the ball when she needs to. In the fourth quarter, a *Rocky Mountain News* article described, Debbie "caught fire offensively."

Then with only two minutes left in the game, Debbie had double figures in every category except points. She had scored eight points already, but lacked two to complete her quadruple double. The Xplosion had a solid fourteen point lead, so the game outcome was not in doubt. "Go get a basket," Coach Sheryl Estes told Debbie.

Debbie wouldn't have sacrificed a team victory for her individual achievement, but since the Xplosion were obviously going to win the game, Debbie was happy to do exactly what her coach said. All Debbie's teammates knew what was at stake as well. Debbie got the ball, drove to the basket, and scored on a layup.

The coach pulled Debbie out of the game with about 30 seconds to go. Fans rose to their feet, clapping and cheering, applauding Debbie's accomplishment. But what she'd achieved really hit Debbie only after the game. During interviews with media people, she found out how rare her achievement was. Only four NBA players had ever posted quadruple doubles, Debbie learned. Michael Jordan never had.

By the end of the first ABL season, Debbie Black had shown that her quadruple double was no fluke. In the ABL post-season awards, Debbie was voted to the Second-Team All-ABL along with her Colorado teammate Crystal Robinson. Averaging 4.4 steals per game, Debbie was recognized as the Defensive Player of the Year. She had started every single game, stole the ball more times than any other ABL player, and had handed out the second largest number of assists.

The ABL playoffs tested both Debbie and her teammates. They'd come into the playoffs with the best record in the west, an achievement Debbie had celebrated by doing a handspring on the way to the locker room, after the game when the Xplosion won the Western Conference. In the regular season, Colorado posted victories in 21 out of their last 27 games. In December they had an 8 and 0 record.

That hot December, Debbie thinks, might have been part of what undermined Colorado in the playoffs. "This game is about peaking at the right time," she says. Her team, she believes, peaked in December, while Richmond was peaking for the playoffs. The Colorado players may have been mentally tired. "For some reason we weren't at the top of our game," is Debbie's assessment. She knows that no one can totally understand the complex way the mental and physical game of basketball, and the odd card which is luck, come together.

One negative factor for Colorado was obvious. Home court advantage, or the lack of it in Colorado's case. The Colorado players had worked all season to get home court advantage in the first round of the playoffs. With their record as the best team in the west, they should have had that important psychological edge. "That first game at home could have been everything for us," Debbie comments, "as far as winning the first game, getting our confidence going."

But the new league had trouble getting access to the arena in Colorado for the correct date. And for some reason the travel costs were cheaper if the first game was held in Richmond. That's how Debbie understands what motivated the league to make the change. It's an example of the kind of financial and logistical problems that the NBA never has to deal with.

Debbie understood the ABL's position as a new league. But starting the playoffs on the road was still disappointing. It was "probably the toughest thing" about the playoffs for her and her teammates.

In the first game, Colorado came close to beating Richmond on the Rage's home court. The Xplosion were ahead by 15 points at halftime, after what Debbie describes as "a perfect half of basketball." It was such a good start that they couldn't imagine losing the game. But Debbie describes her team "falling apart" in the second half, then coming together but not soon enough. In the end, Richmond beat Colorado by a three-point margin.

The narrow loss was "really devastating" for Debbie and her teammates. In the locker room afterwards, players cried and expressed their anger. The strong emotions were understandable, but what the team needed to do next was to make a fresh start. That was what their coach, Sheryl Estes, told her team the day after the loss. In the best of three semi-final format, they had to concentrate on winning the next game and forget about the last one. It was good advice of course but not so easy to follow. "That's probably one of the hardest things to do in basketball," Debbie comments. It was especially difficult for the Xplosion because of the way they lost, playing such a strong first half and then blowing the game in the second half.

"If we only could have won that game. We had them, we had them," Debbie remembers her teammates saying. The results of that psychological jet lag were probably predictable. "We got killed the next game," is Debbie's terse comment.

In the second semi-final game, the margin wasn't even close, with the Xplosion losing by 15 points. Debbie ended up with six steals in that game, the second highest number of steals for anyone throughout the ABL playoffs. Yet when describing the second play-off game, Debbie doesn't mention that flattering individual statistic. Like many of the women in pro basketball, she's very much a team player, someone who focuses more on her whole team's play than on her individual accomplishments. So she simply characterizes the second playoff game as one where her team couldn't do anything right, a game where they just weren't competitive. Perhaps part of the problem was that they were trying too hard, playing tight rather than loose.

That second and final defeat was tough on Debbie and her teammates. It hurt to be eliminated from playoffs in a home game, stung not to have played as well as they were capable of. Afterwards, Debbie had "kind of an empty feeling" inside. The first ABL season, with all its "ups and downs, and good times and bad times, that particular year will never come up again. It's finished," she thought. Time seemed to zoom by her in that moment.

Players cried in the locker room and Debbie was among the red-eyed crew. There had been so many good times during the season, but it was hard to think of them right then. Players hugged each other, saying things like "gee, I can't believe we're not coming back to practice tomorrow." The coach, Sheryl Estes, hugged players too and thanked them for the good job they'd done all year. The playoff loss was still hard for Debbie to take in. "I was trying to get my head around it," she remembers. "It was so hard to believe that everything's over, finished. It's so final."

As players left the locker room, fans who'd been behind the team all season came up to the players. "You had such a great year," fans said to team members, no doubt trying to encourage them to see beyond the playoff loss.

Debbie and her teammates appreciated the fan support, but came together with each other, as they had all season, to share the ending of one last game. All the players went out to dinner afterwards. Not to talk about the game—they didn't say much about it—just to be around the nine other people who would understand their feelings as no one else could.

There was no Hollywood-style happy ending to the Xplosion's season. No glittering championship trophy. But the women had all fought hard, had shown themselves to have the hearts of champions, And their point guard Debbie Black had revealed herself a winner in more ways than were shown by the post-season awards she'd won. Final scores, numbers and awards didn't tell the whole story, didn't reveal how Debbie was there for her teammates off the court as well as on. For younger players like Crystal Robinson, who came to the ABL straight out of college, Debbie acted as a kind of mentor. She helped younger players understand that they couldn't come into the ABL and count on being "instant superstars." The quality of competition was simply too good in the ABL.

Debbie advised young players to have patience, to let their game grow as they competed against other top players. Keep on working, keep on trying hard, was another part of Debbie's advice. "Don't ever think that you're good enough," she told Crystal. "If you think you're good enough, something's going to happen, someone's going to come and knock you down, so you've got to do . . . a little better next year if you want to stay on top."

In other ways too, Debbie acted "kind of like a big sister" to young players like Crystal. As the oldest player on her team—a switch from her family spot as youngest child—Debbie saw that as part of her role. She even gave Crystal some financial advice. Go talk to a financial adviser, Debbie suggested. Don't run out and buy a big fancy car. "You don't know how long the league's going to last, you don't know how long that money's going to be coming in, so be smart."

Debbie's own post-season evaluation of the ABL is that the league is doing well. "I'm feeling better and better about it," she says about the ABL. The league is re-signing players, getting more backers, and for her personally, being a part of the ABL has been a marvelous experience. "It's really exceeded all my expectations," she says, "as far as the quality of players, the professionalism of the league."

The ABL has given Debbie a chance to be a role model for young people in her own country. She loves meeting children after games, on the road, and at camps. She's pleased when girls come up to her for autographs or send her fan letters. "It would make my day," she comments, "if someone said they want to be like me. . . . Growing up I could never say that about a woman."

Not everything was fantastic about the league's first year, of course, and Debbie is honest enough to spell out some of the difficulties. Some of the ABL coaches didn't have experience coaching the type of top athletes coming into the league, which was the case in Colorado, Debbie feels. But the Colorado coaches, in Debbie's view, adapted well to their new situation, learned from their players and did what it took to help the Xplosion be successful.

The media is another sore point. In Denver, fan support grew as the season progressed; Debbie remembers a home game where 9,000 fans were present. In Colorado, the media covered the Xplosion well, Debbie feels, but many other places in the country paid the team and the league overall far less attention. She has relatives around the country, in cities such as Minneapolis, who complained to their local papers about the dearth of stories on the ABL. Her family in Philadelphia, at least, was able to watch any televised games on their satellite dish.

In, spite of the new league's growing pains, the ABL is where Debbie Black's loyalties lie. "This is the league that got me here and this is the league I believe in," she says firmly. She's a Philadelphia girl, a transplant to Australia, and now, a star in the American Basketball League.

College Stars

In a league filled with savvy veterans of international basketball, younger players were actually in the minority. During the first season, some players straight out of college, or not long away from it, struggled to move from their former roles as college stars to more limited roles on ABL teams. However, numerous young players did make the move to the ABL, and many carved out roles for themselves on their respective teams. Among this group are Kate Paye and Jennifer Jacoby. Natalie Williams, a slightly older player, also belongs among these basketball "novices" because her basketball experience ended with college play before she joined the ABL.

Kate Paye

Kate Paye graduated from Stanford University in 1995, after an impressive career as a point guard for the Stanford Cardinal. The summer of the same year she met Steve Hams.

Their meeting took place in San Francisco, after a Pro-Am basketball game that several Stanford and ex-Stanford players were involved in. A group including Christy Hedgpeth and Kate sat down with Steve at the back of a bar. Steve took out a neatly organized business plan and shared his vision of a women's professional league. The ABL would be a players' league, Steve said. It would have twelve teams. Most important, he argued that with all the attention focused on women's sports, now was an opportune time for a women's league.

Looking back from the perspective of a completed first year in the ABL, Kate Paye is amazed by the way an idea was transformed into reality. "It really is amazing what happened this year," Kate comments.

"I think you have to give a lot of credit to Steve and Gary and Anne," Kate says about the co-founders of the league. "Nobody even thought we'd play a game and they just kept plugging away."

Like the ABL founders, Kate Paye knows what it's like to follow a dream, to take a gamble against what seem like insurmountable odds. She was the starting point guard at Stanford from her junior year on, a fact which might seem like the standard sports success story for an ABL player until you add one more element. Kate wasn't recruited by Stanford. She made one of the top women's teams in the country as a walk on.

At five feet eight inches, Kate Paye isn't tall by basketball player standards. She isn't the fastest point guard in the league, but she's fast enough. She's steady and smart, someone who understands the game and can communicate well with her teammates. One of the younger players in the league, she turned twenty three just after the first ABL season.

Kate is an articulate person as well. After talking with her, it isn't a surprise to learn that her mother is a college English teacher. But while Kate's mother may speak knowledgeably about poetry or novels, Kate's area of expertise is basketball. She discusses the game as thoughtfully as any other student speaking on his or her subject. "Basketball's a game of communication," she might say. Or the point guard is "the main conduit of information."

Stanford University, where Kate first put her basketball "chops" together into a smooth, well-controlled game, had been her dream all along. She'd grown up watching Stanford women's basketball games. Her first hometown was Atherton, California and her family later moved to Woodside, communities which are close to Stanford University. Both her parents and her older brother and sister, John and Amy, all graduated from Stanford. Her father had played football there, and her brother had played football and basketball. Her whole family was "sport oriented." "Ever since I could remember," Kate describes, "I was going to my brother's sporting events and tagging along with my dad and my brother."

Playing sports was a given for Kate as she was growing up. She played softball, Little League baseball, soccer, track, and basketball. Kate is young enough that she received the full benefits of Title IX, and her elementary school emphasized sports for girls as well as boys. In elementary school, basketball and soccer were Kate's two favorite sports, but in high school she focused especially on basketball. Her older brother, John, coached her on basketball fundamentals, helping to build the basketball foundation which Kate thinks allowed her to succeed in the ABL. The Stanford basketball camps Kate had gone to ever since the fourth grade also helped develop her basketball skills.

In high school, Kate played point guard for the girls' basketball team, which won state championships Kate's sophomore, junior and senior years. The excitement of winning three championships helped fuel Kate's love of basketball. The only problem was that her high school was in the small schools division, which meant that their winning record didn't translate into a lot of attention paid to the players.

Kate did receive scholarship offers from a number of colleges, such as the University of California, the University of Arizona, and Northwestern University. She mulled over these offers and considered some Ivy League colleges as well. But in the end she knew that none of those other colleges were what she wanted.

"I just knew deep in my heart that Stanford was where I wanted to be," Kate remembers. She had watched the television broadcast of Stanford winning the national championship in 1990. She had sat in the stands for many other games at Maples Pavilion and seen "the incredible fan support." Her bottom line was simple: she wanted to be a part of all that.

The summer before what turned out to be her freshman year at Stanford, Kate told a man helping her with workouts that she wanted to try out for the Stanford team as a walk on. She had better run that by the coaches, the man advised. He called Tara VanDerveer, got her on the line, then passed the phone to Kate.

Kate knew Tara and Tara knew Kate from Stanford basketball camps. Nevertheless, Kate was still nervous as she spoke with Tara. But Tara didn't discourage Kate. She said something like "well, okay, you've got a lot of work to do," paired with the always useful advice to "work on your conditioning."

At some colleges, making the team as a walk on is not even an option for players, but at Stanford the coaches would usually let a player go ahead and try. Kate knew about another woman, Angela Taylor, who had made the team that way two years before. Knowing about Angela "gave me hope," Kate remembers. "It made me see that, you know, hey, if I can do it and if I'm good enough, they'll give me the chance. So I really just have to do my part."

It was the American Dream of hard work and ultimate success translated into the world of basketball, and Kate was clearly a believer. She started towards her dream by participating in the month-long fall conditioning for the women's basketball team. She ran, lifted weights, played pick-up games. After fall conditioning, the tryouts were the first three days of regular practice, which began October 15th. The women ran through drills on basketball fundamentals—passing, shooting, position work, full court transition drills—and with Tara and her assistant coaches watching, Kate and the other women played games as well. Kate could tell that her skills and conditioning weren't on the level of the women already on the team, but she kept trying her hardest anyway. "If I could stick it out and stay tough," she remembers thinking, "I was bound to improve."

After the third day, Tara VanDerveer and Kate Paye sat down together just outside the locker room, on the steps leading to the main floor of Maples Pavilion. The arena where Kate had sometimes imagined herself playing. "You made the team," Tara told Kate. Tara's expression was serious, a basketball coach's version of a poker face. She didn't spend time congratulating Kate. "You need to improve your conditioning, your skills," Tara advised instead. "Keep working harder and don't be satisfied."

It was, Kate feels looking back, "Typical Tara." Self-satisfied basketball players didn't fit with Tara's vision of athletic excellence. "If you did one thing, go ahead and shoot for something higher."

Kate was ready to shoot as high as she could. Even the fact that she didn't have a scholarship yet, that she would have to pay her own way, didn't change her enthusiasm. Luckily, her parents were able to help with the costs. And beginning the spring quarter of her freshman year, Kate did receive an athletic scholarship.

As a student athlete, Kate didn't neglect academics. In fact, in her junior year she was recognized as a second team Pac-10 All-Academic player. Yet she also learned a great deal from the athlete side of the equation. "Some professors might cringe to hear me say this," she comments, "but, you know, I really feel that my participating in basketball for four years, that's where I really learned the most in my college experience." That doesn't mean she didn't enjoy or learn a lot in her classes, but playing sports, Kate says, "you learn so much about life, about people, . . . about competition, about excellence, about winning, about losing."

Of course, all that learning didn't come easily. Kate speaks glowingly about her Stanford coach, Tara VanDerveer. "I think Tara's the best coach in the country." Playing under Tara, Kate found, "was just an incredible learning experience." But Tara has a reputation as a tough coach, and according to her players, the reputation is deserved. Kate laughs now as she recalls the way Tara pushed her players. "Tara's always striving for perfection," Kate describes, "and as we all know, there is no such thing. And no matter what you give, . . . she's always asking for more, and you . . . learn to demand that of yourself."

When Kate was a freshman, in 1992, Stanford won their second national championship. Kate only got to play a few minutes in the semi-final game, but she still found winning the championship "completely thrilling." She might have also expected that it was something which would happen again. But even as Kate built up her basketball skills, playing more minutes and starting at point guard beginning with her junior year, Stanford never went all the way again. "I had to wait for the disappointment of the next three years," Kate recalls, "to really understand and appreciate how fortunate and incredible" winning the championship was.

That realization hit Kate again in March of 1996, after the end of the first ABL season, when she went to the NCAA finals. Stanford had an incredible team, with Jamila Wideman at point guard and Kate Starbird at shooting guard, and Stanford was favored to win it all. When the team lost in a closely contested semi-final game to Old Dominion, Kate felt her former teammates' pain. Even watching from the stands, Kate found the Stanford loss to be "excruciatingly painful."

Graduating from Stanford, ending her involvement in a top college program, was painful too. "So much of who you are and what you've done is tied up in . . . that team," Kate describes. "It's always tough to . . . separate yourself and to move forward."

It helped that she could play pick up games with other current and past Stanford players all summer long, until practices started in the fall. And by then, the fall of 1995, Kate knew about the ABL. She was waiting for the league to begin play, and hoping that that would really happen. In the meantime she took a job as an assistant coach at San Diego State.

Kate liked coaching but in her heart she still wanted to be out on court herself. She still wanted to grow as an athlete, to become the best player she could, just as Tara VanDerveer had taught her. When training camp began for the Seattle Reign in the fall of 1996, Kate felt her competitive pulse quicken. She was competing with and against players who might be eight or nine years older than her, who might be veterans of basketball overseas.

At only 22, Kate was going to be the starting point guard, the person who would have a large responsibility for setting up the offense and getting the ball to the right players. It helped that she felt confident in her basketball background and in her knowledge about the game. It helped that she was willing to learn from the more experienced players. And it helped that she kept her cool. The teasing remarks that players often addressed to each other essentially rolled off Kate's back.

Another positive for Kate was her experience playing for three years at Stanford with Christy Hedgpeth, the shooting guard on the Reign. Kate not only liked Christy, she knew a lot about her basketball moves. But Kate had everything to learn about her new coach and the other Reign players. Her new teammates, Kate comments, were "interesting people with a lot of interesting backgrounds." All the women, in fact, "got along off the court extremely well." On court, however, as the season moved along the dynamics of the team weren't always that good. "There were some strains and there were some tensions," Kate says simply and diplomatically.

Her year of coaching probably helped Kate understand just how important and also how difficult to achieve good team chemistry can be. "Team chemistry," she says wryly, "is always kind of the X factor and if anybody knew exactly how to make it right or could bottle it up, you know, they'd be extremely successful."

Kate understood that the success of the whole league mattered as much as the performance of individual teams. Speaking with fans, players learned what the league meant to them. "I can't tell you how many women have told me," Kate recalls, that "the first game they saw, they cried, just because it was so moving to see woman actually playing professional basketball and it was an opportunity they did not have."

"You guys are great," little boys and girls would say. Their parents would tell players like Kate how glad they were that their kids had such positive role models who would take a few moments to chat with their children.

As a player at a top college, Kate had previously gotten attention from fans, but there was something different about the ABL experience. Day to day she would be focused on practices and games. But every now and then the significance of the new league would hit her. It could happen when a fan would come up to her and tell her, "You know, I just saw you guys run out on the floor and I just burst into tears."

The fans were there in force at Seattle's home opener. On October 27, after playing their first three games on the road, the Seattle Reign came home. Mercer Arena was sold out. "Little Girls Dream Too" T-shirts were sold out. No doubt inspired by all the fan support, the Reign played a strong game.

Kate Paye was one of the stronger players. "Paye Brightest of Seattle Stars" a *Seattle Times* headline read about the game. She was in the thick of the action, going to the floor after loose balls, demonstrating a deadeye aim at the free throw line as she made eleven out of twelve free throws. By the end of the game, Kate's 19 points and four steals were highest on the Reign. She also contributed five assists and had a scanty four turnovers as the Reign beat the Power 83-70.

Dick Rockne of the *Seattle Times* described Kate as a strong floor leader for the Reign. He quoted coach Jacquie Hullah giving Kate's first Seattle performance a glowing review. "She's a winner," Jacquie said about Kate. "She's a quarterback. She's a thinker of the game."

Kate continued to play her solid, intelligent game as the season continued. She would read the offensive and defensive patterns unfolding on court, respond to her coach's signals. She wouldn't yell at players—"I'm not much of a yeller or a screamer," she says— but she would shout instructions to players on court or take someone aside after a dead ball and advise, "On the next play, screen up and then roll to the basket."

Kate might not have been lightning fast, but she could push the ball down the court, play tight defense, and always seemed to have a good sense of what was happening on court. She showed a steadiness out on the floor, an ability to get the ball where other Reign players needed. And she could demonstrate some offensive firepower of her own.

In early December, the Reign were riding the wave of a seven game winning streak at home. As Seattle beat Richmond on December 6th, Kate was an important part of the victory. Her average points per game had been 7.7, a respectable total for a point guard whose main role on court is usually not scoring. But the best point guards, such as Richmond's Dawn Staley, can put in the baskets when their team needs that to happen. Kate demonstrated that she belonged in that elite group by scoring 23 points, a career high for her. Most impressively, she connected with six out of eight three-point attempts.

The reason why she made so many three-pointers, Kate told a reporter, was that she had "a lot of open shots . . . a lot of good looks at the basket." But what Kate didn't say was that she herself was simply an excellent long-range shooter.

As the season wore on, and Seattle fought hard to make the play-offs, Kate continued to do her best for her team. On January 31st, Seattle played San Jose, the other team fighting for the second Western Conference playoff spot. Kate made the crucial basket that gave the Reign a paper-thin two-point victory over the Lasers. She took the ball to the basket, and put in a close shot with a scanty 21 seconds remaining in the game. Even in games where the end result didn't go Seattle's way, Kate was still a solid presence. On February 1st, the Reign played the Colorado Xplosion on Seattle's home court, and Kate logged long minutes, alternating between point guard and shooting guard. In the first quarter she hit two three-point shots.

Kate almost won that game for her team. In the last minute Colorado had a three-point lead, a devastating turn of events for a Seattle team which had led by 16 points at the start of the fourth quarter. As Kate headed down the court with the ball, she was deliberately fouled at midcourt by a Colorado player. The Colorado coach, Sheryl Estes, then called a twenty-second timeout so Kate would have time to sweat those free throws.

There were only 40.9 seconds left in the game. Kate Paye is "a very solid player in this type of sitation," the TV announcer commented, mentioning her 83 percent foul shot percentage. Solid was a good description for her performance then. The pressure was on. Her hands may have been sweaty as she gripped the basketball. But she sank first one, then the second free throw.

Now the Colorado lead was only one point. After a Colorado missed shot and Seattle rebound, Kate brought the ball slowly up the court so that the Reign would take the last shot of the game. But this time the Seattle offense didn't work. A last second shot missed its mark, and Seattle lost the game. As stunned-looking Seattle players left the court, Angela Aycock, the player who had missed that last shot, appeared ready to burst into tears. Kate didn't show a lot of emotion, but teammate Rhonda Smith must have understood her feelings. Rhonda gave Kate a hug.

Kate's teammates knew that she had tried her best that game, as she did all season long. By the end of the ABL's first season, Kate had the sixth highest number of assists in the league and was the seventh highest in free throw percentage. She had also set something of a record for durability, a mark her young legs may have assisted her in reaching. Kate was the only player on the Reign to start in all forty regular season games. All in all, Kate's performance as a player left no doubt that she could play a strong role in the league.

Unfortunately, the Seattle Reign didn't finish as strongly. The Reign never made it into the playoffs—a turn of events which Kate calls "extremely disappointing." The losing streaks the Reign went through mid-season and then later in the season were tough on her and her teammates as well. But even though the Reign didn't end the season as strongly as they would have liked, they kept on winning over fans. Throughout the season, even when the Reign lost games, the crowd would stand and clap for the team as they headed to the locker room. Support like that meant a lot to Kate and other Seattle players.

"The intensity and the enthusiasm (of the fans)" Kate recalls, "picked up throughout the year and . . . reached a climax there for our very last home game." The Reign had already been eliminated from the playoffs at that point. But the crowd was so enthusiastically supportive that Kate describes the game as a "great big love fest." After Seattle beat the San Jose Lasers 85-62, Seattle players mixed with the crowd, shaking hands, exchanging high fives, thanking their fans for all their support. Kate remembers it all clearly. "It was just a really incredible night."

Jennifer Jacoby

It was cold sitting on the bench while the Portland Power played. Wearing her shiny royal blue warmup jacket over her basketball jersey, Jennifer Jacoby did whatever she could to stay warm. But feeling cold wasn't the worst part of sitting on the bench, day after day, game after game. Her team wasn't winning and yet Greg Bruce didn't gave Jennifer, a small but hot-shooting point guard, a chance to play.

Some of the time she wasn't physically able to be out on court. Kidney stones put her on the injured list for a while in the early part of the season. But other times she was there, ready for action, and yet the action never came her way. The games unfolding in front of her, as she sat on the team bench in her courtside seat, featured exciting, high-intensity basketball. Jennifer fought off feelings of detachment, of frustration at her seemingly cast-in-stone status as permanent bench warmer.

During timeouts, she'd stand on the edge of the huddle, seeming to only half listen to the coach's instructions. He wasn't really talking to her anyway. He thought she was too small, and wasn't going to give her a chance. So Jennifer would chew her gum, gaze slightly away from the huddle of players, her expression detached and a little bit bored. She waited for a chance to play, but as the days passed the chance seemed more and more unlikely.

A personable, friendly young woman, Jennifer looks as if she could be cast in an episode of "Little House on the Prairie." Her blonde hair, blue eyes, and freckles fit with her family's roots in rural Indiana, as does the smile that can light up her whole face and her friendly, unassuming manner. At 5'7", she's taller than the stereotypical girl next door but not overwhelmingly so.

When she stays after practice with her teammate and friend, Natalie Williams, to take some extra time to practice shots, Jennifer can appear almost frail compared to the stocky muscular Natalie. But Jennifer has her own areas of strength. She can get the ball to her teammates in just the places where they like to receive passes. And when she catches a pass herself or sees an open shot, she can make an opposing team wish that hadn't happened. Jennifer launches three-point shots with a smooth, sure motion that leaves the ball arcing its way perfectly through the net.

Jennifer isn't a selfish player. She didn't want to light a fire for her team all by herself, but it was extremely hard for her to sit and wait for someone else to supply the tinder, especially since the team didn't have a winning record. Like other women in the ABL, Jennifer had always been a sports achiever who had helped the teams she played on overcome their opponents. Basketball had been central to her life as she was growing up—basketball is "just in my blood now," she says—and the ABL meant a lot to her. After college, before a single ABL game had been played, Jennifer had volunteered her time to help spread the word about the league. In her home state of Indiana, Jennifer had a receptive audience. Indiana has a reputation for being basketball crazy, and Jennifer doesn't try to deny the stereotype. "Being from Indiana, you grow up around basketball."

Jennifer grew up on a dairy farm in rural Indiana where she fed calves, milked cows and helped take care of pigs, sheep, and other animals. One advantage of living on a farm was that there was plenty of space for basketball to happen. There were six basketball goals on the family farm, and a full but somewhat unusual basketball court. Jennifer developed her basketball moves on a gravel court which her father refused to pave. "If you can dribble on rocks, you can dribble on anything," her father would say.

When Jennifer was about four years old, the age when some future musical prodigies are first picking up a violin, she started playing basketball. For Jennifer, basketball was more in tune with her surroundings than classical music. Her father was a coach. Her brother Jon, who was three years older than Jennifer, got lots of positive reinforcement for playing with that large orange ball. Watching her brother, Jennifer decided that she'd follow in her brother's footsteps on the basketball court.

Away from her somewhat rocky home court, Jennifer played in a Boys' Club league where her dad was the coach and she was the only girl. While other ABL players have played in all boys' leagues without any problems, in rural Indiana that mild form of gender bending didn't go over as well with the local folks. Some of the boys' parents didn't like the fact that Jennifer would get playing time while their sons sat on the bench. Pre-Title IX, maybe Jennifer would have been transformed into a cheerleader or sent off to do "girl things" while the boys had their fun. Post Title IX, however, after enough complaints came in about a girl in a boys' league, a girls' league was started with Jennifer one of its charter members.

In fact, the girls' league was fine with Jennifer and she had a good time playing with other girls, yet she didn't agree with the people who had complained about her presence in a boys' league. "I love to play against guys" she says, "because they don't let you get by with anything. They try to block your shot all the time." It's a point of view echoed by many other women in the ABL. Katy Steding, in fact, advises the girls in her basketball camps to play against boys sometimes to strengthen their game. Women who play top-level basketball don't seem to need the rigid boundaries between girls' and boys', mens' and women's sports, which some people want to maintain.

In the girls' league, on school teams, and on AAU basketball teams, Jennifer continued to develop her sport. With Jennifer leading her team, her small high school, with only 38 in her graduating class, provided a real life version of the movie "Hoosiers" for girls' basketball. Jennifer had torn an ACL in her junior year and had the surgery the summer afterwards, but she had worked hard to get ready for basketball season. She wore a knee brace for the first eight games her senior year, then could discard the brace. Unlike in the movie, Jennifer's team didn't go all the way to the championship, but they did advance to the second level of the state tournament, quite an accomplishment for such a tiny school.

From that same year, 1991, Jennifer has an individual accomplishment to boast about. She was voted Miss Basketball of Indiana for the year, no small honor in a basketball crazy state. And throughout her high school career, the 2,343 points she put in made her the state's second highest high school scorer ever.

Although nowadays colleges can't write to players until they're juniors, Jennifer received her first recruiting letter from a college when she was only in seventh grade. Numerous other scholarship offers followed, but Jennifer eventually decided to stick close to home. She'd go to Purdue University, a college her brother had also attended where Lin Dunn, her future coach on the Portland Power, was then women's basketball coach. "I wanted my parents to be a part of my college career," Jennifer recalls. "My parents put out all kinds of money for me to go to camps, and they travelled, you know, took me everywhere during the summer." Jennifer wanted to return the favor by choosing a college close enough that her parents could attend the games and cheer their daughter on from the stands.

There was plenty to cheer about while Jennifer was at Purdue. In her junior year her team went to the Final Four, upsetting Stanford at Maples Pavilion, Stanford's home court, to do so. "I think we were the last team to beat Stanford on their home court," Jennifer recalls with pleasure. Purdue went on to the Final Four and then lost to North Carolina, the eventual national champions. In Jennifer's senior year, Purdue made it up to the Elite Eight before losing to Stanford, in a kind of balancing of the scales of basketball justice which went unappreciated by Jennifer and her teammates.

For Jennifer as an individual player, her college basketball career moved upward from the major setback she experienced in her freshman year. She tore an ACL for a second time, in the ninth game of her freshman year. She still remembers exactly how it happened: "I was dribbling down the court," she recounts, "and went one way and the girl (I was defending) went the other. So I tried to go back quick and my kneecap slipped out." Although she couldn't play the rest of her freshman year, she didn't think about giving up basketball. In fact, she took on the reponsibility of coaching an AAU team of high school age girls, most of whom eventually went on to Division One colleges. That kind of bench sitting was overall a positive experience for Jennifer, something she might return to some day, especially at the college level. "It was a blast. I just loved (it)," she says about coaching. She wanted to pass on the opportunities which she'd had to learn about basketball.

After graduating from college in 1995, Jennifer played for Athletes in Action, a Christian athletic group, and her basketball team competed against Division One colleges. She also went to Brazil for a basketball tournament and to Taiwan with a USA Basketball Jones Cup team for which Lin Dunn was the coach. But all that didn't take up enough of the spaces she was used to basketball filling. So when the ABL called her in the summer of 1995, the league found a willing participant.

If she committed herself to the ABL, the league told Jennifer, she would join a small group of the ABL's top players. These women would be guaranteed a place on a team even before the draft. Jennifer was glad to sign on with the ABL. She had been considering going overseas, and had some offers from Switzerland and other countries, but the ABL was much more of what she really wanted. "Just to be able to stay in the United States," she comments. "That's where I wanted to be." She may not have fully realized just how lucky she was, compared to older players, to have that opportunity straight out of college.

Then again maybe she did. On her own time—she wasn't on the ABL payroll yet—Jennifer called college players she knew about the league, and told them about the tryouts. She gave talks about the league throughout her home state of Indiana. Jennifer was willing to do all that because she believed so strongly that women like her should have the opportunity to play for American audiences. And obviously, when a former Miss Indiana Basketball spoke about the ABL, people were interested.

Yet if Jennifer was well known in Indiana, the same could not be said for her in Portland. For a good chunk of the season, newspaper accounts of games contained almost no references to her. While she was on the injured list because of her problems with kidney stones, and while she sat on the bench after that because Coach Greg Bruce didn't include her in his playing rotation, Jennifer became a practically invisible member of the Portland Power. A player seen standing on the outside of the huddle during timeouts. A player seen in street clothes or warmups on the bench.

Greg Bruce, the first Power coach, didn't have the highest opinion of Jennifer. "He thought I was too little, and he really never gave me the chance," she comments. That was especially frustrating for Jennifer because her team was losing lots of games and she thought the coach should give some other players, including herself, a try. Once in a while certain fans remembered her. "Jacoby, Jacoby," fans would call out, asking the coach to put her in. Jennifer must have appreciated that fan support, that break in her pattern of anonymity, even if her coach didn't seem to be influenced by the fans' opinions.

Jennifer wasn't the only one on her team who had a tough time. The way Jennifer describes it, during the long Power losing streak, team harmony was definitely fraying around the edges. "We started getting at each other and complaining about every little thing," Jennifer recalls. "If someone missed a layup, instead of helping each other, . . . we were like, 'man, how could you miss something that easy?'"

On the Christmas break for the team, Jennifer thought things over and realized once again how dismal both her team's and her own situations were. Then in January, when the almost unremitting cloud cover and rain in Portland didn't contribute to raising anyone's spirits, a Hollywood-style ray of light appeared. It was the cavalry to the rescue, the white knight from outside the kingdom, in the form of new coach Lin Dunn.

If all the Power players felt rescued by Lin, Jennifer must have been the most enthusiastic. Lin had been Jennifer's coach for all four years at Purdue, and Jennifer's coach again when Jennifer travelled to Taiwan with a USA Basketball Jones' Cup Team. "She's always made me a better person and a better player," Jennifer says.

With the coaching change, Jennifer seemed to metamorphosize before the Portland fans' eyes into a better player almost instantly. She knew Lin Dunn's system after all. That was an advantage both for Jennifer and for her new coach. Unlike Greg Bruce, Lin Dunn put Jennifer into the game. According to an *Oregonian* article on the Power's first game with Lin as coach, "The most glaring difference . . . was guard Jennifer Jacoby."

Jennifer's time on court for all the games previously totaled only 41 minutes—not even long enough to make up one good practice session—but with Lin Dunn making her coaching debut and with usual point guard Michelle Marciniak sick with the flu, Jennifer stayed in the game for a respectable 28 minutes. She did get tired—she hadn't played enough all season to be in top shape—yet she was excited to be out on the court for solid minutes. Her suddenly visible smile lit up the basketball court as she dished off assists and hit two three-point shots. "It was awesome," is Jennifer's own comment about the change. "I was just excited to be able to get the chance."

For a number of subsequent games, Jennifer received substantial minutes on court and made a solid contribution. In a game on February 2nd, she had 9 points, 5 rebounds, 5 assists, and hit a perfect a six-for-six free throws. Then later in the season, Jennifer's basketball fortunes declined again. Lin Dunn ended up playing two other guards, Coquese Washington and Falisha Wright, much of the time although Jennifer still got into games some. Lin talked with Jennifer about the change. "It has nothing to do with your ability," Lin told Jennifer. It was simply that Coquese and Falisha were playing well together and doing a good job for the team. Jennifer wanted to be out on court, of course, but she was able to accept still another role on her team, especially since Lin Dunn, unlike Greg Bruce, had communicated to Jennifer what that role was to be.

The last game of the season for the Power, February 20, was also a personal milestone of sorts for Jennifer, the day she turned 24. That still left her one of the youngest players in a league where so many players were older and had years of overseas experience. And yet Jennifer feels strongly involved in the league, and even after all the ups and downs of her first season, she remains a cheerleader for the ABL.

For Jennifer herself, playing in the ABL has been "a dream come true." The first game she really got her chance as a point guard, the game against Richmond in January, is definitely a bright moment in that dream. But even before that, there was one other moment when Jennifer's personal star shone brightly.

It was a shooting star, you could say, because Jennifer's moment of glory was during the three-point shootout held during half time of the ABL All-Star game. The game took place in Hartford, Connecticut in mid-December, and three of Jennifer's teammates—Michelle Marciniak, Natalie Williams, and Katy Steding—were on the Western Conference All-Star Team. Jennifer Jacoby was one of four finalists in the three-point shooting contest.

The other three finalists—Shannon Johnson and Katie Smith from Columbus, and Clarissa Davis from New England—all took turns first, and Katie ended up as the leader of the three with 12 points. As Jennifer prepared to take her turn, a TV announcer mentioned the record number of three-point baskets—54 of them—which Jennifer had made at Purdue. The TV cameras and microphone didn't catch fellow competitor Katie Smith's probably half serious, half joking comment to Jennifer. "You better not hit more (than I did)," Katie told Jennifer.

"Now I'm going to just because you made me mad," Jennifer joked back. She was used to competing against Katie. The two of them had been college rivals in the Big Ten Conference with Jennifer at Purdue and Katie at Ohio State.

The cameras focused on Jennifer as she stood just outside the three-point line to the far right of the basket, the first of several positions she would shoot from. She appeared poised and confident as she waited to begin. Then her personal shooting "lesson" started. Pulling basketballs from the racks of balls, she missed her first few shots, but then the balls began to go in for her. She released her shots in one smooth, efficient motion, raining basketballs at the net from several positions, hitting all four of the multicolored "money" balls that were worth two instead of one point. The final score was Jennifer Jacoby at 15 points, making her the winner of the three-point shootout.

Victory was sweet. A wide grin spread across Jennifer's freckled face as she slapped hands with the other contestants, exchanged high fives with Natalie Williams, then received a big hug from Katy Steding. Jennifer posed with a size-large dummy of the actual check for $5,000 she would receive for winning the contest.

The money would come in handy of course, especially with Christmas approaching, but it may have meant less to Jennifer than the vindication. "I love to shoot," Jennifer says about herself. "I think shooting probably is my number one strength." During the shooting contest, as Jennifer's three-point shots found their mark, as basketball after basketball lofted smoothly towards the net, Jennifer had answered the question which may have been in her own heart too. She belonged in the the league she'd given so much effort to. She belonged in women's pro basketball.

Natalie Williams

Natalie Williams is a basketball superstar. One of the physically strongest players in the league, she's a solid 6'2" tall with broad, muscular shoulders and sturdy legs. When Natalie pulls down a rebound, opposing players rarely take it away from her. When she goes up for a basket, she can overpower defenders with her strength.

Natalie has been named by *Sports Illustrated* as among the five top women's basketball players in the world. After the first season she's one of five players named to the First Team for the best women's pro basketball players by Mel Greenberg of the *Philadelphia Inquirer*. Yet she's a fairly young player; she was 25 years old at the start of the first ABL season. And throughout most of that season, with no previous professional basketball experience, Natalie didn't feel entirely confident about her game.

As is true for many of the ABL women, Natalie hasn't confined her athletic talents to just one sport. Growing up in Taylorsville, Utah, Natalie's two favorite sports in high school were volleyball and basketball. Her senior year her teams won state championships in those sports in fact. But Natalie also played softball for nine years and competed on the Taylorsville High School track team. Her events were the 4 x 100 relay, the shotput, the discus, and the long jump. As a senior she was the state long jump champion.

Taylorsville is fifteen miles south of Salt Lake City, a small, mostly Mormon city, and growing up there, Natalie had other differences which distinguished her beyond her athletic excellence. She was a multiracial child in a mostly white town. And she was raised by a single mother in a time and place where that wasn't the norm.

Natalie's mother, Robyn Barker, met with family pressure not to keep her baby when Robyn became pregnant as a college sophomore at Utah State in 1970. Complicating the family situation was the fact that Natalie's father, Nate Williams, was African-American. Robyn Barker's father, Vaughn, as a *Sports Illustrated* article describes, was one of the signers of a legal agreement which didn't allow Nate Williams to see Natalie until she had reached adulthood. However,

Robyn did keep her child, quitting college to go to work as a secretary, and Natalie grew up surrounded by a loving extended family.

"We told Natalie how beautiful she was a lot," Natalie's mother Robyn commented for the *Sports Illustrated* article. "I don't remember her ever realizing she was a different color from the rest of her family."

Natalie's perspective as an adult woman confirms her mother's view. "When I was growing up, I pretty much considered myself white," Natalie says. "My whole family is white . . . all my friends were white. . . . And just people, as they got to know me, they didn't see a color either." In high school, where differences can seem magnified and peer pressures intensify, Natalie continued simply to be herself. "I didn't really date that much," she describes. "I just mostly hung out with my friends. I was just always an outgoing, very athletic person. That's how everyone thought about me."

Understandably, Natalie wondered about the father she had never met. The father who played for nine years in the NBA. When Natalie was 16 years old, father and daughter finally met. A friend of Nate Williams who lived in Utah told Nate that his daughter was interested in meeting him. Not surprisingly, the meeting was far from easy. Natalie was returning from a basketball camp, and both her mother and father met her at the airport. "It was weird," Natalie says about that first meeting with her father. "At that time I wasn't around very many black people." Her father, she adds, is "an extremely large black person." He's 6'5" tall in fact. "It was weird. It was different," Natalie says again. It took her a while to develop the good relationship with her father which she now has.

It was Natalie's mother, however, who provided the central figure during Natalie's childhood. Even though her mother didn't have a lot of money, she paid for Natalie to go to sports camps. Her mother didn't teach her how to cook—an omission Natalie laughs about—but she taught Natalie to lay sod and to put together a sprinkler system, to do crafts like macrame. Her mother, Natalie sums up, is "an amazing woman."

Natalie also looked up to an amazing female athlete, college basketball star Cheryl Miller. When Natalie was about 14 years old, she met Cheryl at a basketball camp held at the University of Southern California. Cheryl took the time to talk with Natalie, giving her some helpful advice about a decision that would loom large in her future—which college to choose. "Just go with what your heart feels,"

Cheryl told Natalie. "Don't let other people pressure you into doing something you don't want to do."

That was useful advice for a highly recruited high school athlete. In her senior year, Natalie followed that advice and chose UCLA, a college which "just felt right" to her. Making that decision early in her senior helped take the pressure off of her during her last year of high school sports.

Natalie played five years of sports at UCLA. She redshirted in basketball her freshman year, played four years of volleyball and four years of basketball starting with her sophomore year. However, she was more serious about volleyball in college, a fact that may seem ironic now. Perhaps her stronger commitment to volleyball came about because her volleyball team played at such a high level, going to the NCAA Final Four every year. "It was extremely high intensity level," Natalie recalls. In 1990 and 1991, Natalie was chosen MVP of the Final Four as her team won national championships.

It was the second championship, which the Bruins won at UCLA in front of their home crowd, which Natalie describes as "probably the most memorable sports experience of my life." Her team lost the first two games, then won the last three. In the final game, Natalie had the last kill. And then as she was jumping up and down to celebrate, and her teammates were celebrating too, Natalie came down awkwardly from a jump and sprained her ankle. It all made for a season finale she will never forget.

So far Natalie is the only woman to be selected as an All-American in both college basketball and volleyball. In volleyball, she won the Honda Award twice, which designated her as the best U.S. female player. In basketball, she was an All-Pac-10 player for three years, named as the Conference Player of the Year as a senior, and a finalist in her junior and senior years for the Naismith Award, which recognizes the nation's top college player.

Natalie's basketball awards, perhaps even more than her volleyball honors, reveal Natalie's talents as an athlete. The recognition Natalie received as an excellent basketball player came even though she was less involved in the sport than in volleyball, and in spite of the fact that her college basketball team was less competitive, less high level than her volleyball team. Some of her basketball teammates, Natalie found, "didn't have that mentality of a Final Four athlete." In fact, Natalie's team only went as far as making it to the

Sweet 16 in NCAA tournament play Natalie's junior year. "I was there . . . just to have fun" is how Natalie describes her own attitude about basketball at the time.

The fun ended when Natalie tore an ACL in her right knee during a basketball game against Stanford in her senior year. She landed wrong and the ligament tore. The injury "was a hard thing for me," Natalie says. "It was probably one of the hardest things to recover from. But it made me stronger."

It took her nine months to fully rehabilitate the injury. Afterwards, since she was more serious about volleyball, it made sense that volleyball was the sport Natalie went on with after she graduated from UCLA in 1994. She played with the Utah Predators for two years, a semi-professional volleyball league which had four teams in California and a team in Salt Lake City. At the same time, as a member of the U.S. National Team in volleyball, she trained with the team and travelled all over the world to compete against national teams in Japan, Switzerland, Italy, Canada, and other countries.

Natalie's goal was to win a place on the 1996 Olympic volleyball team and to win gold with the team. But with one Olympic position available for Natalie and two of her U.S. National teammates, the competition was intense. In the end, Natalie didn't make the team, and was named as an alternate instead. "It was very disappointing when I didn't make it," Natalie comments, "but things happen for a reason."

The many current fans of Natalie Williams would be quick to conclude that the reason was basketball. Women's professional basketball, that is. Ironically once more, in light of Natalie's stellar performance in the ABL, she was assigned to the ABL's Portland Power as something of an after thought. Not until September 3, 1996, at the start of ABL training camps, was Natalie designated as the Power's second premiere player, after Olympian Ruthie Bolton didn't sign with the team.

Natalie hadn't played basketball since college except for a short stint with the Jones Cup team in the summer of 1996. Although her many basketball strengths became evident early in the first ABL season, Natalie herself didn't feel totally confident about her new role. Basketball still felt a little foreign to her, a sport she was revisiting after her intense focus on high level volleyball.

That volleyball experience, however, certainly helped Natalie excel in basketball. "It helps in jumping, quickness, getting to the ball, getting off the ground very quick, and I think that helps in my rebounding," is Natalie's own assessment. It undoubtedly helped Natalie achieve the vertical jump of 31 inches which assists her in both rebounding and shooting. Volleyball, she adds, is "a game of least errors." There must be a good dig to the setter, for example, for the offense to run successfully. That concern for details and attempt at error free play has, Natalie thinks, transferred to her basketball game.

During much of the ABL's first season, even though Natalie didn't feel entirely confident in her game, she quickly became her team's

Jennifer Jacoby

leading scorer and rebounder, a central player for her team. It was a role that she'd often had on the various teams she'd played on growing up, a role she essentially accepted. "I don't mind the pressure," she says. "I'm used to it. I've always had it growing up, and I like being the go to player."

However, the Power's weakness at the guard position, and lack of sufficient outside shooting, led to an extra amount of pressure on Natalie with defenders from other teams collapsing on her. The pressure she was used to often changed to what she describes as "Not a fun pressure. It's just an agonizing, okay, great, I'm going to have four people on me. There's nothing I can do."

But Natalie hung in there. By early November she was the top rebounder in the league as well as her team's highest scorer. Then on November 9th, Natalie was injured, tearing the meniscus in her right knee in a game against Atlanta. Fortunately, it wasn't a season-ending injury. Unfortunately, it meant she wouldn't be able to play for about a month.

While Natalie sat on the bench, her team's fortunes plummeted, with the Power setting an ABL record for its losing streak. It wasn't until Natalie returned to action, on December 5th, that she and her teammates finally won a game. After the game, as an *Oregonian* article describes, Natalie leapt up to the rim of the basket, a crowd pleasing move that celebrated not only the win but her own return to basketball.

Natalie could have celebrated again when she was named ABL player of the week in early January. On January 17th, an *Oregonian* article described Natalie as not only the "team's leading scorer and rebounder" but also "the emotional glue that keeps the team together." In the previous day's game, Natalie told a reporter, "I felt like I needed to pick up my game for us to win." In fact, her game had been strong all along. A few days later, Natalie earned her fifteenth double-double for points and rebounds in the season.

But talented people in any field typically set their personal goals high. In spite of all her achievements in the first ABL season, Natalie still didn't feel as if she'd hit her stride as a player. Not until the very end of the season. It wasn't until the last two games, she describes, that "I really started coming into my own and feeling very confident and comfortable. And knowing that every single time I took the ball to the hole that I could put it in."

Of those last two games, Natalie's personal best certainly was the season finale, which the Power played at home. "That was the game," she comments, "where I finally felt like I was comfortable as a basketball player." The 30 points she scored that night, a team and personal best, confirmed Natalie's own feeling. She had finally reached a place where she felt she was playing "my best at my game" and where "no one could stop me."

While Portland fans celebrated the team's season-ending victory and Natalie's achievement, some worried that she might choose to leave the team. A WNBA team in Salt Lake City was rumored to be a possible option for Natalie. "Natalie, say it isn't so—don't go," a sign pleaded.

It probably wasn't the sign which made the difference in Natalie's decision to stay in Portland and with the ABL. Most likely it was Natalie's strong feelings for her teammates, her coach, and the league. ""I think the league's great," is how Natalie sees the ABL. "The players are only getting better. . . . The competition is tough every single night. I think it's just going to grow."

Natalie Williams is one of a select group of ABL players who have replica jerseys for sale with their name and number. Early in the first season, on October 21st, 1996, she received the singular honor of being recognized as Utah's Woman Athlete of the Century. At the ceremony held in downtown Salt Lake City, Natalie gave a personal tribute to her mother. "Thanks for choosing to keep me," Natalie said. "For that you are the most important person in my life."

Just as Natalie has a strong role model in her mother, and later found an inspirational female athlete in Cheryl Miller, Natalie is willing to be a role model for others now. "We have tons of little girls who ... want to be like us," she mentions. And that isn't something she takes lightly. "Sometimes you forget why you're (playing basketball) until you see how excited you make these little kids."

Molly Goodenbour, who played for the Richmond Rage in the ABL's first year, agrees that the ABL players are role models. "People do look up to us, kids do look up to us, and especially with more and more girls playing basketball younger and younger, . . . they want to grow up to be like Katy Steding or like Teresa Edwards."

Like Natalie Williams, Molly could have added. The college volleyball and basketball star, the aspiring Olympic volleyball player, has become one of the brightest stars of women's pro basketball.

Players, Coaches and More

"You can't tell the players without a scorecard" is an often re-peated refrain at professional sporting events such as major league baseball games. Yet it seems fitting that at the onset of a new profes-sional league, ascertaining identities wasn't as easy as all that.

The opportunities opened up by the American Basketball League changed lives and changed roles for a number of women. The re-sulting kaleidoscopic landscape of women involved in professional athletics included former players who became coaches, players who went into coaching and then became players again, and former play-ers and/or coaches who worked at many other sorts of jobs for the league. The league made good use of all those different experiences and kinds of basketball know-how. Two players—Sheila Frost and Tara Davis—and one Media Director—Tonya Alleyne—provided part of the color and design in that kaleidescope of changes.

Tara Davis

"I'm one of those people who love to play. I could play all day," Tara Davis says.

Tara's love of basketball took her from collegiate basketball at the University of Washington to a position as reserve shooting guard on the Seattle Reign. With Tara's easy smile, and her agile, 5'10" body, it's easy to picture her doing what she says, taking pleasure from basketball and other sports.

Although Tara played the violin as a child and enjoys reading, sports have been her main interest for many years. In the Seattle area where she grew up, Tara started soccer at the age of seven, started running track a few years later, and began playing organized basketball when she was twelve years old on community center teams. At Ranier Beach High School, she ran track and played both soccer and basketball. "I was very active as a youth," she remembers with a smile, echoing a theme many other players repeat. "I didn't have time to get into any trouble."

If sports was one of the pillars of Tara's world, her mother was the other. When Tara's father died, she was only eight and it hit her hard. She was, she recalls, "mad at the world" for a while after her father passed away. Formerly a good student, her grades dropped precipitously. "I remember my mother looking at my report card," Tara describes, "like, is this the same person?" But fortunately her mother hadn't changed. She was still the same strong woman who kept the family going.

"My mother, she's a superwoman," Tara comments. Her mother worked to support the family but managed to be there for her children. After Tara's father died, it was her mother who gave Tara the feeling that her family still had a strong center, and that things would be okay. She also modeled achievement for Tara and her sister and brothers. When Tara and her sister received their college degrees, their mother received her undergraduate degree too. She is now working on a masters in psychology. When Tara looks at her mother, she receives a simple yet powerful message: "She did it, and if she could do it, I can."

With her mother's example to inspire her, Tara went on to excel in athletics at the University of Washington. In her four years on the basketball team she helped her team go to the NCAA tournament twice. She became the thirteenth highest scorer for the Washington Huskies, with 1,143 points, and pulled down 551 rebounds. During Tara's last year of basketball, and for another year after she completed her basketball eligibility, she competed on the university track team. She still holds the school record for the triple jump—41 plus feet—and she took the long jump title in the Pac-10.

After all those successes, after college, like many female athletes, Tara had no clear path to follow. When she graduated from college in 1994, she could have played basketball overseas but chose not to. The lack of a professional league in the United States was her main reason why not. "Seeing that there wasn't a league back in 1994," she comments, "there wasn't nothing really to come back to or necessarily to look forward to." She didn't want to play overseas for years the way some women had.

When Tara heard about the ABL, however, her vision of her personal future became clearer. If she could make it into the ABL, that was what she wanted to do. She contacted Christy Hedgpeth, stayed in touch with her, and eventually went to the tryouts in Atlanta. For Tara, coming through the tryouts, then making it into the ABL draft pool, felt like a significant personal accomplishment. The Reign only drafted Tara as an alternate, but since one of the players drafted ahead of her didn't end up signing a contract, Tara made the team.

Tara's situation on the Reign is a perfect example of what routinely happens at the professional level of sports. When everyone is highly talented, a player who starred on her college team could find herself relegated to the role of reserve on a professional team. As a league media guide describes, Tara is a good defensive player who can play two positions and also shoot the three. Yet with all those skills, in Seattle Tara was a bench player all year, playing in 36 of 40 games but never starting, averaging only 2.9 points and accumulating one of the lowest totals of minutes played on her team. The adjustment to bench player wasn't easy of course. "It wasn't an ideal playing situation," Tara comments. "You always hope as a player that you'll play more and you work for that and when it doesn't happen, I mean, you're somewhat bummed out about it."

Giving herself positive messages helped. "Your time will come," she would tell herself. "Just keep playing, keep working hard." A mature awareness helped as well. Tara could see the big picture. This wasn't just her personal basketball year but the first year in a whole new league. "It needs to be successful. No one needs to bring it down with negativity," she would remind herself. "So just stay positive."

Her teammates would help along Tara's positive feelings by offering her words of encouragement. "Just keep working hard," teammates would say. "Just keep your head up."

The Seattle fans were always supportive of the Reign, even during their losing streaks, and both Tara Davis and teammate Rhonda Smith were local girls familiar to Seattle fans from their play at the University of Washington. Tara's family provided support as well. Her mother and her mother's fiance had season tickets to Reign games, and Tara's sister and brother attended often. Friends were there too, making up what Tara describes as "a very big support cast" she most definitely appreciated.

That support cast couldn't watch their personal favorite player star for the Reign, because that wasn't ever Tara's role. But they could and did cheer her on when she was on the floor. In the second game of the season, against San Jose, Tara played 25 minutes, her personal longest of the season. She had a personal best of 9 rebounds, three field goals, and ten points total.

In late January, an injury to Reign guard Christy Hedgpeth forced some changes in the Seattle lineup. Tara Davis was one of the beneficiaries, and stayed on court for quite a while as the Reign competed against the Lasers. In the second half especially, Tara was out on court long enough to really get into the rhythm of the game. She was active on defense, stole two San Jose passes, and made an athletic move to the basket, hitting her shot. When she went to the bench late in the fourth quarter, the crowd applauded her.

Fans might not have noticed that Tara did her a lot of applauding herself, acting as a cheerleader for her team mates. Tara showed the same winning attitude even later in the season, when the Reign played the Xplosion on February 1st. At the end of the third quarter, as Tara waited on the bench, she didn't act disgruntled. Instead she exchanged high fives with Seattle players coming off the court. In the fourth quarter, Tara came in for a little bit, then was taken out. She trotted off court, looking composed although she surely would have rather stayed out there, and even slapped hands with Jacquie Hullah, the Seattle head coach she sometimes had difficulties with.

That personal strength was something Tara could draw on in the non-basketball role she also took on during the first ABL season. She became the assistant coach of a high school track team, a position that Tara describes as "really challenging."

She coached mostly girls and some boys, including some quite talented young athletes. Like many coaches of young people, she experienced the challenge of seeing the potential in her athletes and trying to get the young athletes to see it as well. She also had to deal with athletes who waffled about being on the team, boys and girls who didn't do all of the workouts Tara assigned, and young people who didn't respect their elders the way Tara had been brought up to do.

"When I was growing up," Tara recalls, "if I was in the company of an adult or adults, I wouldn't even think of cussing . . . (or) talking back. You know, it was yes, no, thank you." The high school girls and boys she coached, however, would indulge in what Tara describes as "just sailor talk." She would say to them sometimes, "Do you talk like that at home in front of your mother? I don't want to hear it. I'm not your mother, I'm not your father, but I don't want to hear it."

After the inaugural ABL season, the Seattle Reign chose not to re-sign Tara Davis, and she wasn't drafted by any other ABL team. A few months after the season, she considers her future. Playing basketball overseas for a while, to get more basketball experience, is a possibility. Now that women's pro basketball in the United States is an option, Tara doesn't mind the idea of playing in another country for a while.

She can also see a future for herself in coaching, perhaps at the collegiate or even the professional level.

As a high school track coach, she has already seen how certain moments can reward a coach for all her hard work. Those are special moments when after encouraging her athletes, telling them what they could accomplish, all of sudden a young athlete would put it all together. "When they finally get it," Tara describes, "that light goes on and you look at them, and their eyes. . . they're just gleaming."

Sheila Frost

Sheila Frost also knows about the rewards of coaching. And like Tara Davis, she's experienced the dual roles of coach and athlete. But more than Tara, Sheila stresses the distance between the two. Playing and coaching basketball are "like two totally different worlds."

Sheila is certainly qualified to have an opinion on the subject. Her collegiate career was at the University of Tennessee, one of the top programs for women's basketball. She followed that with a short stint overseas, then spent six years as an assistant coach at Old Dominion, another college with a tradition of high-powered women's basketball. When the ABL started up, Sheila made another career shift. She traded the job of coaching college women for another sort of position: putting her own body on the line as a player once again.

The "career change" wasn't without its difficulties. Sometimes Sheila would do a kind of mental flip-flop about what her role should be. When she first started practicing with her new teammates on the Portland Power, she couldn't always keep the two roles straight.

"I still had the coaching mentality in practice," Sheila describes in her soft, Tennessee accent. "I would come out and I would want to correct my teammates. Like 'wait a minute, you should . . . . ' and then I'd stop myself and say wait, you don't have to do that anymore."

At the ABL tryouts as well, Sheila's coach and player "hats" rubbed against each other. Sheila was out on court, playing with and competing against some of the women she'd coached at Old Dominion. As Sheila and her temporary teammates ran up and down the court, one of the Old Dominion graduates kept calling Sheila "coach."

"Coach, give me the ball," the Old Dominion player would shout.

"Don't call me coach now," was Sheila's response. "I'm not a coach anymore. I'm a player."

Actually, although Sheila doesn't expect to ever get coaching out of her psyche—"Once you've been a coach, you've always got the coach mentality," she says—she's spent more years of her life as a player. "I was destined to be an athlete with my height and all," Sheila says. Sheila is 6'4" now, a center's height in women's basketball. When she was growing up, other people would glance at Sheila and make the same assumption: "Well, you're a basketball player," they would say.

In basketball and other sports, Sheila's always been competitive. As with other players in the ABL, competitiveness is a fundamental part of who she is, a character trait that seems as if it's encoded in her DNA. "I'm upset if I don't win," Sheila says about herself. "If I go out and golf, I'm mad at whoever beats me. I don't care if they're a pro. I just always want to be a little better than I am."

The sports she's tried to be better at include softball, volleyball, golf, bowling, waterskiing, tennis, racquetball, and snow skiing. At Giles County High School, she was a member of the softball and basketball, and track teams. She could practically have been a whole track team by herself. She ran the 100, 220, hurdles, 880 and mile relays, high jumped, threw the shotput and the discus, her efforts resulting in some state-wide records. In basketball, she received *Parade Magazine*'s All-America honors for three years. The number of colleges interested in her made Sheila one of the most sought after players ever in Tennessee.

The University of Tennessee was Sheila's college choice. For someone with her sports abilities and competitive spark, Pat Summitt at the University of Tennessee was probably the ideal college coach, someone who would teach Sheila about both playing and coaching basketball. Pat herself had been an Olympic basketball player as well as the coach of the 1984 U.S. women's Olympic basketball team. She's coached elite athletes for years, and knows the kind of effort it takes to excel. Sheila's description of Pat's coaching style makes her sound something like a Marine boot camp drill instructor, a description other former Tennessee players second. "Just when you thought, I can't run another sprint." Sheila laughs a little. "Well, you ran another sprint."

The lessons Sheila learned from Pat Summitt are still with her. She learned offensive and defensive strategies. She learned to believe in herself as a player. And she learned to persevere: "You never say die, you never say I can't, you never say I quit," Pat taught all her players.

Pat herself is a woman so determined not to quit that while pregnant with her son, she went ahead with a recruiting visit even after her water broke as she was getting off an airplane. Only when she began having contractions in the living room of player Michelle Marciniak, a first year teammate of Sheila Frost's on the Power, did Pat decide to end a visit which will surely become legendary in the history of recruiting.

Not all the young women whom Pat Summitt recruited for Tennessee turned out to be made of such stern stuff. A few players did quit, transferring to other schools because they didn't like the pressure Pat put them under. But Sheila stayed at Tennessee all four years and won two national championships in the process, in 1987 and 1989, her sophomore and senior years. Sheila's personal record of five blocks in the 1989 championship game helped that winning effort. As did the never-say-die attitude of all the Tennessee players. As a senior, Sheila recalls, she and the other two seniors had a similiar attitude. "We know what I took to win. We'd been there before, we'd won it once before, and we just had a mind set that we were going to win it our last year at Tennessee and we did."

Sheila has only one significant regret about her college years. Her basketball activities kept her so busy that she didn't make many friends outside her basketball world. In the summers, she played on summer teams and worked at basketball camps. During the school year, practicing, playing, lifting weights, and travelling to away games left her with too little time to connect with people outside that intense yet narrow world.

Paradoxically, though, basketball expanded as well as constricted

Sheila's world. She played for USA Basketball teams that went to Russia, Yugoslavia, Taiwan, and Canada. And she went to Ancona, Italy after she graduated from college—only five days afterwards in fact—to play for a professional team there.

While she was in Italy, Sheila taught English to Italians, learned some Italian herself, and made the adjustment to a different style of play. At Tennessee, she'd been accustomed to playing an up tempo game with defensive pressure. In Italy, Sheila recalls, "One of the first things I was told in practice was I go too fast." When her coach told her that, she gave him a confused look and asked him to explain. All he did was repeat that she was too fast. "I've never been told that before in my life," Sheila told her coach.

Sheila's role on court changed in other ways. At the University of Tennessee, as is typical for women's basketball, team play is emphasized, with everyone making a contribution. But in Italy, the foreign players, in this case Sheila and one other American, carried the main load. "We were pretty much expected to do it all," Sheila recalls. "It was . . . Sheila get the putback, score inside, get the rebounds, block the shots." She laughs when she remembers. "If I had twenty rebounds a game and the other person had one, I didn't have enough."

Sheila injured her back in Italy—post players are typically at higher risk for injuries because of all the banging inside—and doctors thought her playing career was over. "They pretty much told me not to play again," Sheila says. But she put the never-say-die philosophy she'd learned from Pat Summitt to good use, rehabbed her back injury, and a year later went to Russa and Yugoslavia with a USA Basketball team. In fact, she hasn't had any problems with the back injury since, something she mentally knocks on wood about.

Although Sheila moved on to coaching basketball back in the states, she made a promise to herself that she would remember a few years later. If a professional basketball league started up in the United States, she was going to go for it. The ABL turned out to be the new league Sheila had hoped for. She went to the tryouts and then hoped for the best in the ABL draft. Actually, she wasn't at all sure whether her dream of playing in a pro league was going to come true. On draft day, Sheila confessed to a reporter much later, she was definitely sweating it. "I haven't played basketball in six years," she thought, "Why would anybody pick me?"

After Sheila got the good news, that she'd been drafted by Portland, she knew she had some hard work in front of her. As a coach, Sheila hadn't been the type to just sit around on the sidelines. She'd typically found a way to play basketball herself at least three days a week. But Sheila knew that she needed to do a lot more to get ready. She was 29 years old after all, so she'd be one of the older players in the league.

It was hot in Richmond, Virginia, where Sheila made her home, hot and humid enough to make T shirts stick to overheating bodies. The combination of temperature and humidity could result in a total heat factor which was easily over 100 degrees.

On those blistering hot days, Sheila would be running around the track, drawing incredulous stares. "People look at you like you're crazy," is how Sheila puts it. She had to give herself a pep talk, motivate herself to keep on going. "I'm going to be playing basketball and getting paid for it," Sheila told herself, over and over. That was the broken-record message that kept her working hard on the track and pumping iron in the weight room.

It wasn't just money that motivated Sheila though. The money represented the new role she'd be playing as a professional basketball player in her own country. Sheila was very much aware that she and the other first year ABL women would be playing a pioneering role. "That was one of the things I was most excited about," Sheila comments. "I'm one of the first. One of the 80 first players to come out here and start this league."

Sheila vividly remembers the opening game. Describing her feelings during the pregame activities, Sheila sounds almost like an excited young girl. "Oh my gosh," she recalls, "I was as excited then as I think when I was going into the national championship game (in college). Now walking out on the floor with all the to-do around— we had the fireworks and the spotlights—I felt like a little kid all over again. I was so hyper, so excited, my adrenalin was about as high as it could be for that game."

After the fireworks and the speeches, the two teams, the Power and the Atlanta Glory, took the floor. Sheila wasn't actually out on the floor when the first basket was scored, but she was there. She was making history along with her teammates and the women on the Glory. She was carving out a place for women's professional basketball in the United States.

Sheila's own place on the Power, however, was far from clear for much of the season. Early in the season she was injured, in something Sheila describes as a "freak acident" during a Power practice session. She went up to block a shot, was undercut by an opposing player underneath the basket, and fell hard to the floor, landing on her head and the middle of her back. The resulting problems with her neck did not heal completely during the season, even though she did take off a little time, a week on the injured reserve list after the initial accident. It didn't help matters when she received further injuries during a game later in the season against Seattle.

But the injuries were only one of her problems. Her other main problem was with coach Greg Bruce, a difficulty many Power players shared. Even when Sheila was back on the active list and ready to play, she never knew what her role on the team would be from day to day. Not knowing, playing longer minutes one game and not at all or very little the next was "a mental disruption" for Sheila. She remembers a game against Columbus where she played 15 minutes. Then the very next game, she didn't even get out on the floor. While teammate and fellow post player, Natalie Williams, was injured, Sheila started and might play 30 minutes a game. She wasn't surprised that when Natalie returned, her own minutes were cut back, but she never had a clear sense of how much or when or why she would play.

The fluctuation was even harder for Sheila because she looked at her situation with a coach's as well as a player's eye. She wanted to understand her situation, wanted to understand what Greg Bruce's game plan was. "What's going on here?" Sheila would think. "What did I do? I didn't go out and get a speeding ticket. I didn't get thrown in jail. Is that why I'm not playing? What's the deal?"

All the uncertainty frustrated Sheila, for her teammates as well as herself. Greg "didn't come in with a plan. He didn't stick by it," Sheila thinks. Her years of coaching taught her that a coach has to sound certain, at least in crucial situations. "You go into a situation where it's two seconds left in the game and you're tied, . . . you need to have a play and say, this is what we're running. This is how we're going to run it." As a coach, you may doubt yourself, but you shouldn't let the team know it. Greg Bruce, in contrast, would say things like "well, maybe we should, but I'm not sure."

With the injuries and the coaching problems, Sheila actually thought about quitting but didn't want to do that. Fortunately, what Sheila describes as the "mental flip flops" during the season and "playing with my head" got dramatically better when a new coach, Lin Dunn, took over the coaching reins for the Power. Sheila appreciated Lin's consistency, and the fact that at last she knew her role on the team. She would come in off the bench, for a few minutes here or there, whenever she was needed. In spite of the never-fully-healed injury, that consistency was a big part of why Sheila feels that the second part of the season was when she really came into her own as a player.

Lin Dunn knew that Sheila had been a coach, and when Lin first joined the team, she asked Sheila for her perspective on the team. Lin would sit on the bench next to Sheila and say to her, "I want you to give me some of your points," or "Help me out with these plays." Sheila hadn't lost her coach's eye view of the game, and yet as a player she didn't think in the same way. By mid-season, her player persona was dominant, and when Lin asked for her coach's perspective, Sheila found it very hard to give. "It was a struggle for me to do both at the same time," Sheila describes, "you know to play and to come over on the bench." The "two totally different worlds" Sheila had lived in didn't blend very well.

Even though Sheila didn't feel especially able to help Lin out, she appreciated her style as a coach. She respected Lin's toughness, the way she would tell players their roles and give them both positive and negative feedback. Sheila liked hearing about what she'd done wrong. It fit with her own style as a player anyway, a style that was undoubtedly affected by her years of coaching. After a game, she would think about her mistakes. If only she'd stepped one way, or slid another way. She was hard on herself as a player, and she liked a coach who would let her know what was what.

Sheila remembers a game which the Power won and her postgame feeling of dissatisfaction with her own perfomance. She'd missed a couple of fairly easy shots. Afterwards in the locker room she wanted to apologize, wanted to say "I'm sorry, I should have focused more on hitting those shots." But before she could say anything, Lin Dunn verbally took the floor. "Well I've got something to say," Lin said in her typical assertive manner. Sheila and the other Power players were listening. Then Lin turned and looked right at Sheila. "Sheila," Lin said, "if you don't start making those easy little putbacks, I'm going to cut your ponytail off and shove it"—here Sheila switches to a euphemism—"where the sun doesn't shine." Sheila laughs remembering that moment.

Sheila's personal version of the ABL season had both high and low moments. On the court, there was her return to the University of

Richmond, the college where she'd coached for the previous four years. Playing in an ABL game at the college's Robins Center, Sheila put in ten points and grabbed ten rebounds in only 19 minutes. Off the court, travelling could be a little hairy, like the Power's trip east where they played all four Eastern Conference teams in a single week, a less than ideal type of schedule which all the first-year teams experienced sometime during the season. On another trip the team left Denver, flew to Seattle, played that night, and returned home right after the game. "You forget where you are," Sheila recalls. "You kind of panic when you wake up in a hotel room and have to think about where you are." Always being on a tight schedule could be tough too. But Sheila got used to finding a window seat on planes or buses so she could lean against the window and catch a "power nap."

Sheila feels positive about the way she and the other first-year pioneers dealt with all the stresses and presented themselves to the public. The players' manual included pearls of wisdom such as that players should conduct themselves "in an orderly fashion." But Sheila doesn't think that the league was ever really sweating it about the players' on-and-off-court conduct, something that's in glaring contrast to the way some male basketball players can behave. "I guess this is a sexist comment," Sheila says, "but I think they knew that females were going to perform up to a little higher standard. They didn't have to tell us not to go out drinking and getting in trouble. We know those kinds of things." Players would use common sense, like deciding to wear sweats if they left on a trip at five in the morning and to dress more nicely if they left at noon. And the players were all well aware that what they did mattered. "This being the first year of the league," Sheila says, "we didn't want to jeopardize the ABL."

By the season's end, Sheila was looking forward to returning to her home in Richmond, to her two cats, and to friends and family there. She was looking forward as well to having some unscheduled time, a summer with no obligations aside from her workouts. She would have the time she needed to heal from injuries and prepare for more ABL basketball.

If Sheila had been 32 or 33 when the ABL started, she thinks it might have been too late for her to make a comeback as a player. She might have stayed with coaching for good. But the league came just in time for her. The league gave her, and other players like her, a second chance.

Tonya Alleyne

Like Sheila Frost and Tara Davis, Tonya Alleyne has coaching in her blood. In Tonya's case, she left a coaching position to join the ABL as media director for the Richmond Rage. After the first year, she made a tough decision to leave the league in order to accept an assistant coaching position at the University of South Carolina. She has vivid and mostly positive memories of her ABL year.

While Jackie Joyner-Kersee played for the Richmond Rage, Media Director Tonya Alleyne was an especially busy woman. Richmond, Virginia is only the 59th largest TV market in the United States and Jackie is, as Tonya puts it, "a world wide superstar" who came "into this little market." Tonya did the best she could, and she's the kind of energetic, outgoing, high-achieving person whose best is pretty good, but it wasn't an easy situation.

Having Jackie on the team "rocked my world," Tonya says. It's easy to guess what part of the rocking was coming from. Was it all the media and fan attention directed Jackie's way? "Oh girl, you don't even know," is Tonya's quick response. "My voicemail got full in 20 minutes. Everybody from Dateline to Maury Povich to the local church community pastor." Tonya imitates their voices. "Can Jackie come do this? Can Jackie come do that?"

Tonya liked and admired Jackie. When Jackie left the team, because the Rage's schedule was too much for her along with her other commitments as a world-famous athlete, Tonya both understood and regretted Jackie's decision. "Her champion mentality," Tonya feels, "added a whole lot to the team." But Jackie's departure did make Tonya's life a little easier.

Of course, Tonya wasn't looking for easy when she took the job of media director with the fledgling Richmond Rage. She wanted a challenge, a job she would both enjoy and find meaningful. And even though her description of what she actually did on her job reads more like several people's jobs, she's still very positive about her experience with the Rage.

Tonya's 28 years old, a friendly, good-with-words, high energy person. She's a native of Philadelphia who describes herself as "a product of Philadelphia basketball," and who played with Richmond Rage star point guard Dawn Staley in summer leagues when they both were growing up. Tonya is also a former player who ended her playing career with no regrets after college. At 5'6" tall—"I'm like skinny, I'm a little girl," Tonya says—she didn't think she'd have very good opportunities overseas. But the basketball career she did have took her a lot of places she wanted to go. It got her a scholarship to Seton Hall, where she received both her bachelor's and master's degrees. A knee injury her senior year meant that she took that year off from playing and finished her last year of eligibility while she was in graduate school.

After graduate school, Tonya worked as an account executive for a Philadelphia radio station before taking a job as head coach at Beaver College, a private Division Three school in Glenside, Pennsylvania. Tonya enjoyed coaching, and thought that working through basketball she could have a positive effect on young women's lives. Basketball, she felt, had given her a lot and she wanted to pass that on. "I just want to make sure other young women," Tonya explains, "specifically African American women, to be honest with you, really get those opportunities."

Tonya is idealistic enough to want a job where she feels she's making a difference. And she wants a job she enjoys personally as well, not 100 percent of the time—she's enough of a realist not to go for that—but say a good eighty percent or so. She wants to be able to feel that "I love what I do every day. I love waking up in the morning."

Coaching was that kind of job for her. And when Tonya heard about the ABL, she had a hunch that being a part of a new professional league would also give her that day-well-spent feeling. She was at the women's 1996 NCAA Final Four in Charlotte when she saw the listing in the schedule for an information session on women's professional basketball. Her reaction was instantaneous. "Ooh, that's something I definitely want to go to," she thought, even though she hadn't heard anything about the ABL before that moment.

Gary Cavalli and Anne Cribbs were there on the panel, along with Debbie Miller-Palmore, who at that point was the first general manager hired. Gary and Anne and Debbie spoke about the league, and as Tonya listened she was quickly sold on the idea. "I just got excited hearing them talk about it," she recalls.

After the information session, Tonya introduced herself to Anne Cribbs, told Anne what her background was, and communicated her interest in the league loud and clear. "I would love to be a part of what you all are doing," Tonya told Anne. Tonya sent her resume right away, but didn't hear anything from Anne until a week or so before the ABL tryouts in Atlanta. Anne had lost Tonya's resume, as it turned out, and asked Tonya to fax her another copy so she could circulate it to the newly hired general managers for the various teams. Tonya faxed the second copy of her resume but didn't leave it at that. "I knew it would be more beneficial to me for them to see my face as opposed to just a piece of paper that could be shuffled away," Tonya explains. With her own money, she bought a ticket to Atlanta and then called Anne Cribbs to let her know she and a friend were available as volunteers. "Anne, I'm going to be coming and you can put us to work," Tonya said.

At the tryouts Tonya was kept busy. She videotaped some of the tryout sessions; she stapled materials, sent faxes, and hung up listings for which players had made it to the next round; and she did whatever else needed to be done. "Just hustled my butt off" is how she puts it. "It was basically something I knew I wanted to be a part of and I just went after it."

When she had lunch with Tammy Holder, the general manager for Richmond, Tonya made the personal connection which got her the job as media director with Richmond. It probably didn't hurt that Tonya knew Dawn Staley, the star Richmond point guard. And Tonya is well aware that Anne Cribbs' assistance helped her as well. Anne gave Tonya the media pass which allowed her to go anywhere during the tryouts. If that hadn't happened, Tonya doesn't think things would have worked out as well. "I kept thinking," Tonya recalls, "if she'd never given me that pass, I never would have been able to volunteer. I would have had to be up in the rafters, up in the stands, and it might not have ever happened for me."

But it did happen though. Tonya's energy, and initiative, and just plain chutzpah had landed her a place in the new pro league. It was a place where she felt she belonged, and a new job where Tonya's energy was a good match for the demands of her job.

In the budget-conscious new league, all the teams were understaffed the first year, which meant that people holding positions like Tonya's had to juggle so many job hats they were in danger of scalp burn. In the Rage office, aside from the general managers, there were only six other people, a small number to do whatever needed to be done for a professional sports team. Just for Tonya to run through the list of what she actually did takes her several breaths. She was of course, the person media people came to with interview requests and for press credentials for games. She also assisted the press during games, kept game notes, and kept some team statistics. Additionally she made up the press releases about the team, started a data base system for a fan club, and was in charge of setting up photographic sessions for the team. She did hire a local person to do the media guide, which she was officially in charge of too, because otherwise that project in itself would have taken all her time. And time was very much a factor. She was hired in August and the season started in October, which meant the media guide, like so many other vital tasks, had to be done right away.

After delegating the responsibility for the media guide, Tonya could get on to still more responsibilities. She coordinated team public appearances, which she both set up and attended. She dealt with community requests for appearances from team members. And she travelled with the team whenever they went on the road, because she needed to assist the press with setting up interviews with team members. She also made herself available to share information and anecdotes with the press to help them cover the team. On the road, she even had the job of scouting out restaurants if the team wanted to eat together.

Going on the road with the team was a lot of work, but it could be fun as well. Tonya remembers everyone playing cards a lot for entertainment, and when the women were waiting for their bags to appear at an airport luggage carousel, the "action" switched to another sort of gambling game. "We'd take bets on whose bag would come out first," Tonya describes. "Okay, I got five dollars on mine," someone would say. "Okay, I got your five dollars," someone else would put in. The team member whose bag came out first would be the lucky winner of the moment. "That was pretty cool, pretty interesting," Tonya recalls. "It kind of lightens things up."

That lightening up could make a difference when everyone was tired out from travelling, like the time when players flew on a red eye flight from San Jose to Richmond and didn't arrive until eight o'clock in the morning. That was also a time that Tonya felt her separation from the players. After that long flight, the players went home and mostly slept all day. Tonya, on the other hand, went to the office and put in a full day of work, getting out the team statistics and doing whatever else needed to be done.

All that first year, Tonya's job was tiring, and rewarding, and frustrating at times as well. Money was always an issue—unlike the other women's pro league, the WNBA, the ABL didn't have the NBA as its financial big brother—and the lack of money to do things the way Tonya wanted to definitely frustrated her. "With the Rage," she comments, "I had all kinds of great ideas, but we could never do anything. We couldn't spend any money."

All profits and losses were made by the league as a whole, and since the league lost about four million dollars the first year, money was always tight. In Richmond as with all the other first-year ABL teams, the marketing budget was small. There wasn't enough for TV ads—the Rage did very little with TV—so Tonya went for news-paper and radio ads which reached and persuaded fewer people but were cheaper to buy. The Rage couldn't go out and purchase a bunch of billboards either to advertise their team. And even when money was spent on marketing, sometimes the centralized struc-ture of the league resulted in poor communications about what was done. "We had a billboard in Richmond that the league bought," Tonya remembers, "and we didn't even know where it was. None of us on staff ever saw it." That might have seemed like a funny situation if the stakes, the survival of a new team and a new league, hadn't been so high.

Tonya understood the situation of course, but still found it frus-trating. Starting out with the Rage, she'd figured, for example, that in some way the team could produce its own video and sound tapes for commercials. As a media director, she'd thought that even if she didn't have her own video equipment, she could rent equipment or bring in a production house so the team could make a highlight video and a commercial for the team, and she'd planned on doing about the same for radio. "Then when I got there," she remembers, "all these realities just kind of came into effect and it was like, no we can't do that because we don't have enough money."

Tonya's other main area of frustration had to do with the play-ers. As the media person, she was the one who made connections between media representatives and players. For a brand new league and a new pro sport for women, those media connections were vi-tally important. "We all knew this was year one," Tonya says. "In order for us to survive . . . we needed to do as much (as we could), you know, get out to every birthday party, everything and anything."

The majority of the players cooperated fully with the media. But Tonya found that some of the Richmond players were less helpful, and from media directors around the league she heard that the same was true for other teams. Leaguewide, media directors, Tonya com-ments, were frustrated by "how fast like the superstar mentality kicked in with these women." A minority of the ABL women were reluctant to talk with media people, or make the public appearances, or sign the autographs or perform the other PR functions which the league needed. At times, Tonya wished that she could get those superstar wannabes to understand just how important it was to act as role models, and also to understand that they should be grateful for the opportunities the league had given them because "at the drop of a hat it could be gone." As in fact it was gone for some of the players who weren't re-signed after the first season.

Yet in spite of her difficulties with some players, overall the connections Tonya made with the Rage players, the friendships she established, were one of the most rewarding parts of her job with the league. Even though she chose to leave the team after the first year, she expects that connection with the players to endure. "I will always have relationships with them," she says. "We'll always have that experience that we've had together."

While she was media director, Tonya thought about helping to form a kind of political connection among players as well, some kind of Black players council. She saw the league as a good opportunity for African-American players like Dawn Staley and Teresa Edwards to form that kind of a group because the league did provide opportunities for so many African-American women. And that kind of a group would have neatly dovetailed with one of Tonya's own key interests. "I don't think you could call me a feminist," she comments, "but I'm very much into women, especially black women . . . really making strides professionally and making strides in society."

On a less political level, Tonya appreciated the basketball strides which the Richmond Rage made towards the end of the season by making it into the finals of the ABL playoffs. "It was very exciting," Tonya recalls. "I was extremely psyched." The playoffs only increased her duties as media director—she now wishes she could have taped the whole playoff series so she could have watched it all afterwards at a less frenetic time—but it was all worth it for her team to have a shot at winning the first ABL championship.

The playoff series had its ups and downs. Richmond lost the first game, then won the second at Columbus, then came home and won the third game as well. When Columbus evened the series with a win, the fifth and deciding playoff game, which Richmond lost, was held at Columbus. That loss in the final game Tonya describes simply as "real disappointing." Yet in the locker room afterwards, she sensed that the women were okay, that they were "able to sit back and finally just reflect" on their experiences that year.

Since the season ended, and since she's moved on to her new job as assistant coach at the University of South Carolina, Tonya has done some reflecting herself on her intense ABL year. "It was a bittersweet feeling" for her to learn that the team would be moving to Philadelphia, since she was from that city, had worked for the radio station there, and had the kind of media connections that could have helped the team. "Bittersweet" is a good adjective as well for her feelings about the Richmond fans. On the one hand, the attendance at games was never high enough. On the other hand, Tonya comments, "the fans that we did have were excellent, I mean die hard, dedicated." She wrote a letter entitled "Thank You Rage Fans" for a women's newsletter to express her appreciation for fans who did support the Rage.

After reflecting about her experiences, Tonya moves on to thinking more globally, about the future of women's professional basketball overall in this country. Her outlook is a positive one. "I think women's professional basketball will be here forever," she says confidently. "Whether it's called the ABL, whether it's called the XYZ, whether it's called the WNBA, I think that it's here for good."

With the Division One coaching experience she'll get at her new job, Tonya has hopes of someday returning to professional women's basketball in a coaching capacity. Meanwhile, she feels proud of having been a part of a new league's startup year. And she knows that she herself personally and many others gave their best shot to difficult jobs. "We all the did the best we could during the first year," Tonya says simply.

Two Eastern Conference Coaches

Head coaches in pro sports never suffer from a shortage of attention. Head coaches run the show, earn the kudos and take the blame. Assistant coaches, although very important to a team, can sometimes seem invisible to the public. But both types of coaches are very important in the day to day life of a basketball team. In the ABL, two of these coaches are Lisa Boyer, head coach of the team known as the Richmond Rage during the league's first year, and Kelly Kramer, assistant coach for the Columbus Quest.

Kelly Kramer

Kelly Kramer speaks in positives about her experiences as a first year assistant coach in the ABL. "It was really a thrill just to be a part of the league in any sort of capacity," Kelly says. "It's just such a dream come true for any woman or any person involved in women's athletics and women's basketball to see all this come about and to see it be successful."

Then Kelly qualifies her statement. "You know," she adds, "I can't even really say it was a dream come true because . . . I never really dreamed that it might happen." Growing up in Miami, Oklahoma, she hadn't pictured there would ever be such an opportunity for women basketball players.

Now that women's pro basketball is finally a reality in the United States, now that top women basketball players finally have the chance to star in their own country, Kelly Kramer is glad to be a part of making that happen. She's glad to have the opportunity to be an assistant coach for the Quest, and doesn't seem to worry at all about the fact that she's not the head coach. Or about the fact that when TV cameras focus on head coach Brian Agler and his players in a timeout, Kelly's face appears, if at all, seemingly by accident.

Kelly has the kind of friendly and simply nice personality that those adjectives don't do justice to. She's someone who will go out of her way to help a writer interested in the league even though her only connection with the writer is over the telephone. She's 5'8" tall with a trim athletic build, short sandy hair, and a warm smile which must have contributed to the positive team chemistry on the Quest. And she's a self-defined jock. "Your typical tomboy," she says. As a girl, she recalls, "ever since I could remember I was outside playing with the fellas."

It makes sense that growing up Kelly didn't envision players like the ABL's Teresa Edwards or Dawn Staley lighting up a basketball court. Even though Kelly is only 35 years old, she's old enough to have experienced a time when girls' and women's sports simply weren't a priority. Yet she's also young enough to have grown up when times were beginning to change. They had just started girls basketball and other girls' sports in her town when Kelly was in the seventh grade, only a year before she started playing on the girls' basketball team. "I was just really lucky," Kelly says. "It was the right time for me, and it's too bad that women that came just a few years before me missed out on it."

Kelly knows just how lucky she was. "There's just, gosh, countless women like that," she adds. Her own mother is one of them in fact. Like so many other girls' mothers, she grew up before the impact of Title IX and didn't have the opportunity to participate in sports.

Kelly herself lucked out on two counts. Time was a factor. She started in high school in 1977 and graduated in 1980. "I just sort of came in on the heels of when Title IX was introduced," Kelly comments. The other part of Kelly's good luck was growing up in what you could label a sports family. Her father was a football and track coach and sports were simply part of normal family activites. "I grew up around athletics," Kelly recalls, "and my dad included me in all that."

In grade school, Kelly attended a school located only about half a mile from the college where her father was football coach. During football season, she'd walk over and watch the practices, while her younger sister, Kirsten, took the bus home from school. And even though football has the reputation of being a macho, quintessentially masculine sport, Kelly was always made welcome by the team. In fact, she didn't just watch from the sidelines. She became a ball girl for the football team.

During the crash and thunder of football games, Kelly stood on the sidelines, ready to do her part. She kept the extra footballs dry. She caught passes thrown out of bounds and tossed the football back to the referees. She fetched an extra ball when it was needed. It was a small role, light years from being the starring quarterback on a football team, but it was a role Kelly enjoyed immensely. "I just loved being there," she remembers, "I wanted to be a part of it."

She was a part of sports activities in other ways too. In her neighborhood, she played pickup games of baseball, basketball, and football with mostly boys all the way through her high school years. "I was never made to feel like I shouldn't be out there," she comments. Playing tackle football was part of the picture for her from a fairly young age. When she was in the first or second grade, her father bought football uniforms—helmets, shoulder pads, the works—for Kelly's older brother Kirk and for Kelly as well. A photograph in the family album shows Kelly and Kirk dressed up in their football gear.

Kelly's father continued as a high school coach for several years, and then became the football and track coach for Northwestern Oklahoma Junior College in Miami, Oklahama the smallish city—population of about 14,000—which Kelly calls her hometown. Meanwhile, Kelly herself started playing girls' basketball in the eighth grade. In junior high she ran track in the spring and played basketball in the winter. Once again, having a father who coached was helpful. When Kelly was a junior and senior in high school, her father coached cross country as part of his job and Kelly started working out with her father's cross country runners to get in better shape for basketball.

Kelly's father's supportive attitude, directed towards a daughter as well as towards his son, might have been influenced by his own family history. His mother, Elsia Kramer, played basketball in Missouri in the 1920's, the same era when Grace Sullivan Bell was playing basketball at the University of Oregon. Elsia, who still stays active with exercise classes, has pictures of her basketball team and a team trophy. Elsia's experience helped lay the groundwork for women's pro basketball, Kelly understands. "She's one of those women that did have a chance to play, and, you know, she's one of the pioneers," Kelly says about her grandmother. About the ABL, her grandmother's opinion is that it's "fantastic."

Kelly's father continued to be supportive of his daughter's sports interests and Kelly continued to find sports exciting. Basketball was the sport Kelly liked the best, and she was fortunate that Oklahoma had been a relatively good state for girls' basketball for a long time. In the 40's through the 60's, Oklahoma small towns maintained the tradition of girls sports, and after Title IX, schools in bigger towns and cities followed suit. Oklahoma, however, was also the last state to put an end to what had become a basketball relic: the six-on-six style of girls' basketball where three offensive players, called forwards, and three defensive players, called guards, on either side played a half court game with no roving players permitted. At least there weren't any restrictions on dribbles when Kelly was growing up, which was a lucky thing, because the six-on-six, half court game was what she played until she went to college.

"I appreciate the game," Kelly says about the six-on-six style. "It was really a fast game. It was very offensive minded." When she began coaching, she coached six-on-six ball in fact. However, she prefers the modern five-on-five game which she started playing in college. "I didn't like missing half the game, which essentially you did when you played six-on-six," she says.

In high school, Kelly was a forward on the basketball team and also ran track. The boys at her high school had baseball and football teams too, but at the time Kelly didn't question why the boys had more sports opportunities than the girls. After all, it hadn't been that long, only in 1975, when girls' teams had been started—a state of affairs Kelly now calls "absurd" and "just crazy." So the girls were glad that they got a chance at some kind of sports. "When we finally did get started competing," Kelly remembers, "we were just so happy to get to do it that I didn't really think about fighting for more."

Kelly's junior year, her basketball team made it to the state tournament in Oklahoma City, a tournament that received plenty of attention in a state where girls' basketball has a solid even if somewhat interrupted history. After high school, Kelly moved on to Seminole Junior College, where her play on the basketball team was recognized with All-region and All-Conference honors, and then to Crowder College, in Missouri, where she was the captain on a basketball team which went 29 and 2 that year.

For her junior and senior years, Kelly transferred to Oklahoma Baptist University, a college close to Oklahoma City, where she received a basketball scholarship. The school was solid for academics and had a good program for women's basketball, even though it was a NAIA (National Association for Intercollegiate Athletics) rather than a more prestigious NCAA school. But prestige wasn't what mattered to Kelly. What she wanted was the opportunity to play, and that was what she received at OBU, where she was a bench player her junior year, a starter as a senior, but totaled plenty of playing time both years. She was a guard at OBU, someone seen as a "defensive specialist or role player," and during her two years there her team had a 51-14 record and went to the finals of the state tournament both years. They didn't play at the Division One level, but "It was a really good brand of basketball," Kelly recalls.

After college, Kelly saw her next life step as clearly as if she'd possessed a crystal ball. She'd grown up with a father who coached, in a sports loving family where going to games was part of the normal routine and where Kelly wasn't the only athlete among her siblings—her brother played football and ran track. Ever since she'd been in junior high school, Kelly had known that she wanted to coach.

She started out her coaching career in high schools and junior high schools, working at three different small schools. She juggled those demanding jobs for five years. "When you're in that situation," Kelly describes, "you coach every sport, you coach every grade, I mean, you don't get a break all year long." She taught classes in history, geography, health, and physical education as well during her stints as assistant girls basketball coach and head track and softball coach at Pawnee, Oklahoma Senior and Junior High Schools, and then as assistant girls basketball coach and head track and cross country coach for the Schulenburg, Texas Independent School District and later for the Jay, Oklahoma Senior and Junior High Schools.

Then an opportunity came for Kelly to move to college basketball. Ironically, it was a version of the old boys' club, a traditional avenue for young men to get ahead, which helped out Kelly. Brian Agler, now head coach for the Columbus Quest, had been an assistant men's basketball coach at the junior college where Kelly's father was and is a teacher, Northeastern Oklahoma A & M Junior College. When the head coaching job for the women's team opened, Brian got the job. And that was where the old boys' club type connection came in, or perhaps it would be more correct to call it an old boys' and old girls' connection, since Brian Agler was friends with both of Kelly's parents through his work with the women's booster club.

When Brian had an opening for an assistant coach, Kelly applied for the job and got it. She'd been thinking about trying to move up to the college level, and since she knew Brian and he knew her, that undoubtedly gave her a leg up over other applicants. Actually, she became the only full time assistant Brian Agler had, even though Division One programs would typically have two assistants. But this was women's basketball after all. "The women's program and the budget . . . was far below that of the men's," Kelly remembers.

Both in the ABL and at the collegiate level, some people question the idea of a man coaching women's basketball. Historically it has been true that at the collegiate level, since the NCAA replaced the AIAW as the governing body for women's collegiate sports, and since women's sports became relatively more prestigious, the ranks of women coaching women's collegiate sports such as basketball have thinned. But Kelly Kramer doesn't find any problem working together with Brian Agler as the two coach women's basketball. "Brian's focus is women's basketball," Kelly comments. "He's made a commitment to that."

Working as a team, Kelly and Brian moved up the coaching ladder. At Northeastern Oklahoma A & M, in spite of a low budget, the women's basketball program at least had the use of the new athletic facility because the men's team preferred to practice in the old gym, which they could close off to outsiders. Then Kelly and Brian moved on to the University of Missouri-Kansas City in 1988, and to Kansas State University in 1993. There they played in the Big Eight Conference, which later became the Big Twelve, which Kelly describes as a "great women's basketball conference" and a "great opportunity."

But since this was women's basketball, the great opportunity still had some drawbacks. There were excellent athletic facilities, but the men's teams had first crack at practice times, a situation which has often been true in college athletics. "We sort of worked around them," Kelly remembers about how the women's team scheduled practice time in relation to the men's team. While the mens' coaches had nice cars to drive on recruiting visits, Kelly describes the car she received as "this jalopy that I wouldn't take ten miles out of town." However, once more Brian and Kelly worked hard and well together and improved the women's program "to a level of respectability."

The idea of a women's professional basketball league kind of snuck up on Kelly and Brian. When the two first started coaching at the University of Missouri-Kansas City, there was a semi-professional women's league getting going in midwestern towns, such as Kansas City and St. Louis. The emphasis was on the "semi" rather than on the "professional" because players received pay only for expenses, only practiced about once a week, and just played on weekends. Still, that got the idea of a women's league percolating in Kelly and Brian's heads. He'd like to get involved in a professional women's basketball league, Brian told Kelly. He thought such a league would really happen at some point.

Of course, Brian and Kelly weren't the only two to have that kind of a discussion, and a few years later, they read about how the ABL was being formed and was going to have a team in Columbus, Ohio. Since Brian is from the Columbus area and a big fan of women's basketball, he was strongly interested. He contacted the league and flew out to California to interview with Gary Cavalli and Steve Hams. Even though Kelly had moved with Brian to coaching positions at three different colleges, the ABL was a different can of worms. It was a risky attempt at a women's pro league, and certainly no one would have questioned Kelly's decision if she had decided the ABL wasn't a good career move for her. She might have thought about trying for a head coaching job of her own instead, somewhere within the collegiate game. Initially, Kelly was in fact somewhat sceptical about the ABL, due to the history of women's leagues in the past that didn't work out. But she was impressed by the fact that many of the women on the U.S. National Team supported the league.

When Brian got the job of head coach and general manager for the fledgling Columbus Quest, Kelly decided to take the gamble and move with him as his assistant coach once again. "It was taking a chance," she recalls. "It was kind of a leap of faith. But what a great opportunity and sort of an adventure."

The adventure started at the ABL tryouts in Atlanta, where close to 600 women attended. "That was a great thing," Kelly recalls, "to see all those women there with all their dreams." But the dream of a new women's pro league might have seemed shaky, to say the least, when Kelly and Brian were first setting up their offices in Ohio. For the first staff meeting, Kelly remembers, there was a folding table and about seven folding chairs. The only other addition to what could be loosely called office furniture was a telephone somebody brought from home which was plugged into a wall outlet. It was "literally starting from the ground floor," Kelly recalls. Actually, that was already an improvement from when Brian first went out to Ohio in late May and early June, and the two women he hired had to get started working in someone's kitchen.

The Columbus Quest as a team at first didn't seem that promising either. During training camp, an article appeared referring to the team as the "Columbus Questions." The team had stronger guards than post players, for one, and many people's assumption was that strong post players would be necessary for success in the ABL. But the lack of respect for the team, Kelly feels, actually became a positive—something that motivated the team.

She remembers a pre-season exhibition game played in Springfield, Missouri against the Colorado Xplosion. Since two Colorado players had played collegiate basketball in Springfield, the crowd was rooting for Colorado. Another strike against the Quest was that they only had seven players available to play. Katie Smith had just signed with the Quest, but she was attending the NCAA Women of the Year banquet in Kansas City. Andrea Lloyd was recuperating from knee surgery and La'Shawn Brown was sick. Certainly no one would have been surprised if Columbus had lost the game, but that wasn't what happened. While about 5,000 fans watched, the seven Quest players made their stand. "They weren't going to lose," Kelly remembers.

Kelly enjoyed working with Brian Agler and she enjoyed being assistant coach for the Columbus Quest players. Brian, she felt, "established a great rapport with his players. He always was respectful with them and he gave them a lot of input." About the team, she describes them as women who "love to have fun" and who didn't get too deeply into their own egos. The women "gave each other a hard time, all the time, like sisters would do, but they were respectful of each other and our staff and just good people." What that meant was that both Kelly and Brian could be friends as well as coaches to their players. That must have been especially natural for Kelly to do, since she is not only an outgoing person, but she's basically the same age as the oldest player on the team, Valerie Still. Kelly also smiles a lot more easily than the somewhat dour head coach Brian Agler. After games, Kelly and the players, and often Brian as well, would often go out to eat or just hang out together.

Travelling with the team could be tiring but it could enjoyable as well. During a ten-day road trip, the Quest played Colorado and

Portland, and then had three days off before a game in Seattle. Rather than flying back to Columbus, they took a side trip to Moscow, Idaho, the home town of Quest player Andrea Lloyd. The town put on an Andrea Lloyd night, paid for the team's airline tickets, meals, and hotel rooms. In return, the team played an exhibition game against people from the town and put on some basketball clinics. Kelly remembers driving forty miles out of town, through a blizzard, to get to a clinic. "That was fun," she recalls about the whole experience, "to take the ABL to a part of the country that otherwise . . . would never be a part of it."

The "Columbus Questions" ended up burning up the league, establishing the best record by far. They played what Kelly describes as "Quest basketball," which she characterizes as "playing together as a team" and "just sacrificing everything for the good of the team and doing whatever it takes. . . screening out, diving on the floor for loose balls, setting picks for your teammates," all the crucial actions which aren't necessarily reflected in basketball statistics. It all ended up in "great team chemistry." Even though the players were together, their supporting cast of fans in Columbus, Ohio took quite a while to climb on board. Over the whole first year, Columbus had the lowest attendance average in the league. "We struggled to sell tickets," Kelly recalls. But gradually fan support improved. By the time the Quest played their last game of the season, the final playoff game against Richmond in Columbus, the arena, which seats about 6,500 was sold out. People were buying tickets from scalpers for $30 just to see the last quarter of the game.

The game Kelly remembers the most, however, wasn't that last playoff game. It was the one right before it, the fourth finals game which was held in Richmond. That game was "probably the neatest experience that I've ever had," Kelly comments.

For the game, someone might have chosen to revive the nickname Columbus Questions. After all, things didn't look good for Columbus. They had lost the previous game, game three of the series, and had only won one game to the Richmond Rage's two. After losing game three, they had to play Richmond again in game four the very next afternoon. Richmond, of course, would be playing to win the championship, an outcome that seemed highly possible.

Kelly remembers waking up that morning in her hotel room in Richmond but not getting ready to go to the usual shootaround on a game day. Instead, players and coaches had a team meeting in a room at the hotel. All ten players and two coaches were there and everyone spoke, sharing their feelings about the team and the upcoming game. Kelly herself didn't speak for very long, but she did make an important point. The way the team had fought back at the end of playoff game three gave them momentum for game four. Kelly reminded the women of their collective strength. In the last game, the Quest women "showed what they were made of and they hung together and fought and competed like crazy," Kelly told the players. "That's what our team's all about," she added. "We got back to playing the basketball that we played all year."

When coaches and players finally headed out to the gym for shooting practice, a couple of hours before the game would be played, the mood was both determined and mutually supportive. Brian Agler was out on the floor in his game-day suit rebounding free throws for Tonya Edwards. Other players came out on the floor to take shots as well. At the same time, ABL officials stood on the middle of the court, discussing logistical matters like , "Okay, if Richmond wins today, here's how we want the trophy presentation to go." The league had the trophy out on court at one point. Yet the Quest players continued their shootaround.

As both an assistant and head coach, Kelly had done her share of trying to motivate teams and players. But that day no motivational speeches were needed. "We didn't have to say anything," she recalls. The Quest players saw the preparations for the trophy presentation to Richmond, heard about the team party and parade planned for after the game, and shared the same feeling. "There ain't no way that this is going to happen," was the Quest women's attitude.

Brian Agler did retell some basketball history to the team before the game. About a time years ago when the Celtics were up against the Lakers in a playoff series, and the Celtics like the Quest were behind in the series. The Celtics had to play in Los Angeles, the Lakers' home court, and hear all about the Lakers' plans for their victory celebration, but the Celtics ended up winning that playoff series. The moral was clear. Obviously the same role reversal could happen for the Quest.

By telling that story, Brian included a women's pro team in an ongoing narrative about basketball great players and teams that often has seemed to include only male athletes. And the women of the Columbus Quest came together in a way that justified their inclusion. It was something that happened before the fourth game of the finals actually began, before the starters ran onto court as their names were announced by the loudspeakers, before the opening tip-off.

Kelly Kramer remembers "the feeling in the locker room." It was a determination, a coming together, a kind of collective energy and emotion that was hard to describe. Yet it was something real for players and coaches alike. "I just knew going into that game," Kelly says simply, "our team wasn't going to be beaten."

Lisa Boyer

At critical moments in games, Lisa Boyer huddles with her players in front of the team bench. She diagrams plays on her basketball board, gestures with long fingers as she explains plays, makes eye contact with players, extends her hands to the pile of teammates' hands before players go back on court. She looks intense, high powered, as she communicates with her players in the huddle, and as she walks the sidelines during games, sometimes shouting instructions to players.

At games Lisa is always nicely dressed, in well cut blazers and trim slacks. Her collar-length hair has a styled, blow dried look which would fit as well on an account executive or salesperson. Yet Lisa Boyer wouldn't want to make the switch to another field. She thrives on the excitement of close, competitive games, of elite athletes competing against each other. Coaching in the ABL, she says, has been "an incredible opportunity to play with some of the best women's basketball players in the world."

For Lisa, the game Richmond played against Colorado, on Friday, November 1st, was one of the memorable moments of the season. It was early in the ABL season; the Rage had only played four previous regular-season games, and had lost three of them. Two of their first four games had been on the road, the first two back to back, and now the Rage had to play five of the next six games on the road, including their game against Colorado. It was a tough schedule, especially for so early in the season, and Lisa describes her team as "still struggling at that point."

Lisa got up at six o'clock on a cold fall morning for the team's flight out west. When the Rage arrived in Denver, they had a long ride from the airport to the city. The gym the team would practice in was less than ideal. It was in "some YMCA thing" Lisa remembers. The gym didn't even have a full-size basketball court, and the players had to change in a boys' locker room. Everyone was tired, hungry, and the practice didn't go well. Lisa was left with a bad feeling about the upcoming game.

The first half of the game confirmed Lisa's feelings. Colorado had a solid lead at half time. But "when the going gets tough, the tough get going" is more than a cliché. It also describes Lisa Boyer's style and philosophy as a coach. At half time she talked with her team about basketball basics—rebounding, defense, execution. She talked about the mental game too—the "will to win, willingness to compete." And she also brought up a perhaps touchier subject, the players' confidence in her personally.

"Humor me," Lisa said to the women. "Just listen to me and let's try to see if we can get this done." When her team took the floor, Lisa remembers, "it was a whole new team." They played with more energy and cohesion, and Lisa felt excited watching them. By almost the end of regulation, the Rage were down by only three points.

Lisa called a time-out. In the huddle, as players listened and watched intently, she diagrammed a play. Marta Sobral, a tall, long-limbed woman who had played for the Brazilian team in the 1996 Olympics, was to attempt a three-point basket.

As the basket swished through the net, tying the score and sending the game into overtime, Lisa Boyer had a sense that she had scored points with her team as well. She was a fairly new coach after all to this group of elite athletes. She had something to prove and at that moment she felt that she had done just that. The play she'd diagrammed had worked wonderfully well. "It was kind of like you're proving that maybe you do know something," Lisa comments.

The game—still far from over—would end up going into triple overtime, becoming an endurance contest for players and coaches on both teams. By the final seconds of the second overtime, the Rage had reached a basketball déjà vu experience. They were once again down by three points. Then Dawn Staley managed to get a shot off in time against tough defense. Lisa watched in amazement as Dawn's shot went in. "It didn't even look like it was going to hit the rim, much less go in the basket," Lisa remembers. "It looked like it was way off."

When Dawn Staley pulled off the magical shot, the game went into its third overtime. Everyone was exhausted at that point. Players would come in off the floor, towel off sweat, grab a drink, and make comments like "I can't take it." But Dawn Staley, who had been on the floor for the entire game at that point, is a don't-say-die player just as Lisa Boyer is a don't-say-die coach. "We're going to win this," Dawn told her teammates. "We're going to win it and we're going to stay in it."

Lisa still remembers those time-outs as the game came to a close. "Sometimes the energy in those huddles," Lisa describes, "It's trembling, I'm shaking, it's a high." Those are the kind of intense moments Lisa wouldn't want to live without. "That's the love of the game," she comments. "These are moments that you live for."

Lisa Boyer and her team will probably never forget that game. Perhaps many of the fans won't either. At the end of the third overtime, Richmond finally pulled ahead. The deciding margin was only three points. "It was a team win," Lisa comments. She and her team had come together and pulled out the victory.

Of course, sports victories weren't new for Lisa Boyer. Growing up in Ogdensburg, New York, a small town near the Canadian border, Lisa played practically any sports and games she could find with other neighborhood kids. Kick the can, kickball, tag, basketball, and football. She didn't play baseball though, a game she describes as "a dumb sport" and "like watching paint dry."

Lisa was born in 1957, and the newspaper in her hometown describes her as "one of the North Country's first standouts after girls sports were established in the early 1970's." In high school the basketball team she played guard on was undefeated in Lisa's sophomore year. She also played soccer, volleyball, softball—a sport she was unenthusiastic about—tennis, and ran track.

When Lisa went to college, AIAW was the ruling body for women's collegiate sports and there were very very few athletic scholarships for women. At Ithaca College, in Ithaca, New York, Lisa played college basketball anyway, received a degree in physical education, then obtained her masters degree in physical education as well at the University of North Carolina at Greensboro.

After graduating from the University of North Carolina, Lisa became an assistant coach whose motto should have been "have resume, will travel." She was an assistant coach at Davidson College, Converse College, East Carolina, Miami of Ohio and Virginia Tech, changing jobs every year for six years in a row. "I should have had stock in U Haul," she comments dryly.

In 1987 she made the step up to the head coaching ranks, becoming head coach of women's basketball at Bradley university in Peoria, Illinois. Bradley is a private school which plays in Division One and has a strong tradition of basketball. Hershey Hawkins, who played for the Seattle Supersonics, is a Bradley alumni. In Peoria, "Bradley basketball . . . is the show," Lisa comments. But she hedges her description with a refrain familiar to coaches of women's college teams. It's the men's game that has the strong fan and financial support, not the women's. "No way," is Lisa's terse answer to whether Bradley gave equal support to women's sports.

In spite of inadequate funding, Lisa managed to have a fair amount of success at Bradley. In 1990, Lisa was selected Gateway Conference Coach of the Year. In the 1991-92 season, the 17 wins posted by the Bradley Lady Braves were the second-largest number of wins ever at Bradley by a women's team. During Lisa's time at Bradley, she became the coach with the most wins in the college's history. But as much or more than the wins and the honors, Lisa valued her players. "I had some of the best kids come through my program," Lisa describes, "women that still stay in touch with me."

She's proud to report that all her athletes graduated, a statistic many men's coaches can't duplicate. She obviously cared a lot about her players, and as a college coach, she spent lots of time with them. Not all of that was peak moments of course. Sometimes she'd get angry with players. Sometimes players were angry with her. Through it all players and coach forged a strong bond. "When they call you three years later and say 'coach, I'm getting married, will you come to my wedding?' those are real special things," Lisa comments. "Obviously you've touched their lives and more important, they've touched your life."

Lisa Boyer just plain loves coaching basketball. "No day is ever the same, no game, no year, no team. Everything is always changing and there's so much energy around the people that play this game. You know, you can get addicted to it."

Coaching in the ABL has been as rewarding as college coaching for Lisa, yet different. In college, coaches do a lot of monitoring of their players. When are the players at practice, when are their classes, how much do they study? In the ABL players are adults who go where they want to go off court, make their own decisions. After one season in the league, Lisa hasn't had the chance to work with the same players over several years, as she would in college. And elite athletes won't necessarily accept a coach's decisions as easily as college players will. Working with them can be challenging, but it's a challenge which Lisa loves.

On the Rage, one of those elite players is Dawn Staley, a member of the 1996 Olympic team. Lisa's glowing description of Dawn makes her sound something like a gifted chess player. Dawn, Lisa describes, "has an uncanny gift of being able to read the floor. She is usually thinking maybe three to four plays ahead." Other outstanding athletes on the Rage include Brazilian Olympian Marta Sobral, and international veterans Taj McWilliams and Adrienne Goodson.

Players like these are a special group. The first year ABL coaches, Lisa Boyer feels, are also special. When the ABL was first looking for coaches, no one knew for sure if the league could even survive its first year. The first year coaches were all, in a sense, gamblers. "All eight of us came in and took a great chance, took a great risk," Lisa comments.

Lisa made the initial contact with the ABL, then spoke with the ABL co-founders at the NCAA Final Four in 1995, and decided to go for broke with the new league. It certainly wasn't anything she had to do, nothing like the equivalent of a shotgun wedding. She had a secure job as a coach and an administrator at Bradley. Of course, at Bradley, as she puts it, "I was getting a little tired of banging my head against the wall." The college still didn't see the light about providing equal funding for women's sports. That made the ABL, which was all about promoting women's sports, seem even more attractive.

Playing the new game involved plenty of challenges. "All eight of us basically jumped in with both feet," is Lisa's description of herself and her fellow new coaches. The waters ahead were essentially uncharted. The new coaches navigated as well as they could the "waters" of a new league where many concerns had to be worked out during the course of the season.

Coaches and general managers came together in Atlanta for the week-long first ever ABL tryouts. After every practice session, coaches and general managers were together in a room. "Keep, cut, keep, cut" were the words which signaled necessarily quick decisions about players. One "keep" would move a player along. Along with their general managers, the coaches were the ones who decided who, out of all the players at the tryouts, would be part of the first ABL draft pool.

Both before the season began and during the season, coaches would call each other frequently. "What are you doing about this? What are you doing about that?" they would ask. "We were all in the same boat," Lisa describes, "and so there was a lot of comraderie there and a genuine concern and care for each other."

It was the ABL coaches, concerned about too loose officiating, who voiced their concerns in a conference call, spoke with league officials, and managed to get referees to call the game more tightly. When the ABL was laying out its first year schedule, Lisa points out, many top Division One referees were already booked for college games. The ABL had to pull together a pool of referees, and these refs had to adjust to the ABL game. "Some of these officials were seeing moves by these women that they could never have anticipated because they're very talented," Lisa comments.

Not surprisingly, the coaching changes made during and immediately after the first year have been difficult for Lisa. "I liked Jan very much," she says about Jan Lowrey, the San Jose coach who was replaced after the season. Lisa sympathizes with Jan's big problem, which was losing one of her best players, Jennifer Azzi, to a season-ending injury early in the season. That could happen to any coach, Lisa knows.

"I liked them all," she adds about the first year coaches in general. Her bond with those first year coaches was special, a bond that will probably never be as strong among coaches in following years. The first year coaches all shared the difficult and exciting experience of guiding players and shaping policy in a brand new league.

As the first Rage training camp began in early September, Lisa spoke with a reporter about the difficulties she faced. "We all come from different systems and different backgrounds – the coaches, the players, all of us," she pointed out. Defense was an area of particular concern for Lisa. Many of her players had played overseas, and defense isn't stressed in leagues overseas. "We want to pull our players away from that kind of thinking," Lisa told the *Richmond Times-Dispatch* reporter. "We want them to understand how intense they're going to need to be; how important it is that they get it done at both ends of the floor."

The Rage played their season opener on the road, at New England. It was a Saturday night. The New England Blizzard, which had the highest attendance leaguewide all season, brought out 9,800 fans. That meant almost 10,000 people cheering for the Blizzard and rooting against the Richmond Rage. Then on Sunday, the Rage played another road game against Columbus. As Lisa describes it, the combined picture wasn't a pretty one. We "literally got our brains beat in both games."

After those first two games, understandably, she felt "a little concerned" and "a little nervous." But she also felt that the team's problems were fixable. The Rage were allowing other teams to score easy buckets on them. They weren't playing tight defense or getting back fast enough on defense. They weren't rebounding strongly enough. Her players had more than adequate skills, Lisa knew. The problem she felt, "was getting everybody on board and committing to what we needed to do."

One of Lisa's strategies was to hold team meetings. Losing games, something elite players on the Rage didn't have a lot of experience with, was a major focus of discussion. Lisa, her assistant coach, and the players would discuss team weaknesses such as rebounding and transition on defense. They would talk about team strengths like athleticism and speed.Lisa Boyer is a clear communicator, and her players must have listened to her. As the season continued, things got better for the Rage. And as the team started winning games, players felt more committed to the offensive and defensive system Lisa was trying to put into play. The defense and the half court offense improved. "The more success that they had, the easier it became," Lisa summarizes.

Easier but not easy. For Lisa, being the head coach could still be a tough and somewhat lonely job. Players are bound to have disagreements with their coaches. Coaches' decisions won't please all players. And ABL players, of course, were used to high level play and high-powered coaching. Lisa recognized that ABL rosters were filled with "Olympians and All-Americans and All Conference players." All the players could be defined as stars.

Put that star power together, Lisa feels, and players don't adjust right away. They instinctively try to play the role they've always played—carrying the team, being the go to person. But basketball is a team game, and even at the professional level women's basketball is especially team-oriented, much more so than the NBA game. It simply didn't work for every ABL player to play as if she were still the "main woman" for the team. Gradually, players got used to their roles.

After the first season, Lisa continues to feel extremely positive about the challenge of coaching in the ABL. "To be able to come to a team and coach the kind of players that I've been able to coach. It's unbelievable," she comments.

Her enthusiasm doesn't mean Lisa Boyer is naive, or blind to the larger picture. The ABL has had more success in its first year than anyone might have expected. The league, Lisa feels, is establishing a more solid foundation. Yet, the WNBA is a complicating force Lisa is well aware of. "The WNBA is lurking out there," Lisa comments. "It's not like we don't know that there's a big pink elephant in the room."

In Lisa's view, the "zillion times" the WNBA's games are on TV will be more publicity for the women's game and could actually help the ABL. On a less optimistic note, Lisa knows that the WNBA has a lot more money. Yet she is confident that the ABL has more of one very important resource. "Without question we have the best players," she asserts.

Those top quality players were on display as the regular season ended and the ABL playoffs began. Richmond and Atlanta had competed for the last Eastern Conference playoff spot—Columbus had sewn up first place and New England was solidly in last—and Richmond had won the coveted position. The team would go to the first-ever ABL playoffs. In the semi-finals, they would compete against the Colorado Xplosion.

The first game of the playoffs should have been held in Colorado, since they were the top team in the Western Conference and had a better record than Richmond. But in a new league, things don't always happen in the most predictable fashion. Colorado had scheduling problems with their arena and so the first game was set for Richmond. That was an advantage for her team, Lisa Boyer felt. It meant that the team wouldn't have to cross time zones from east to west and end up playing late at night according to their internal clocks.

Even with the lucky break the Rage were 15 points down at the end of the first half. "It was gut check time," Lisa remembers.

Her team knew what was at stake. Lisa didn't have to lay it all out for them or diagram a huge number of plays. Little but important things were what she talked about in the locker room. Driving harder to the basket, getting back more quickly on defense, playing tighter more assertive defense. "We're either going to go out and play or we're not," she told her team in the locker room. "And if they're going to beat us, they're going to beat us because they're more talented not because of lack of effort."

As her players gathered their energy for the second half, Lisa stood in front of them. "It's about your effort and how much do you want this," she told her players. She spoke clearly and emphatically. It must have been obvious how much she wanted the game.

Her team responded, fighting their way back. By the end of the third quarter, the Rage had tied the score. "It was still a very close game," Lisa remembers, "but I truly believe we had control of the game from the end of the third quarter on, from a mental stand-point." Lisa's experienced perspective as a coach proved correct when her team won the game.

When the series moved to Colorado, for the second semi-final game, Richmond played a good game and Colorado didn't. "They really came out flat," Lisa remembers. "They couldn't get anything to fall." The hoop seemed to have an invisible shield around it for Colorado. Richmond, on the other hand, shot well and ran up a lead that was sometimes as high as 25 points. "Which was incredible in this league," Lisa comments. All the ABL teams were so competitive all season long that huge leads were relatively rare.

As competitive as her players, Lisa was glad to get the win, yet she sympathized with the Colorado first year coach, Sheryl Estes. "I'm sure that Sheryl was probably disappointed that it wasn't a better game."

The semi-final playoff format was two out of three, so with two victories Colorado was ready to move on to the finals. Their opponent in the finals, the Columbus Quest, had also overcome their semi-final opponent, the San Jose Lasers, in two games. Both teams were feeling upbeat and reasonably well rested when the ABL finals began.

This time the playoffs went according to plan, with the first game at Battelle Hall in Columbus. It was "just a really odd game," Lisa remembers. Columbus three-point shooters like Shannon Johnson and Tonya Edwards shot the lights out and Richmond couldn't stop them. The Rage got to the free throw line a large number of times and were "unconscious" from the line, making an amazing 34 out of 35 free throws.

At the half, Columbus led by five points, 48-43. "I think we've weathered the storm," Lisa told her players. She expected the Quest's hot outside shooting to cool at least a little. Then in the third quarter, Dawn Staley, Lisa Boyer's star point guard, came up limping. Dawn bent over, grimaced, had to limp off the court. Lisa substituted Dena

Evans for Dawn, and probably said a mental prayer that Dawn could come back into the game.

Dawn did return and the game remained close. In the fourth quarter the fans were loud as the teams took a time-out. In the huddle, Lisa gestured to her team, her expression not anxious but intense. "Let's go," she encouraged as her players headed back onto the court.

Lisa's description of the end of the game makes her sound like a sportscaster, a role she obviously could play with ease.. "It's a one-point ball game with 12 seconds to go in the game. And we probably didn't get off the shot we wanted to get off, and lost the game by one."

Frustrated was how Lisa and her players felt after the game. Her team hadn't played particularly well, Lisa thought. Columbus shot very well and Richmond didn't. "I don't think we ever felt like we got on track," Lisa comments. Richmond's free throw shooting kept them in the game but they couldn't build a lead over Columbus. In the end, they couldn't stop the Quest.

Coaches and players watched film of the first game. Lisa read-

Lisa Boyer

ied her players to make a comeback. "It really comes down to determination," she told herself and her team. In the second game, the Rage played with an intensity that matched Lisa Boyer's own. They played strong defense and, Lisa feels, took control of the game, winning by a comfortable margin.

After the second game, coaches and players shared the same goal—to win the ABL championship with the next two games. Since they were both held at Richmond's home court, it was a good opportunity for the team. Having a few days off before their next game helped a lot too. All along, the playoff competition between Columbus and Richmond had been "very physical," Lisa describes. "It was two very experienced teams using everything in their bag to try to win the championship." No one would try to hurt an opponent—

the way NBA star forward Karl Malone described himself as willing to do during the 1997 NBA playoffs—but players weren't giving an inch.

The third and fourth games were back to back, on a Saturday and a Sunday, a schedule better suited for television coverage than for players who would put out their maximum effort for every game. Of course, the less than ideal schedule affected both teams equally, but Lisa thought her team had something of an advantage. They were older, somewhat more athletic. Perhaps that was what made the difference on Saturday, when Richmond came up with the win.

Both teams were tired on Sunday. "I thought maybe we could outlast them," Lisa remembers hoping. But one of those intangible mental factors was working against Richmond. The Rage were ready to have a party to celebrate their championship. Columbus knew that, knew that their season could come to an end. Metaphorically speaking, they had to their backs to a wall they didn't want to define them. Perhaps because of that they were even more strongly motivated than the Rage. At any rate, the final result was that the Quest simply "had much more control of the game" on Sunday, Lisa feels. The Rage had to postpone their victory party.

Once again players and coaches shared the same emotion. They were "extremely disappointed" that they hadn't won the championship in Richmond. Instead, both teams would play one last game, a game that would be held in Columbus.

Playing on the road didn't concern Lisa very much. Her players were all professionals. They knew what it took to win an away game. But "the fatigue factor" was something she knew would have an effect. After the disappointment of losing the last game in Richmond, the team had to board a plane the very next morning for Ohio. "That isn't exactly what we had in mind," Lisa comments dryly. Partying would have been more like it, celebrating the championship that could have been theirs after the fourth game.

Columbus fans came out in force for that fifth and deciding game. Television cameras focused on the shiny trophy which would be awarded to the winning team. For coaches and for players, this would be the go-for-broke game.

Lisa Boyer was looking sharp in a black blazer, with white pants and a white blouse. Her expression was focused as the starters were announced. As play began, she couldn't just sit on the bench and watch. She would walk along the sidelines sometimes, calling instructions to her players or just seeing the game from another angle.

That angle must not have been a good one at the half, with Columbus holding an eleven point lead. As Lisa headed for the locker room she looked tense, perhaps angry as well. But she wasn't ready to hand the game to Columbus. Not at the half. And not with only about five minutes to go in the fourth quarter when one of her best players, Adrienne Goodson, stepped on a teammate's foot and turned her ankle, the pain causing her to roll a kind of somersault on the floor.

Coaches have to think on their feet in situations like these. Lisa hadn't subbed in the fourth quarter yet, but now she had to. She put in Rehema Stephens, a good player but not nearly as much of a go-to player as Adrienne Goodson.

Lisa Boyer hadn't given up and neither had her team. Dawn Staley hit a three pointer to cut the Columbus lead to nine points. With under three minutes to go in the game and a time-out called, Lisa squatted in front of her players. She drew out a play on her basketball board and explained what she had in mind. She gestured with her hands to help make herself clear. Anything is possible in basketball, and Lisa could visualize plays which would work for her team.

But the anything possible didn't work in the Rage's favor. With slightly over a minute left, Columbus had an insurmountable lead of 13 points. Television cameras focused on Columbus players starting their celebration, on Columbus fans on their feet.

A television camera did focus for just a moment on Lisa Boyer. This time she was sitting on the bench, just taking everything in. She would have to talk to media people soon and explain what went wrong in the loss. Shake hands with the winning coach. Spend time with her team after one last game which nobody on the Rage would celebrate.

"I want to congratulate both teams," League CEO Gary Cavalli said after the game.

Probably not many people congratulated Lisa Boyer afterwards. Within the winner-loser framework which is part of sports, she and her players weren't the heroines of the moment. But something inside of Lisa Boyer, either after the game or not long afterwards, must have told her she'd done well at a tough job. She'd brought a team together during the first year of a new league. She hadn't led her players all the way to the "promised land" of an ABL championship. But she'd brought them almost all the way there.

The Second Oldest Player

Thirty-seven year old Laurie Byrd was and is the oldest player in the ABL. That makes Valerie Still the second oldest. She turned 36 in May, a couple of months after the ABL season ended.

Valerie hadn't expected to play in the league at all. After 12 years of basketball in Italy— the most years of play overseas for any U.S. woman—Val had retired from basketball. She and her husband, Rob Lock, were the proud new parents of a baby boy, Aaron Still Lock, who was born in February, 1996, just about six months before ABL training camps began. Valerie had planned to take off something like five years to care for her son.

The change in her plans started happening when a woman involved in marketing the league, one of the assistant coaches from her college team, began talking to her about the league. Valerie and Dotti Berry, the former coach, were working on Valerie's self-esteem program for kids called SKIP, Still Kids Improvement Program. The goal of the program was "to teach kids to dream again."

It was in August, the summer before the new ABL teams would begin play, when Dotti mentioned the league to Valerie. "There's this opportunity," Dotti said, "It's a professional league that's going to get started."

Valerie was sceptical. She knew about other attempts at leagues that had started and then folded. "No, I don't think so," was her basic response. She hadn't played for two years. She'd just had a baby. She wasn't in any kind of shape for basketball.

But Dotti was persistent. "Every time I'd come in," Valerie recalls, "Dotti would say things like, 'listen I talked to the coach and I've talked to the league and it's a great opportunity.'" Val continued to listen sceptically. She wasn't buying what Dotti was trying to sell her. "I just thought she was crazy," Valerie comments.

In Italy, Val was well known for her basketball feats. In the United States, she'd been away for so long that most people didn't remember her. Dotti singlehandedly spearheaded a Valerie Still "revival." She sent out a packet of info about Valerie—her photos, some basketball stats—and talked to Brian Agler, the head coach of the Columbus Quest. Brian, it turned out, had a pressing need for an post player. A number of players supposed to be on the Quest roster either didn't sign or ended up going to other teams. Brian Agler "needed a big person desperately" was the way Dotty portrayed the situation to Valerie.

Dotti sold the league in other ways as well. Here was a new pro basketball league starting up. "You'll be making history," she told Val. "It's new, it's going to go." Plus playing for the ABL would only be a five or six month commitment, and Columbus, Ohio was only a three-hour drive from Lexington, Kentucky, where Valerie and her husband and son made their home.

Only partly convinced, Val decided she'd make a trip to Columbus. She, Dotti, and Rob drove there together, along with baby Aaron, whom Valerie was still nursing. She would meet Brian Agler, the Columbus coach, and have a mini-tryout. Since she didn't even have basketball shoes any longer, she and Dotti made a quick shopping run to a mall in Columbus, where Val bought shoes and warmups.

The Columbus Basketball Club, where the Quest typically practiced, was a chocolate brown, barn-shaped building. Inside was a small, hot gym. There was no air conditioning to fight against the late summer humid heat. Only the early evening air cooled the gym a little.

The Quest players had already run through some drills. Valerie did a few stretches, then joined the other women for a full court scrimmage. These other players were all younger than she was, all in better shape. Halfway through the workout, Val was ready to leave. She hadn't lost her ability to do the basic moves of basketball. The fundamentals—like blocking out and rebounding—were still there for her. But she was way out of condition, not the player she'd been.

It was hard for her to keep running up and down the court. She was short of breath. Her heart pounded. Why was she putting herself through this, she wondered. But she didn't quit. She kept on guarding players, putting up shots, and hustling for rebounds.

Afterwards Brian Agler came up and shook her hand. Brian had wanted Valerie to come try out, but now that he'd seen how out of shape she was, she was prepared for the brush-off. "Well thanks for coming out. See you sometime soon," was what she was prepared to hear.

Brian's actual words were different. "Can we talk in my office?" he said simply. So Valerie, Dotty, Rob Lock and Brian all trooped into Brian's small office. There was a desk, two chairs, one small window—nothing which resembled the more luxurious digs of NBA coaches. Brian Agler's approach was typically straightforward. "Listen, we want to sign you right now," he told Valerie.

Valerie couldn't believe what she was hearing. She looked at Brian. Had he really just said that? She looked at her husband. Disbelief was written on his face too. "We both were just so shocked," Valerie remembers. An offer to join the team was most definitely not what she was expecting.

Columbus, Ohio wasn't on Val's future itinerary. She and Rob had a trip to California coming up. "Give me four or five days," Valerie told Brian. "I'd like to talk it over with my husband."

Valerie, Rob, and baby Aaron went out to California as planned, but her California vacation must not have been a very relaxing one for Val. While she, Rob, and Aaron were there, the ABL faxed her various contracts. After only four days, Valerie and Aaron went back to Columbus. While she was there, she signed a contract with the Quest.

Valerie's decision flipped around the more common husband-wife scenario where a family relocates because of the husband's new job. Valerie's husband Rob had some trouble taking everything in. "Rob was in shock," Valerie recalls. "He couldn't believe it. He's like, only you could do something like this, only you."

Valerie might not have quite believed it herself. Joining the ABL was a major change in her plans. But it wasn't as if she didn't have reasons for her decision.

That summer she'd seen the Olympics on TV. She saw the U.S. women basketball players block shots, steal the ball, swish three pointers. As she nursed her baby, she'd watched women like Teresa Edwards and Ruthie Bolton and Katrina McClain take the world to school for women's basketball.

"It's too bad," Valerie had thought. "I'm this old. I've put so much into women's basketball." She'd been one of the best known female players in Italy as well as in Europe overall. "I didn't have the opportunity in my own country," went through her head. "I wish I had the opportunity." But she had told herself it wasn't going to happen. "That's just a dream," she said to herself.

But dreams were turning to reality in women's basketball, and Valerie could feel the change. Thirteen or fourteen years ago, she remembers, "there was no television coverage and you had to convince people that you could be sweaty and have muscles and still be feminine." In the summer of 1996, the world watched strong women, their faces shining with sweat, drive to the basket.

The television reporting of the 50th anniversary of the NBA also struck a chord with Val. Players from the early days of the NBA were featured. "What if the ABL becomes like the NBA," Valerie thought. "I would be one of the pioneers."

Could a new mother also be a basketball pioneer? A professional basketball player? Male players in the NBA never seem to worry about the reverse situation, but when the basketball player and new parent was also a woman, things seemed different. Caring for her infant son while also playing high level basketball would be a personal challenge for Val, perhaps the toughest one she'd ever faced. But she's the kind of person who likes meeting challenges. And then she thought about the U.S. kids who would watch her if she played basketball in the states. She could be a role model for them, especially for girls who played basketball.

Problems and possibilities cycled through Valerie's mind as she changed Aaron's diapers and spooned him baby food. Should she go for broke, give the ABL a shot? "It would be great if I could pull this off," she considered. On the other hand, she had plenty of doubts. What if she messed up big time on the basketball court? What if the new league was too late for her, if she really was too far over the hill?

"I didn't want to go in and not produce and not perform like I knew I could ten years ago," Valerie recalls. She didn't want people watching her and laughing a little. She didn't want to overhear people saying, "Oh my goodness, look at this girl. She can't play."

Mixed feelings and all, Val signed her contract. Training camp was going on right then, so she didn't have time to mull over her decision. She packed her bags, literally, with enough things for herself and Aaron to survive for a while. For much of the year she would bring things up to Columbus whenever she drove from Kentucky to Ohio. Meanwhile she and her infant son moved into a hotel.

Those first few weeks of Valerie's new life weren't easy. Rob was still in California. When the team practiced, Valerie had to ask friends of her teammates to watch her baby while she worked out with the team. After a hard practice—the kind of tough workout her body hadn't had for a while—Valerie plunged into another tough job, that of new mother. "I'd go home tired, broken down because I hadn't played in so long," Val recalls. And then she'd nurse her baby, change his diapers, be the mother that he needed. She felt guilty for spending so much time away from Aaron, so she'd focus her attention on him no matter how tired she was.

Living in a hotel didn't cut it for Valerie. And she wasn't an unattached young woman straight out of college who could just move into a little apartment. As well as a husband and a baby, her family included three dogs who were still in Lexington, Kentucky. Finally Valerie found a house in Ohio. When Rob returned from California, the family—dogs and all—moved into their temporary new home.

Like Valerie, Rob had also been a professional basketball player. He knew the kind of effort playing professional sports demanded and overall he was supportive. Valerie's coach, Brian Agler, was supportive too. "Don't push yourself," Brian advised. "We know what kind of shape you were in when you got here." By December, Brian figured Valerie would be much more fit. After December, Brian said to Val, "we're going to want you to take a bigger role in playing.

Valerie appreciated Brian's attitude and his clear expectations. Meanwhile, while she was working herself into better shape, she did what she could for her team. Once the season started, she played a limited number of minutes in each game, but she helped her team in more than just games.

With ABL teams not having top priority on arena or gym scheduling, sometimes the team had early practices. At 7 or 8 in the morning, everyone on the team was tired. Val might have been up with her baby until three or four in the morning, but she'd come onto the court and work hard. Actually, with all the stress of her life, sometimes she really did feel best out on the basketball court.

Val didn't try to act her age with her new, mostly younger teammates. Far from it. "I would go out and I would be goofy," she recalls. She and a teammate, Sonja Tate, would mimic a professional wrestling act. They'd roll on the floor, body slam each other. When the rims were lowered on the baskets, along with her new teammates, Valerie took part in slam dunking contests. Valerie's high spirits, and her warm, somewhat comical smile, helped create the good chemistry on the Quest.

As the team came together, Valerie kept on working hard. Gradually, she sweated herself back into playing shape. Her new life in the ABL got easier but it still wasn't easy. After about a month with the Quest, one night she called Dotti Berry, who was now her agent. "I was crying," Val recalls, "I can't do this," she told Dotti. "I can't believe you talked me into this."

Valerie had plenty to cry about. "I wasn't happy with the way I was playing," she describes. "I had pains all over. I mean if there was any part on my body that could ache, it was aching."

Some athletes—male and female—would undoubtedly have packed it in at that point. Decided that 35 years old was too old to be making a sports comeback. The body is less forgiving after 30. Aches take longer to fade away. Muscles have a little less spring in them, a little less resiliency. Injuries happen more easily.

But Valerie had a mental toughness that helped her keep on going. That inner strength was as much a part of her as her strong, athletic body. It was something she'd learned growing up in Camden, New Jersey. Something she'd learned from her mother Gwendolyn, who had ten children by the time she was 32 and raised them almost completely on her own.

Valerie was the next to youngest of the Still children. Her father was mostly away from home, working at whatever jobs he could find until he became disabled. Their neighborhood was poor, with most neighborhood families on welfare, but Valerie's mother and father tried their best to stay off public assistance. Their family was a strong one. "We may not have had gourmet meals but we had a meal," Valerie recalls. "We may not have had the best clothes in the world, but we had clothes on our backs, and we had a lot of love."

Valerie's mother was the central figure for the family. As a mother herself now, Valerie can understand what her own mother went through raising Val and her sisters and brothers. In the 1996-97 media guide for the Columbus Quest, Val describes her mother as the person she admires most. "She was just so strong," Valerie recalls. "She instilled in us . . . the courage to go on in front of adversity."

It was an example that shaped the pattern of Val's own life. "There's nothing that will just knock me down," Valerie says. "I'm always going to try to get up, dust myself off and go on. And mainly that's because of her, you know, watching what she's done."

"Dare to be different," Valerie's mother told her children. Be strong, stay out of trouble, be yourself. "You should have dreams and go for them and nothing should keep you down." Not peer pressure, not teen pregnancy, not crime or drugs.

The "different" part of Val's mother's message hit home for Val in still another way. She grew up in a multiracial family, with her mother a mixture of Irish and African-American, and her father American Indian and African-American. Their lighter skin tones and multiracial parents could make Valerie and her sisters and brothers the targets of hostility from other kids in the neighborhood. Valerie remembers being called names, being chased home from school. "Half breed" other kids sometimes called her.

Valerie can laugh now looking back, but it wasn't so easy when she was a child. She was different in lots of ways. She was an athletic girl, a girl who played sports. She was tall, the tallest boy or girl in her middle school class. She was of mixed race. "There was no way that I was going to fit into any one category," she sums up.

Other than within her family, basketball might have been the place where Val fit in most, where she could use both her height and her athletic ability. Her father was too busy working to come watch Valerie play basketball and other sports, but her mother encouraged her, coming to just about all her high school games. Since her mother liked the Still children to stay busy, Valerie was involved in other activities too. She played in her school band from middle school through high school and eventually learned to play the piano, guitar, saxophone, and trumpet. She was talented enough that her mother imagined music as a future for her.

Valerie's family situation changed radically when she was an older teenager. Her older brother, Art Still, signed with the Kansas City Chiefs, a NFL team. When Art joined the Chiefs, all of a sudden the family wasn't poor anymore. Art bought the family a home in the suburbs, so Val changed schools her senior year, moving from an all black high school to the basically all white Cherry Hill East High School.

Once again, it helped that Valerie played basketball. At the new school, she was the star player. Her teammates and other students at the school were excited about how Valerie could change the school's basketball fortunes. Probably because of her special role, Val doesn't remember racism directed at her. Her outgoing personality probably helped too. So new school and all, she had a good time playing basketball her senior year.

The University of Kentucky, which Val describes as "basically a white school," at least at the time, was where she went to college. Once again racism wasn't really an issue for her. Her status as a basketball player may have been the main reason. Being reasonably light skinned probably helped too. And perhaps it was also that she'd learned to present herself as simply a person, simply herself, as someone who dared to be different.

On the basketball court, her "difference" meant knocking the socks off opposing players. The 2,763 points she scored in college are still a record at the University of Kentucky for any basketball player—male or female. She helped her team win the Southeastern Conference Tournament Championship in 1982. During her four years in college, she also racked up individual basketball honors. She was twice named a Kodak All-American, three times a *Street and Smith* All-American, twice was named as an all conference player, and was named in *Basketball Weekly* as an All-American also.

Valerie Still

In spite of her basketball achievements, if Valerie wanted to continue playing after college, she had only one option—to go overseas. Her older brother could sign a pro football contract in the states and buy his family a house. Family and friends could watch him play on television. But while Valerie played ball in front of fans overseas, she would be mostly forgotten as an athlete in her own country.

Val paid that price because she loved basketball. She got herself an agent, and the agent received an offer for her from an Italian team. Italy was where many of the best American players went.

Uncertain what she should do, Valerie talked things over with her mother. "If you really want to do this, just take it for a year and have fun with it," her mother advised. "It's only a year and see what happens and then make up your mind." That trial year stretched into twelve. Valerie became a true basketball expatriate, someone who essentially lived her life overseas.

She played for Italian teams in Schio, Cesena, Brianza, Como, Magenta, and Sesto San Giovanni. When she played for Como, her team won the championship in their league. As a Magenta player, in the 1989-90 season, Valerie ranked second for scoring in her league. Over the next few years she was once again scoring champion or runner up in scoring as she played for Sesto San Giovanni and GBC, a team located near Milano.

At first, Valerie wasn't thrilled by life in Italy. Lots of things—too many things—were different. The Italians were too laid back, she thought. If she called a plumber, he might come in two or three weeks time. The same could be true for phone repair or new phone service. But the worst part was being lonely. She badly missed family and friends.

Italy was beautiful though. During her first year, when she stayed at the home of her company president in Monza, near Milano, she could look out the window and see burnt orange terra-cotta roofs. In Como, where she lived a few years later, she lived in an old fort with more terra-cotta on the roof and thick stone walls. She could walk along the shores of picturesque Lake Como, where famous actors and actresses like Elizabeth Taylor maintained homes.

As Valerie connected with people and places, she began to enjoy some of the things about Italian life she had disliked at first. After games, teams often sat together and had dinner for three hours or so. They'd enjoy good pasta, wine, and conversation. "It's no rush, it's like enjoy life" is the Italian attitude, Valerie describes. She came to like that way of living. She could be as laid back as the Italians off the basketball court, and a fierce competitor on court.

Living in Italy had another advantage for Valerie. The girl neighborhood kids had called "half breed" didn't run into that kind of attitude overseas. Nobody asked Valerie if she was white or black. Race wasn't an issue there the way it is in the U.S. In Italy, Val recalls, her identity was simpler. "I can just be me, an American."

Valerie enjoyed some of the best parts of living in Europe. She went skiing, to museums, to beaches. When she played in European

Cup competition one year, she and her teammates travelled to play different teams in France, Spain, Yugoslavia, and Russia. In the summers, she travelled around Europe on her own. Her parents insisted that she come home each summer for a month, but the rest of the time, Valerie stayed in Europe. "The summers were the best," she recalls. "I could just vacation, go from beach to beach."

Italy was essentially becoming Valerie's home. She dated an Italian man and considered marrying him. A skilled pianist and vocalist, with a background in both classical and pop music, Valerie started a music career in Italy—singing in nightclubs in the town of Pavia and on two disco albums. A multi-talented person, Valerie's off court activities weren't limited to music. She did some modeling of sports clothing like ski wear and warmups, and she had her own television show about women's basketball, making her the first foreign player ever to host an Italian TV show. It was that varied background which inspired a writer for the *Richmond Times-Dispatch* to describe her as "the closest thing the ABL possesses to a renaissance woman."

By the time Valerie hosted her TV show, her Italian was fluent. "I probably speak Italian better than I do English," she jokes. On her TV show, she would interview players from opposing teams and from her own team as well. She'd also have special guests like Daryl Dawkins and Tony Kukoc, and one day she did an interview with a basketball player named Rob Lock, the man who was to become her husband.

Rob had played for a year with the NBA Clippers, then gone overseas to play professional basketball in Italy, and then France and Spain. After meeting Rob, Valerie was definitely smitten. "It was love at first sight," she describes.

Rob Lock is 6'10" tall. He has strawberry blonde hair, blue eyes, and a quiet, introverted personality very different from Valerie's. He introduced Valerie to items of ordinary American life which weren't part of her expatriate awareness. On Rob's satellite dish, or on tapes his mother sent, he and Valerie watched "Cheers"—a show she'd never heard of—and David Letterman. Little by little, Rob reintroduced Val to American culture.

Val's deepening relationship with Rob led to another change in her life. For a couple of years she put her own basketball career on hold while she travelled and stayed with Rob. She missed basketball sometimes but kept busy with gigs singing at clubs. It seemed as if she was turning into the musician her mother had pictured.

Actually, Valerie might have been forced to give up basketball before she voluntarily took a break from the sport. In 1991 her team in Como won the championship. She then switched to a team in Brianza. At about the same time, her father was diagnosed with cancer, so a lot was happening in Valerie's life the night of November 25, 1991.

That night she went out after a game with some friends. Afterwards, Valerie dropped off her friend and teammate, an American woman named Vicky Orr who had played for Auburn in college. Valerie was heading home herself when a car pulled out in front of her. Just that quickly, the accident happened. Valerie had no time to brake. Her car hit a tree and wrapped itself around it.

Valerie wasn't wearing a seatbelt since they weren't required in Europe. The impact flung her into the back seat and knocked her shoes off. It crushed the windshield and flung glass fragments like shrapnel into Valerie's face.

The driver who hit her kept on going, but a man who witnessed the accident came to Valerie's aid. He thought she was dead at first, but she regained consciousness, somehow managed to get out of the car and actually walk to an ambulance the man had called.

Her strong, athletic body had been hurt badly by the crash. In the small hospital she was taken to, doctors put her broken wrist in a cast and repaired her nose, which had been almost severed in the accident. She had fractured her first cervical vertebrae, but the Italian doctors only put her in a neck brace rather than completely immobilizing her neck. Days later doctors discovered that her pelvic bone was broken in six places.

One of Valerie's sisters, who was a nurse, came over to Italy to help take care of her. Lying in her hospital bed, Valerie thought she was going to die. She was in enough pain that at times she might have wished to. After she was released from the hospital, her sister took her to see the car. "Val, you've got to see it," her sister insisted. Val cried when she saw what was left of the car she had been driving. The main impact had been on the passenger side. If her teammate Vicky had still been sitting there, Val realized, Vicky would surely have been killed.

When Val finally was able to return to the United States, a doctor examined her and gave her some non-medical advice. "You need to go to the first church you see and say a prayer," the doctor told her, "because there's no way you should be here."

Doctors in Italy had already told Valerie that she'd never play basketball again. But Valerie wanted to prove them wrong. In February, she went to the gym and began shooting foul shots. When her teammates saw her, "it was like they saw a ghost or something," Valerie remembers.

She wasn't a ghost though. Even though she wasn't quite the same physically—her nose healed a little differently; her bones warned her of weather changes—she regained her strength and mobility. She did play the next year, for Cesena, another Italian team.

A couple of years later, after Valerie and Rob decided to marry, they discussed future plans. Rob hated living in Europe and wanted to return to the United States. Valerie liked Europe but wanted to be with Rob. Their geographic loyalties in the states conflicted too. Rob was from California, Valerie from New Jersey. In the end, they compromised by moving to Lexington, Kentucky, the town where both had gone to college and played basketball for the University of Kentucky. In February, 1996, Valerie gave birth to a son, Aaron Still Lock. She planned on being a full time mother for a while. And then the ABL came calling.

The Columbus Quest didn't sign Rob Lock to a contract, but it wouldn't be incorrect to label him a basketball husband. Probably Valerie couldn't have achieved as much that first ABL year if it hadn't been for the support she received from Rob. On most road trips, he travelled with the team to take care of Aaron. He logged plenty of childcare hours at home in Ohio too. Once in a while, when Rob really needed a break, Valerie's sister or someone else would come in to help for a week or two.

Initially it seemed as if Valerie's new team, the Columbus Quest, needed help too. More help than any one player could provide. The media labeled the team the "Columbus Questions," and when Valerie considered her fellow teammates, she could understand the label. Star players like Michelle Marciniak, the MVP of the 1996 Final Four, and Carla McGhee, a 1996 Olympian, who were originally supposed to be with Columbus ended up playing for other teams. The women Columbus actually had seemed like a mismatched bunch.

Nikki McCray had been on the 1996 Olympic team, but she was seen as a defensive specialist rather than a key player. LaShawn Brown was missing fingers on her right hand from a lawn mower accident she suffered when she was a child. Katie Smith, who had starred at Ohio State University, didn't sign until very late. Meanwhile, Brian Agler had signed three alternates to fill in his roster.

Valerie has always been a positive thinker. She is a realist though too. "I'm thinking in my mind this team is doomed to lose," she remembers. Her own label for her new team was "The Bad News Bears." "These girls just didn't look like they could play basketball," was Val's assessment. "I said to myself, if they pick a 35 year old mother that hasn't played for two years, they're in bad shape."

It's one of the ironies of the first ABL year that the team which seemed headed for the bottom of the standings ended up being the best team in the league. Coach Brian Agler used other people's low expectations to help motivate his team. The Quest, he reminded his players, were expected to come in last in the Eastern Conference.

None of the Columbus players took that sitting down. All of them, including Valerie, were strong competitors. "Our practices were like just a dog-cat fight," she recalls. "It got really nasty."

The fierce competition in practice helped the Quest to come together as a team. As Valerie struggled to get into basketball shape, she gained a new perspective on the mix of players on the Quest. Mature players like Valerie and Andrea Lloyd, whom Valerie had played with in Europe, helped steady the team. Younger players like Shannon Johnson stepped up too. And attitude helped as well. The mental game is an important part of basketball. "We knew we were underdogs," Valerie describes, "so we would go in there just loose, laughing, and probably, if you asked other teams, just goofy."

She remembers a half time show in Atlanta where there was a Double Dutch jump roping contest. The Quest had the lead, but leads can disappear fast in basketball and this was an important game. Instead of resting, however, Shannon Johnson, Sonja Tate, and Nikki McCray began to jump rope along with some local girls. Brian Agler stood on the sidelines, just watching and holding his head.

Valerie's baby son Aaron's frequent presence was another thing that made the Columbus team a little bit different. Aaron was there at practices, on the team bus, at team meetings, on team flights to other cities. Many coaches, certainly many if not most male coaches, would have taken a hard line. Valerie imitates a typical coach: "You players need to concentrate on basketball. We don't need any distractions around here." That was what Brian could have said and probably no one—except perhaps Valerie herself—would have argued. Babies are simply not an expected part of professional teams.

Actually, Aaron's presence may have helped the Columbus team come together, helped the players bond into a kind of family. "Everybody became Aaron's sister," Valerie remembers. "They would take care of him in the airport and they would play with him." For a pregame warmup, LaShawn Brown would often put Aaron in his stroller and run laps around the basketball court pushing Aaron. All that helped players remember that basketball wasn't the only thing in life, Valerie thinks. They could play hard but also play loose instead of uptight.

More and more Valerie felt the team was fitting together and she was fitting in with the team. All the Quest women played games and tricks on each other just as sisters would. Val was often in the middle of the fun. One night the team was taking a red eye flight from Portland, Oregon back to Columbus. Baby Aaron, who was travelling with the team as usual, had a bowel movement at the airport. After Valerie changed him, she had a dirty diaper to dispose of.

The "lucky" recipient for the diaper became Nikki McCray. Nikki had tons of frequent flier mileage because of all her flights with the U.S. National Team, so she often flew first class. As Nikki stood at the ticket counter, trying to upgrade to first class, Valerie spotted Nikki's bag next to her own. Nikki's bag was the perfect place for Aaron's dirty diaper, Val decided. She slipped the diaper into Nikki's bag.

Unsuspecting, Nikki picked up her bag. The team got on the plane, laughing among themselves, wondering when Nikki would catch on to the joke. When Nikki found her first class seat, the team were watching. "Oh my goodness," Val remembers thinking, "They're going to think that's her smelling like that."

Nikki took her seat, put the bag up, and during the long nighttime flight, she would bring free drinks back to her teammates. The other women on the team were all wondering when Nikki would catch on to the joke.

When the team arrived in Chicago, where they had to change planes, Nikki still hadn't figured things out. She took a teammate, Sonja Tate, with her to the Red Carpet Lounge. "Keep your eyes on the bag," other teammates instructed Sonja.

Later, Nikki took Val aside, "Hey Val, I can't believe you put that in my bag." Perhaps the gag seemed too juvenile to come from one of the team's veteran players. But Nikki didn't get mad about the joke. Instead she confided that she'd switched the diaper to Sonja's bag. What Nikki didn't know was that Sonja had returned the favor. The dirty Pamper went back in Nikki's bag again. "This Pamper is festering. It's like nasty, you know," Val describes. And this time the diaper was inside the case for the pillow Nikki carried with her.

The team finally boarded their flight to Columbus. Everyone was tired but the ongoing joke kept the women's spirits high. Nikki McCray didn't upgrade to First Class this time. As Valerie remembers the sequence of events, "this time she's sitting with us low lives, you know in Economy." Nikki took her pillow out from her bag. Valerie and other women watched as Nikki fluffed up her pillow and rested her head on it. Right away Nikki raised her head up, wondering if one of her teammates had "let a little air biscuit," as the team would put it.

Naturally, all the women cracked up, and Nikki finally discovered the dirty Pamper in her pillow case. "Aaron's dirty diapers," Valerie recalls, "You never knew where they would show up at. We'd always find some creative place to put them."

Dirty diaper jokes, having other sorts of fun, and sharing moments from their lives brought the women of the Quest together. For quite a while, many outsiders still thought the team wasn't for real, that all their wins were some kind of fluke. Valerie and her teammates saw themselves as "David and Goliath"—with Columbus the David—even as they started the season with an eleven-game winning streak, even after they amassed the best record in the league, even as other ABL teams began to gun for Columbus. After December, as Brian Agler had expected, Valerie began to contribute more, to play more minutes.

There are many games Valerie remembers from during the season. When the Quest played at New England, there were always big crowds. For one game, the crowd numbered over 10,000. "Whoa, this is cool," Val remembers thinking.

Another memorable game was against Atlanta. Atlanta had great young centers. "They could run circles around me actually," Valerie recalls. But experience counts in basketball, just like in other sports. NBA veterans can always show rookies a thing or too, and Valerie did the same with the young Atlanta players. She would use her body against the young centers, fouling a little if she could get away with it, and then she'd rub it in. "Old as I am, you're going to let me do this to you," she might say to the opposing player.

By the end of the season, the Bad News Bears, the Davids of the

ABL, had by far the best record in the league, 31 wins to only 9 losses. They defeated San Jose in two straight games in the ABL semifinals. The team won their second game by a sizeable margin and all the Quest players celebrated.

Val couldn't celebrate as much as other players though. When she returned to her hotel room, she found that her infant son had a fever. Valerie and Rob spent most of the night, until about two or three in the morning, in a hospital emergency room. When they went to bed, they barely had time to sleep. At five in the morning, they got up to catch an early flight with the team.

While Valerie continued to juggle her dual roles as mother and professional basketball player—one of only three players in the league to do so—the Quest moved on to the ABL finals. The team they faced now was the Richmond Rage—a team led by former Olympian Dawn Staley at point guard, a team which would challenge them much more than San Jose.

The first game of the ABL finals was held at Batelle Hall in Columbus, Ohio, the Quest's home court. About 4,100 fans didn't fill the arena, which has a 6,500 person capacity, but they made plenty of noise.

Valerie Still was one of five Columbus starters. She looked focused as she came on court during player introductions. Then a big smile spread across her face. She slapped hands with her teammates and even exchanged high fives with the Columbus mascot. The crowd cheered extra loudly as Valerie's name was called.

Valerie made the first basket, a close bucket, of the game. In the second quarter, she showed her hustle and heart by going to the floor, along with a Richmond player, in a fight for a rebound. While Columbus built up a lead and then while Richmond fought back to make it a close game, Valerie demonstrated how valuable she was to her team. She ran the floor efficiently, not lightning fast but fast enough. On offense and defense, she played smart and strong. Her back to the basket, she held her position against opposing players.

Columbus had a five point lead at the half, with the score 48-43. The lead seesawed in the second half. Columbus three-point shooters like Tonya Edwards shot the lights out, but the Rage kept scrapping their way back, getting to the line and making their free throws.

In the fourth quarter, with the game close, Valerie grabbed the ball from Taj McWilliams, a Richmond player, and put it in the basket in one strong motion. Soon afterwards Valerie thought she was called for a foul. She headed for the referee, looking upset, then found the foul was called on someone else. A big smile transformed her face.

Throughout the game, Valerie had pulled down her share of rebounds. But the rebound that counted the most came at the very end of the game. The score was 89-90, with Columbus holding onto a fragile one-point lead. With only seconds left, Richmond had possession of the basketball. They took a shot, missed, and Valerie grabbed the rebound. The clock ran out a few seconds later.

At the Richmond end of the court, Valerie leapt into the air several times, acting more like an excited fifth grader than a thirty-five year old woman. She knew that she'd just won the game for her team, and her teammates knew it too. They ran up to her and hugged her.

Happiness turned sour for Valerie and her teammates with the second game. They lost that at home, really badly, with Valerie playing only 16 minutes in the game, mostly in the first half. But it wasn't a time for her to focus on her personal statistics. The lost game hurt her whole team, taking away the home court advantage they'd worked so hard for.

The playoffs moved on to Richmond and Richmond won the third playoff game as well. One more win was all that Richmond needed to clinch the ABL title. Their victory parade was already planned. Their champagne was on ice.

"We got down in the final series," Valerie recalls, "and had our backs up against the wall." Then the tables turned in the fourth game of the series, with Valerie putting in 22 points and grabbing 16 rebounds. Columbus won that game in Richmond by 95-84. Valerie knew her own play had made a difference. When her teammates "see this old lady diving on the floor and going inside," she told a reporter, "then they're like 'hey, I can do that too.'" Yet typically, Val gives most of the credit to her whole team. "Our character kicked in," she says.

The fifth and deciding game was held in Columbus. For much of the season, fan support in Columbus hadn't been strong, but for the ABL World Championship game, 6,313 fans, a record number of people, filled the 6,500 capacity Battelle Hall. It was essentially a sell-out crowd, the first one the Quest had had at home all year. Fans clapped, cheered, held up signs. They wore strange headgear—birds' nests on their heads—with signs that read "Quest Nest" explaining the odd turn in men's and women's millinary.

Columbus held a lead the entire game, with Valerie jumping for the tipoff and then making the first basket of the game. But the Richmond Rage wouldn't lie down and concede the victory to the Quest. For much of the game, Richmond would make a run and cut the Columbus lead. Then the Quest would pull ahead again.

As usual, Valerie was in the thick of the action. After she made her first basket, a TV announcer, referring to her overall performance in the playoffs, called her the "hottest player thus far for the Columbus Quest." Val played as if she were justifying that description. She went up for rebounds in a crowd of players, using her basketball-smarts as a veteran player to hold her position and grab the ball. She set screens so her teammates could shoot from the perimeter. She played tough defense on the strong, athletic Richmond players Adrienne Goodson and Taj McWilliams.

In the second quarter, Valerie hit a three-pointer, making her two for two from that range in the playoffs. Later in the quarter, she went to the floor fighting for a rebound. In the third quarter, she made a strong, veteran-smart move to the basket, leaning her shoulder against Taj McWilliams, and then lying on the floor for a moment after she tangled with Taj, all of it just enough to get the foul call in her favor. At the line Val looked intense, focused. As she aimed the basketball, her well defined arm and shoulder muscles showed the hard work she'd put in all season.

With slightly under five minutes to go in the fourth quarter, Columbus had a ten point lead. Anything could happen with that much time, and neither team was relaxing. Val caught a pass, cut through a crowd of defenders and took the ball strong to the basket. When a foul was called in her favor, she slapped hands with teammates, then hugged Tonya Edwards before she made the foul shot.

With about a minute left, Columbus had a solid lead. The outcome of the game was now clear. Columbus players on the sidelines exchanged smiles and hugs. Fans were on their feet cheering and clapping. Valerie caught a pass and made a close basket. Afterwards she did a little dance, leading with her hips in what you could call a basketball shimmy. As she headed back down court, she jumped up and down several times, then hugged a teammate at the other end.

It was under a minute when Valerie Still came out of the game. As the crowd cheered, Valerie pumped a fist skyward in a kind of salute and did a little leap-step towards the crowd and the Quest bench. She hugged her teammates, a radiant smile on her face.

Then the game was over, with Columbus winning 77-64. Valerie Still and her teammates were the first ever ABL World Champions. League CEO, Gary Cavalli, presented a shiny trophy, a statue of a woman athlete, basketball held in outstretched arm, to coach Brian Agler. The Columbus Quest women carried the trophy around the court, raised the trophy high.

Valerie herself had another trophy to receive. At 35 years old, she was voted the MVP of the playoffs. Val stood holding her son Aaron in one arm as she received her award. As a young woman who represented Nissan spoke, Val held her head down, her face partly hidden by a tan and red ABL Championship baseball cap. She looked a little teary eyed as she bit her lip and lowered her head again.

"You've had a long journey here," the young woman from Nissan said to Val. "And to enjoy the ride home, I want to give you the key to the Nissan Altima." Valerie smiled as she accepted the gift.

How did it feel to win the championship, another woman, a TV announcer this time, asked Val. "Right now I really can't describe it. Aaron can probably," Val said in a husky voice.

She was able to describe her feelings about her teammates though. "I've played with some talented players, but never with a team that has the heart that they do."

The feelings Val had at that moment, feelings which almost overwhelmed her, tied into many different aspects of her life. Her son Aaron was there when she received her MVP award. "It's going through my mind," Val recalls, "fifty years from now, my son will look back on this and be telling his friends or family about it."

Valerie's husband Rob was there too as well, which meant a lot to Val. "We had a tough time, with everything going on," Val describes, "but we hung in there, we stuck through it, and . . . in the end it all paid off."

She thought about the fans watching her and her teammates, especially the girls. "All these little girls out there," she thought, "you know you're a role model for them."

Valerie's mother was in New Jersey rather than Columbus, watching the final game on TV. But Val could feel her mother's support, just as she had all season. "She's just my best friend," Val says about her mother. During the year Val had called her mother every day, talking to her about baby Aaron, about basketball, about the difficulties Val and her husband Rob sometimes had. So it was fitting that Valerie gave the Nissan Altima she won to her mother Gwendolyn, the strong woman who raised her, who helped Valerie "dare to be different."

In a way, Val's father was there for Val too. He'd passed away a year before but Val still felt his presence. "My dad never got to see me play," Val says, "and I always joke with my family that he was the one putting in all the baskets for me at the end. Because the whole year, nothing went right for me and then everything just clicked."

Winning the ABL World Championship, and being named MVP of the playoffs, meant a lot to Valerie. She was almost the oldest player in the league. Add another year or two, and the ABL probably would have come too late for her. Instead, as her team won the championship, her own athletic talents won recognition in her own country. Family and friends and total strangers could see with their own eyes just how good Valerie was at basketball.

A Future for the Women's Pro Game

"Ladies and gentleman, things are going to get bigger and better next year," is Gary Cavalli's message to fans at the conclusion of the first ABL playoffs. In early May of the same year, the sound of dribbled basketballs no longer reverberates in ABL practice facilities around the league, coaches no longer call timeouts and diagram do-or-die plays, but "bigger and better" is on the way.

On May 5, 1997, the second ABL draft takes place. In San Jose, Seattle, Hartford, Atlanta, Denver, and other ABL cities, general managers, coaches, and other league personnel are linked by teleconference. Computer keys click, telephone lines carry news of draft picks and trades. It's an important day for the league—new players are a big part of the future of the ABL, and in a larger sense, of the future of women's pro basketball. The draft follows on the heels of an invitation-only ABL tryouts, held at the University of San Francisco from April 24-27, where 51 top players, most from the college ranks, some who'd been playing overseas, present an awesome array of talent.

The Power's locker room — formerly used by the Blazers, who now have more luxurious quarters — is the location for Portland's part in the draft. For the occasion, the small, unpretentious locker room is dudded up. Power pennants hang over wooden lockers, Reebok towels are draped neatly within, and red and green Power posters adorn a media table in the front of the room.

At ten minutes after ten Pacific time, the first team to choose, the expansion team in Long Beach, California, selects Yolanda Griffith, a 6'4" center who has starred in college—she was named as a First Team All-American and the Division II Player of the Year — and who played professionally in Germany for the last three years. These top picks have been previously arranged, so only two minutes later, Portland chooses DeLisha Milton. DeLisha, who is the winner of the 1997 Wade Trophy recognizing her as the top woman basketball player among all U.S. college seniors, is dressed brightly for the occasion in orange slacks and a matching orange short-sleeved top. The outfit looks good on her tall athletic body as she stands behind a media table. "I'm so proud of her," DeLisha's mother tells a newscaster. "We're just thrilled that we were able to get DeLisha in the first round," head coach Lin Dunn says. "Words can't describe my feelings," DeLisha herself comments. Her smile is dazzling.

Not long after the draft begins, Falisha Wright comes into the locker room to listen to the draft choices and the trades. She had surgery on her injured left shoulder after the season, and has been working out to get in shape. She expects to be 100 percent recovered by next season and already has received the news that she'll be back next year with the Power. "I'm very excited," she says about her own position. But she can't forget the fact that not all her first-year teammates will join her back in Portland or back in the league at all. "I'm really bummed out that friends aren't going to be back here," she comments. Yet she knows that pro sports teams have to make decisions that won't always leave everyone happy.

Meanwhile the draft continues. It's a little like horse trading at times, and also like a wait-your-turn gambling game where the stakes are high. Will Lin Dunn and Portland go for a guard soon? "I plan to get one this next round," Lin asserts. "If someone doesn't steal her from me."

"Okay Portland, You are on the clock," a voice announces through the telephone. In a clear voice, Linda Weston makes the third round pick, Elaine Powell, a 5'9" guard from Louisiana State. "Portland is definitely prepared today," someone from another team says over the telephone lines. Not every team has been as ready with their draft choices. Meanwhile, Lin Dunn continues to look over her list of players.

A woman's voice from Seattle comes over the telephone wires. "We're involved in a possible trade. We might need a few more minutes." The few minutes stretch on. In the meantime, league people are having problems getting the ABL web site to do its thing. Linda

Weston jokes about Lin Dunn's hunch: "She's pretty sure the WNBA turned off our web site."

Seattle is still working on its trade. "Are they trying to trade for Michael Jordan or something?" someone jokes. But the mood is light. No one really seems to mind waiting. In the end, Seattle trades their third round pick and Charlotte Smith to San Jose for Val Whiting and San Jose's fourth round pick. The complicated player move has taken about 25 minutes to accomplish. Finally, the draft can move along again.

DeLisha Milton and her mother can't stay the whole day. They have to catch a flight back to DeLisha's hometown of Riceboro, Georgia, where the town will be honoring her with DeLisha Milton Days. Before DeLisha leaves, she and her mother are given tan baseball caps decorated with the Power logo, enough caps to cover heads on a sizeable extended family. DeLisha and future teammate Falisha hug, and both Linda Weston and Lin Dunn also hug DeLisha. Lin's farewell has a southern-style warmth to it. "Beverly, it's been so nice to meet you," Lin says to DeLisha's mother. "We can't wait until you come back."

Lunch is wheeled in, chicken pocket sandwiches on Middle Eastern bread. As anyone hungry munches away, the draft continues. With six rounds, and a number of trades, it lasts until the afternoon, a productive day filled with choices that affect lives and enough chaos for comic relief. "Anybody know what we're doing?" a woman's voice asks over the telephone lines. "Anybody know who we're waiting for?" When the six rounds are over, Portland personnel celebrate with champagne. Presumably the same beverage is shared throughout the league. The draft is, after all, a day for celebration, a day for looking forward to a second and future seasons.

The existence of not one but two new pro basketball leagues, the ABL and the WNBA, clouds the picture of what the future will be. Still, there's no doubt that women's professional basketball is getting attention and being taken much more seriously than ever before by fans, the media, and corporate interests. And it's being taken seriously by top women players, who now see a basketball future in their own country.

The ABL has signed many of the best college players graduating in 1997, ten out of the top thirteen the ABL had especially targeted. Among the top players going for the ABL are Kate Starbird from Stanford, the winner of the prestigious Naismith Award and the

NCAA Player of the Year; Le'Keshia Frett, an All-American from the University of Georgia; Portland's top draft pick DeLisha Milton of the University of Florida, who won the 1997 Wade Trophy recognizing her as the top senior in women's college basketball; and Kara Wolters of the University of Connecticut, the Associated Press National Player of the Year.

"The ABL is where it's at," LaTicia Morris, MVP of the Southeastern Conference Tournament, says to reporters.

"The ABL looks at you as a real pro, not just a part-time player," Kedra Holland-Corn, a star guard from the University of Georgia adds.

Top coaches as well are now committing themselves to the ABL. Not surprisingly, there has been a high level of coaching turnover. In San Jose, Portland, Hartford, and Atlanta—four of the eight first-year ABL cities—coaches were replaced either during or immediately after the season. The new coaches who have joined the league seem to signal its increased level of legitimacy. In San Jose, for example, Angela Beck, the coach with the highest number of wins ever for a University of Nebraska women's basketball team, who had been chosen a Big Eight coach of the year, is now the new head coach for the Lasers. In New England, former NBA player and coach, K.C. Jones, is the new head coach for the Blizzard.

Aside from people news, throughout the ABL the level of optimism has also been helped along by news about sponsorships and investments in the league. Although the league lost about four million dollars in its first season, more of a financial loss than it had expected, founding sponsor Reebok has extended its sponsorship to a three-year, seven-figure deal. A new sponsor, Phoenix Insurance, and a Silicon Valley business group have invested six million in the ABL, with Phoenix making a ten-year commitment to the league. Both Reebok and Nike will be doing print and TV ads for ABL players, which should help increase league visibility. Overall, the league's budget has increased from 16 million in the first season to 23 million for the second season, and its marketing budget has doubled.

However, there is no denying the fact that the ABL faces tough competition from the other new women's league, the NBA-sponsored WNBA. On June 21st, as the WNBA plays its opening game at the Great Western Forum in Los Angeles, over 14,000 fans are in attendance to watch the Los Angeles Sparks compete against the

New York Liberty. The nationally televised game is just one indication of the WNBA's strength. Assisted by the strong marketing pull
of the NBA, the WNBA has received a level of television coverage
especially impressive for a first-year league, with weekly games televised by NBC, Lifetime, and ESPN. With a marketing budget of 15
million, as opposed to the 1.5 million the ABL spent in its first year,
the WNBA has drawn impressively large crowds, such as the 18,051
fans at Madison Square Garden on August 24th, and averaged about
9,000 fans per game. By contrast, the ABL's first-year attendance
average was about 3,500. However, a number of ABL cities had stronger fan support and some ABL games have drawn sizeable crowds,
such as the record-setting 11,873 fans who attended a late January
game in Hartford, Connecticut.

The ABL and the WNBA both fill a gaping hole in U.S. women's
basketball, yet the two leagues contrast in many other ways. WNBA
sponsors include corporate biggies like Sears, Spalding, Nike, Coca-
Cola, with the level of corporate sponsorships outstripping that of
the ABL. Player salaries are different as well, but here the ABL does
far better. The ABL's minimum salary of $40,000 and average salary
of $80,000 easily top the the WNBA's minimum of 10,000 and aver-
age of $35,000. The ABL's maximum salary of $150,000 surpasses
the WNBA's $50,000 (which doesn't include the extra money top
stars can make with endorsements).

Both the WNBA and ABL feature exciting basketball, although
many sportswriters agree that in the two leagues' first seasons, the
ABL had an overall better level of play. Perhaps the most obvious
difference between the two leagues is when they do play. The
WNBA's 28 game, summer season contrasts sharply with the ABL's
44 game (40 in the first year) season during the traditional time for
basketball. Clearly, the WNBA's strategy is to opt for a time when
not only are NBA facilities available, but when there isn't much competition from other sports. It's a strategy that may in fact help create
fan interest in women's pro basketball. Yet ABL CEO Gary Cavalli,
speaking on a segment of *Real Sports* on HBO, expresses his heart-
felt disagreement with the WNBA approach.

"If you're going to give women the chance to really have a first
class pro sports league," Gary comments, "don't put them at a time
of the year that's convenient, or when the boys aren't using the gym.
Say that women's basketball is strong enough, is good enough, to be
able to stand on its own." It's a comment which clearly reveals the

division between the two leagues.

Slightly further into the program, the host of *Real Sports*, Bryant Gumbel, considers the question of whether the two leagues will merge in the future, combining their talent and money, as would seem logical. "If it makes sense to sit down and talk merger at some point in the future, we'll do that," Gary Cavalli tells Bryant Gumbel. But WNBA commissioner Val Ackerman has a different response. "We don't see things moving in the direction of a merger."

Whatever the future for the two leagues, the ABL moves forward. Some first year players were not re-signed by the league, usually as a result of a team's rather than a player's decision. With so many top players from the college ranks entering the ABL, the league has become even more competitive. However, many first year ABL players' lives are still connected with the league.

Not long after the first season ends, Valerie Still hasn't yet come down from the "high" of winning the ABL championship when she goes in for a routine gynecological exam. The exam reveals a lump in her right breast. Doctors advise that Valerie have the lump surgically removed.

A lump in a woman's breast is a scary business. "All I could think about," Valerie says, "was not being able to see Aaron grow up." In spite of the fear any mother would surely feel, she is able to joke a little with her doctors. "All my teammates they're having knee surgery, and here I am," she tells her physicians.

A week or so later, Valerie receives the good news. The lump is benign. She can get on with her life. She can enjoy the singular honor she and her teammates have received. They are the first group of women professional basketball players to be invited to the White House.

In early July, the Quest players fly out to Washington, DC. This is the players' first reunion since the end of the season, and it has the atmosphere of a family reunion. Women joke with each other, hug, do a little trashtalking. As the team tours Washington, visiting monuments and memorials, Valerie thinks about what it means to be officially recognized as professional basketball players. It means acknowledgement for her and her teammates' accomplishments, and for the American Basketball League as well. "It made me think that we're going to be a part of American history," is how Valerie sees the visit.

The next day a meeting with Hillary Clinton is scheduled. Everyone comes together in the East Reception Room—including Gary Cavalli, Steve Hams, all the Quest players, Kelly Kramer, Brian Agler, Brian's wife, and the "honorary member of the team," Valerie's son Aaron. While they're there, Aaron embarrasses Valerie by getting crumbs on the East Room rug. Sonja Tate, a Quest player who is nicknamed OC by her teammates, with the initials standing for Out of Control, tries to dance with Hillary Clinton.

Rather than dancing, Valerie shares her feelings with Hillary. She tells the First Lady how much she appreciates the recognition of what the team has done. For her personally, after having spent so many years overseas, the honor is especially meaningful. Hillary Clinton shares her own feelings with Valerie, about how happy she is that Valerie and her teammates can be role models for girls.

The White House visit shows Valerie how far she has come. "I reached my summit. I've made my dream come true," she comments. But she isn't ready to come off the mountain just yet. She is the first Columbus player to sign on the dotted line, to commit to a new contract for future seasons, in Valerie's case for the next two years.

Valerie doesn't make that commitment because she can't face the thought of an October without basketball. She decides to step up and do it for the league. Women like herself whom fans recognize, she feels, need to be out there playing, helping to strengthen the ABL and acting as role models for all those little girl fans especially.

Valerie doesn't look forward to all the travelling next year—some of which will be without her son Aaron. Next season, she feels will "be hard on me, but I think in the long run it's the right thing to do." She does look forward to the idea that ten or twenty years into the future, there will be a women's professional basketball league. She pictures her son Aaron telling someone that his mother had helped to start that.

The future players for that women's pro league are already in training. In mid-July, as the WNBA draws large crowds and while training camps for the ABL's second season are still over a month and a half away, in basketball camps and clinics held across the United States, girls as well as boys are learning basketball skills. Some of the girls in camps now, the most talented few, will become the future stars for women's basketball.

At the Katy Steding Basketball Camp, held at The Hoop in Beaverton, Oregon, a group of eight to twelve-year-old girls are learning the fundamentals of basketball. They aren't long on basketball know how, but their enthusiasm for the game is obvious. They look up to Katy, who is their main instructor, partly because at six feet she's so much taller than them. But the smile on one young girl's face, as she turns her face towards Katy, shows strong touches of heroine worship.

The co-founders of the ABL wanted the players to be role models. There's no doubt that Katy Steding is fulfilling that mission. As she shows a group of girls the correct way to make some perimeter moves, she has role model written all over her.

"Forward, forward, forward," Katy encourages one small girl whose T shirt hangs almost to her knees. The girl hesitates, then moves correctly. She smiles when she gets it right.

"Square up in a good shooting position," Katy advises all the groups of girls who rotate to her station. It was years ago when Katy Steding learned the same basic basketball moves for the first time, but she doesn't seem bored as she explains the fundamentals. In slow motion, she demonstrates facing away from the basket, pivoting on one leg, squaring up and facing the basket, then aiming and shooting. A small girl with a blonde ponytail ducks a flying basketball coming towards her head. With another ball, she takes a shot and misses, the hoop looking way above her.

After the drills, a game begins. Katy moves back and forth on the sidelines, encouraging the girls. "Nice shot," she shouts. "Good pass." No doubt some of the girls are imagining themselves as larger, faster, stronger, or fantasizing that they're really playing with their heroines in the ABL and the WNBA. Certainly many of these girls, and their mothers and fathers, sisters and brothers will be in the stands next season to watch Katy Steding and her teammates, and the players on other ABL teams, perform their basketball high-wire act.

In Philadelphia in later July, Debbie Black speaks at a press conference about the ABL team formerly known as the Richmond Rage, which is relocating to Philadelphia. Since Debbie's from the area, she's excited about the move, which means she'll get to play some games in front of family and friends there. In fact, "excited" is too mild a description. "I'm ecstatic," she comments. But for herself personally, her future is elsewhere, with the Colorado Xplosion, where she's just signed a five-year contract, her personal vote of confidence in the league and one of the multiyear contracts the league has been extending to its top players.

Meanwhile, Debbie is spending the summer at her parents' home in Lancaster, a suburb of Philadelphia, and enjoying her mother's home cooking. In June she worked long days—nine in the morning until eight in the evening, a horrendous schedule she promises herself never to repeat—at a basketball camp for boys and girls. But for much of the summer one of her main activities has been going to nearby parks with her brother to play pickup games.

Other than Debbie, the pickup players are all guys. "You can't walk up anywhere where there's girls playing," she comments. Playing against guys is good for her game anyway. But in spite of her high-level skills, in spite of her role as star point guard for the Colorado Xplosion, it still helps her out to have her brother with her in the park. "We have next, and it's me and her," her brother will say. "It's a lot easier for me to get in the door that way," Debbie comments. This is the same player, of course, who scored the only quadruple double in the ABL's first season, a feat that has been rare in the NBA as well. Women basketball players, it seems, have made a lot of progress but still have a ways to go.

Early in September, in all the ABL cities, training camps begin. In San Jose, California, Angela Beck, the new head coach, leads the Lasers but Australian guard Shelley Sandie finds many familiar faces, such as Jennifer Azzi, the injured player she replaced last year, as she practices with her team. Shelley is refreshed by her time back home in Australia yet glad to be back with the Lasers.

In Long Beach, California, for the ABL expansion team the StingRays, Trisha Stafford relives the experience of her first year ABL training camp by practicing with all new teammates as well as new coaches. She's happy to have a fresh start with a new team she describes as having "sheer basketball talent" on its roster. And she's happy of course that she'll be playing home games in the Los Angeles area, close to friends and family.

In Philadelphia, Lisa Boyer leads her team, renamed the Philadelphia Rage, through drills and scrimmages. Kirsten Cummings participates in only part of the practice. The knee she injured last year needs just a little more time to fully heal, so she takes part in many drills but not in scrimmages. It won't be too much longer, though, before she'll be out on the court for good.

Kirsten Cummings' teammate, star forward Adrienne Goodson, likes her team's new location. It puts her closer to her family in New Jersey and makes it easier for them to come to her games. Adrienne is upbeat about training camp as well and describes her team as "probably about three times as better as we were last year." She also appreciates the fact that this season she won't have to play the role of main translator for her Brazilian teammate, Marta Sobral. This year the Rage staff includes a Brazilian woman, formerly a journalist and sportscaster in Brazil, who speaks both Portugese and English.

As a result, Adrienne will now be able to concentrate solely on basketball. For her, that intense focus begins in the preseason, a time she understands the importance of. That's when teams work on conditioning, offensive and defensive patterns, and get a feel for each other's basketball moves. "It's a really intense time and a time for concentration," Adrienne describes. And it's obviously a time she's glad to be a part of, even though training camp can be tough on players' bodies. "We go with the bumps and bruises," Adrienne says matter of factly, "but it will all pay off when the ball's tossed up on October 17th."

At the Columbus Basketball Club in Dublin, Ohio, Valerie Still and her teammates go through long practices—their first one lasted four hours—and then lift weights three days a week. At 36 years old, Valerie finds tough practices harder to take and minor injuries more bothersome than when she was younger, and she also worries about the time she's spending away from her son Aaron, who is now 19 months. "A lot of women have to work an eight hour job," Valerie's mother reminds her daughter, to help Valerie put her personal situation in perspective.

All the Columbus Quest players, as well as head coach Brian Agler and assistant coach Kelly Kramer, whom Valerie describes as "a real positive type person," have to keep the team's situation in perspective. Positive thinking is in demand as the Quest go through changes. While other ABL teams have already signed the players on their roster to contracts, last year's champions have to live with more uncertainty. Deadeye outside shooter, guard Tonya Edwards, only signs her contract around mid-September and joins training camp very late. By the third week of September, star forward and local college star, Katie Smith, still hasn't signed a contract, and no one knows for sure if she'll be back. Carla McGhee, traded to the Quest, is now pregnant.

Perhaps hardest for the team to deal with, star guard Nikki McCray, the 1996 Olympian who was honored as the ABL's Most

Valuable Player during the league's first season, announces on September 16th that she won't return to the team she helped win a championship. Instead, she has just signed a three-year contract with the WNBA. "I saw what the NBA can do to promote their game," Nikki is quoted as saying. "The WNBA has created a lot of exposure for women's basketball, and I want to be a part of that."

Valerie Still isn't taken completely by surprise at Nikki's decision. During the summer, when Valerie stayed at Nikki's house in Columbus, the two women talked about the possibility of Nikki playing in the WNBA. Valerie told Nikki more than once that if Nikki switched to the WNBA, "she'd be letting the ABL down and . . . she'd be letting the women's basketball cause down."

When Nikki does opt to change leagues, Valerie is disappointed. To some degree, however, she sympathizes with Nikki's position. The contract she's signed includes the kind of personal services deal which has brought WNBA stars Lisa Leslie and Rebecca Lobo a base salary of $250,000. "It's hard for a 24 year old not to succumb to that kind of pressure," Valerie comments to a reporter from *USA Today*, "and that kind of glamour and glitz . . . and the get rich quick type of thing."

Valerie wonders what the WNBA will do with their potential new star, and poses a question which is quoted in *USA Today*. "What is the WNBA going to do, market Nikki McCray as the MVP of the ABL when they've never acknowledged the existence of the ABL?"

Even after the WNBA's successful first season, Valerie has serious doubts about it. The women in the WNBA, Valerie thinks, are "always going to play second fiddle to the guys." Will the WNBA ever give their players a full-length season during the normal time for basketball? "I don't know if their main concern is women's basketball," Valerie wonders.

Valerie Still's strong feelings reflect the uncertainty involved in the existence of two women's pro basketball leagues. Her comments also illustrate the fact that although the two leagues play in different seasons, the ABL and the WNBA are in many people's eyes in competition with each other. Not surprisingly, other ABL players and coaches also have strong opinions about the WNBA vs. the ABL. Whatever happens with the two leagues will affect many people's lives and probably the future of women's pro basketball.

"I think it's great for women's basketball," Val Whiting says about the WNBA. "I used to be like God, they're just trying to steal our thunder. But after a while it was no, this is great for us." She even enjoys the WNBA commercials. But she doesn't appreciate people in her home city of Wilmington, Delaware asking her why she doesn't play in the WNBA.

Kate Paye expresses similarly mixed feelings. About the WNBA, she argues that "It just validates that the time is right for women's professional basketball. I think it only creates more opportunity for players." On the other hand, Kate doesn't like the summer league aspect of the WNBA. Women, she thinks deserve "a full length season played during the basketball season."

It's a theme which Kelly Kramer also echoes. The existence of two leagues shows the progress women's basketball has made, and Kelly is in favor of anything that creates more interest and exposure for the women's game. Yet the WNBA's summer league format bothers her too. Women's basketball, Kelly believes fervently, is done with second class status, finished with being a kind of warm up act for the men's game. "We've been there," she says. "It's time for something different. And I think we've proved this year (in the ABL) that we can be the main show."

Fans of both leagues seem to agree that women's basketball, although different from the men's game, is not a second-rate sport. In both the ABL's and WNBA's first seasons, women and men, gays and heterosexuals, people of all races, children of all ages, and lots of little girls cheer on their favorite teams at games and wait in lines afterwards for autographs. Many fans find that professional women basketball players are far more approachable

Kate Paye

than their NBA counterparts, a difference that should only help to further the women's game.

Meanwhile, women's pro basketball is moving forward. Throughout September, basketball of the training camp variety continues to happen throughout the ABL. In the Power training camp in Beaverton, Oregon, the team with the league's worst record during the first year is in a more stable situation than the first year champions, the Columbus Quest. On the Power, seven players return from last year's team and most draft choices have signed as well.

Head coach Lin Dunn is glad to be coaching in the ABL. "For the first time in my 26 years of coaching, I'm not discriminated against in salaries, uniforms, budgets . . . just because I'm a woman," Lin tells a reporter. "My whole career," she adds, "I've battled against a system where women are perceived as not good enough."

That isn't the case in the ABL of course. And Lin's team should be more than good enough. Overall, she's pleased with the depth on her team and the competition for starting positions. But in spite of the favorable situation, Lin isn't relaxing and her coaching style can not be described as mellow. "Get down here. If that's a scrim, we're in trouble," she shouts at one point; "Bust your butts to get down here. You're not running, you're jogging," she shouts immediately afterwards. But Lin leads her team with a sure hand which inspires confidence among her players.

Natalie Williams is one of the returning players, and the only starter from last year who is certain of keeping that position. The cast of characters this year includes Stacey Ford and Lisa Harrison, both strong contenders for starting positions, who are glad to be back after their summers away. There are new faces but also empty places, like holes in a photo album, where some first year players haven't returned this season. Coquese Washington's bright smile and energetic presence is missing, but Coquese's friend, Falisha Wright, once more speeds down court. Falisha doesn't reveal much emotion on her face, yet her intensity as she distributes the ball and guards other players shows how much being on the team means to her.

A revived looking Katy Steding, focused on the practice yet smiling and joking with her teammates, is out on the court. "I feel a lot more refreshed," Katy says the day before, at a book signing for her ex-coach Tara VanDerveer. At a Power exhibition game in early October, Katy's renewed energy shows up in her hot play. "Resurgent Steding shines in Power win," a newspaper account describes. She puts in 21 points to top all other scorers. Not surprisingly, when the starters are announced a couple of days later, Katy is among them. This year, Katy thinks, she can to try to play up to her potential. And she's not only positive about her own play but about the league she helped to found. She feels "very good about the way things are going."

In training camps and exhibition games, before the second season officially begins, perhaps optimism reigns in everyone's heart. Even setbacks are accepted with good spirits. Jennifer Jacoby sits on the sidelines because she sustained a minor injury to her knee in a recent practice. She sits patiently as the trainer wraps and ices her knee. Sheila Frost also remains on the sidelines for now. She had surgery on a torn rotator cuff in her left shoulder a few weeks ago but should be able to play soon. Meanwhile, she stands along the side of the court or under the basket, acting as a kind of extra assistant coach. "Good shot," she encourages a teammate as she watches the action with her bifocal vision, her coach's and player's eyes.

Training camps aren't the most glamorous aspect of women's pro basketball and typically draw little interest. Yet the media overall are now paying attention to women's pro basketball. The September 1st issue of *Newsweek* has the headline, "WOMEN'S B-BALL ON THE LINE," on its cover. The article within mainly focuses on the WNBA but makes references to the ABL. Actually, the perspective offered by *Newsweek* is a little strange. The ABL, the article states, "offers a better game," yet the article goes on to say, "as a machine for manufacturing celebrities, the ABL can't compete." Why, one might wonder, does creating a celebrity machine come to seem the most important aspect of women's basketball?

One of two new sports magazines featuring women, *Sports Illustrated Women/Sport*, places the headline "HOOP WARS WNBA VS. ABL" on the cover of its Fall 1997 issue. Within the article, the sidebar on "Court Couture" offers a body hugging design for women's basketball uniforms which acts as a small reminder that in some people's eyes, women basketball players still need to create a more feminine image. Yet overall the article takes women's basketball seriously, evaluating both leagues and including a First Team and Second Team of star players from both leagues which has been chosen by Mel Greenberg from the *Philadelphia Inquirer*. Among the players recognized are Natalie Williams and Adrienne Goodson.

Television, of course, is a vital media outlet for any pro sports league that hopes to remain viable. In the high tech oriented nineties, if women's pro basketball can't make waves on the TV waves, it won't be seen as a truly big-time sport. On September 9, the ABL officially announces its new TV package, a deal that might not be all the league could have hoped for but which still represents progress in a vitally important area. Fox Sports Net, which reaches nearly 60 million households, will be televising a game live every Sunday, the FOX Sports Net ABL Game of the Week, throughout the ABL season, and will also cover a good deal of the ABL playoffs. Additionally, Black Entertainment Television, a cable station available to almost 48 million viewers across the nation, has increased its coverage from last year's seven games during the regular season to twelve Saturday night games this year.

There isn't a deal with ESPN or Lifetime such as the WNBA has. In contrast to the WNBA's NBC contract, ABL games still won't be available on any non-cable channels. Still, the expanded TV package is definitely reason for optimism. The ABL's press release about the TV package quotes Gary Cavalli in an understandably upbeat mood. "We're very excited about our new national television package . . . ," he comments. "This is a major step up for the ABL. It provides us with much greater exposure and consistent air times. Fans will now be able to watch the best women's basketball in the world. . . ."

The same day the league announces its TV schedule, plenty of untelevised basketball action is going on. In Seattle, on a warm, somewhat muggy day, the Reign are busy preparing for the upcoming season with their fall training camp. Practice is held in a private health club located on the Ship Canal, which connects Lake Union to Elliot Bay. The gym there is spacious, with a high ceiling, shiny, new-looking basketball floor, and double rows of windows on three walls. Trees thick with green leaves are visible through the windows, as are the masts of boats passing by. Only an occasional breeze stirs the warm air inside the gym, however. Not long into the practice, the players have begun to sweat.

The Reign players are dressed in practice outfits. Black shorts, black sleeveless jerseys with names and numbers in white. Practice players, who aren't actually members of the team, add to the number in attendance, including one male practice player, the only man in the gym. The trainer Robin Moore is there too, as well as the two Reign coaches, head coach Jacquie Hullah and assistant coach Sue Darling. Reign players and coaches smile and joke sometimes, yet the practice is obviously serious business.

As with the other ABL teams, there are faces missing from last year's group. Tara Davis will not be back with the Reign. Instead she's a tryout player with the New England Blizzard. There are new faces as well. Val Whiting, traded from San Jose, is here in the gym, with number 52 on her practice jersey. Early in the practice, Val's shoulders and upper arms already shine with sweat, yet the heat doesn't seem to bother her. Fully recovered from last year's knee injury, Val runs easily down the court with long, strong strides. She's obviously intent on learning her role with her new team. Val is happy to be here in Seattle, she says after the practice.

As the practice continues, the players form two lines for a drill involving layups, other close shots, and sometimes an opponent guarding the shooting player. Christy Hedgpeth, now recovered from the surgery to repair her torn ACL, although not yet back to her pre-injury playing form, dribbles the ball behind her back as she waits her turn. Linda Godby towers over the players near her in line. Two players guard Val Whiting as she weaves her way in and makes a layup. Whenever a player makes her shot, her teammates clap their approval.

The movement of players and balls in the practice flows smoothly, but Jacquie Hullah often stops the action by blowing her whistle to change the drill and explain in her clear, low-pitched, penetrating voice what she's looking for. A new drill, for practicing a pick and roll, leaves a shooting player "rolling" around her temporary team-mate who's setting a pick. Christy Hedgepeth makes her shot, moving easily, and so does Kate Paye. Linda Godby misses hers, seeming a little off balance as she shoots, then makes a face afterwards. This is only practice, but the players are focused, obviously trying to do their best.

Jacquie Hullah's flow of instructions continues, all in the somewhat arcane language of basketball. "Basket, cut, player, give and go." "Good pick and roll." Assistant coach Sue Darling claps to encourage players. Nobody watching the drills looks bored.

At 2:00, a half hour into the two-and-a-half-hour practice, the players form a large circle in the center of the court as they do various stretches. There's a quiet meditative feel to the moment. The players remain mostly silent as they stretch shoulders and other upper body muscles, bend over to stretch calve muscles, then move onto the floor for a variety of leg stretches. Jacquie stands at one point on the circumference of the circle, talking quietly and joking with one of the younger Reign players.

After the quiet moment there's action again. The players run from one end of the court to the other, stopping and starting and stopping again. With arms bent and hands held up in the air, the women have the look of miniature airplanes as they run and stop, run and stop. Their movements are punctuated by the sound of team-mates clapping and the squeak of basketball shoes on the floor.

The emphasis on basketball fundamentals gradually segues into work on plays instead. Often they're done first in slow motion, so everyone can absorb the complex motions of each particular basket-ball ballet. Jacquie is patient and clear as she explains plays. "We're isolating so and so," she explains in a teacherlike way. She could be in a college classroom diagramming angles in a geometry problem.

Just after four o'clock, the running and shooting stops and ev-eryone clusters at center court. They talk about mundane but im-portant details like the need to drink enough water during prac-tices. Then everyone extends arms and touches hands. "Team," the players chant before breaking the huddle.

After the practice Jacquie Hullah is relaxed, glad to talk for a few minutes. She's upbeat about the second year with this some-what changed Seattle Reign team. "The level of play last year around the league was just so fine and so exciting," she says. "And when I think that we have even another group of more talented players who have joined what we had last year, I expect this season's play to be even higher."

Jacquie laughs when she's asked if she feels like a survivor, after all the coaching changes of the ABL's first year, but that's in fact what she is. She's definitely glad that she remains the head coach of the Reign, but knows the reality of coaching pro sports. "I think there's very little security at the professional level for coaches," she says.

The competition between the WNBA and the ABL could create a sense of insecurity as well, yet Jacquie focuses on positives. With its large marketing budget and extensive TV coverage, and resulting strong attendance at games and good TV ratings, the WNBA, Jacquie thinks, has proved that there is an audience for women's pro bas-ketball. The two leagues, the WNBA and the ABL, "should build off each other's momentum." "I think there's plenty of room for both of us," Jacquie adds. She obviously isn't interested in warfare be-tween the two leagues. "I think there only needs to be one winner and that is women's sports," she says firmly.

Tara VanDerveer, the Stanford and 1996 Olympic coach, also envisions a positive future for women's professional basketball. At a reading and signing for her new book, *Shooting from the Outside*, when asked about the new pro leagues Tara compares women's professional basketball to a "runaway train on a track." Regarding the future for it, "there's no going back," Tara says with conviction.

The women of the ABL have hitched their professional futures to that runaway train. As the second ABL season begins, in teams across the country players burn shoe rubber on the hard, polished floors of basketball courts, shoot the ball in graceful arcs that swish through the center of the net, make slick, behind-the-back passes, set hard picks and dive to the floor for loose balls. Coaches diagram plays and explain the tactics which should work best against particular teams. Other league personnel—general managers, media directors, trainers, and more—are also busy.

First year ABL players received gold pendants with a wagon wheel on one side and the inscription "ABL Pioneers" to commemorate their role in the ABL's inaugural year. With the confidence that befits pioneers, the women of the ABL, and the men involved in the league as well, share a vision of the basketball future. Women's pro basketball, these pioneers are betting, is here to stay, a permanent part of the sports landscape in the United States. Kate Paye from the Seattle Reign expresses an opinion others have echoed: "In five years, whether it's the WNBA, the ABL, or a combination of both, there will be a league for women to play in."

The women of the ABL are doing their part to make that happen. They're working for a future where little girls can grow up to become professional basketball players, where grown women won't have to leave their own country if they want to play professional basketball. They're playing for fans across the United States, bringing them a fast-paced, exciting, highly skilled game that has broken through the constraints of the past. And they're playing for themselves, because they're women who love basketball.

Epilogue: ABL All-Stars

Emerald green lights thread through the darkness, spelling out players' names on the arena floor. As disco type music fills the arena, green lines of light rove around the floor and the stands in a visual counterpoint to the music. When the light show concludes, the arena remains in darkness. Then bright white spotlights shine down near an entrance to the arena as the players from the 1998 All-Star teams are introduced.

The ABL All-Star game is a Sports Entertainment Event. It takes place on January 18th at Disney World near Orlando, Florida. In the Wide World of Sports complex, the Fieldhouse is full of cheering, clapping fans ready to watch some of the best women basketball players in the world. The basketball luminaries celebrated as All Stars include three of the 1996 Olympians: Teresa Edwards, Jennifer Azzi, and Dawn Staley. Another Olympian, Katrina McClain, was named to the All-Star team but will not play due to injury. But the other players who run on court to the cheers of the crowd are stars in their own right as well. For the Eastern Conference, they include Adrienne Goodson of the Philadelphia Rage and Valerie Still of the Columbus Quest. Among the Western Conference All Stars are Debbie Black of the Colorado Xplosion and Natalie Williams of the Portland Power. Among the four coaches who have earned the honor of coaching the All-Star game is Portland Power coach Lin Dunn.

With the arena lights on again and the stands almost full, the game is ready to begin. Valerie Still jumps for the opening tip off for the East team and she makes the first basket for her team as well.

Partway into the first quarter, when she hits the floor to fight for the ball, she smiles as she gets up even though she's called for her first foul. This year Valerie is among the league leaders in scoring, rebounding, and blocked shots. It's also her first time to be selected for the All-Star team—an honor she appreciates. "Playing with the best players in the world," Val says before the game. "For a professional player that's the ultimate."

Natalie Williams is most definitely one of those top players. The ABL's current top scorer and second best rebounder, Natalie makes her presence known as she goes up strong to pull down rebounds.

Debbie Black

At the start of the second quarter, when she comes back into the game, she scores the first basket for the West. In a trademark Natalie Williams move, she grabs a loose ball and jumps high and strong into the air as she lays the ball into the basket. "Natalie Williams is a thing of beauty to watch in the low post," a TV announcer comments. Late in the quarter, after Natalie hits another close shot, she raises her arms in triumph.

A group of late elementary school age girls clap and cheer throughout the game. All members of the Martin Luther King Pep Squad from Springfield, Massachusetts, the girls look sharp in their yellow and black jackets and skirts. "Take the ball to the hoop, hoop" or "Take that ball away, say, take that ball away," the girls chant. At time-outs, the girls clap and dance.

Later in the first quarter, during one of those timeouts, both teams make substitutions. As Debbie Black, a reserve player for the West, and Adrienne Goodson, one of the reserves for the East, enter the game, they both demonstrate that among the All-Star players, the distinction between starters and reserves is essentially meaningless.

Debbie Black, the ultimate hustle player, is third in the league in steals and fourth in assists. Right away she puts her hustle to work for the West team. In quick succession, Debbie steals the ball, drives to the basket and tries hard although unsuccessfully to make a shot before the buzzer sounds. Soon after she races down court and rifles a quick pass to a teammate. The teammate, Shalonda Enis from Seattle, hits a three-pointer and Debbie is credited with her first of several assists. "I love playing, so I just really enjoy being out there," Debbie says before the game. Her high energy and enjoyment can be seen in the second quarter also as she works hard on defense, steals a ball thrown in by East star Dawn Staley, grabs rebounds, and makes two baskets of her own.

Like Debbie Black, Adrienne Goodson is having fun at the All-Star weekend. "It's good to tear down the barriers," she says, "and come out on the floor and play with people that you're going against all year long." The third ABL player to score more than 1,000 points, in the All-Star game Adrienne is much more focused on how her team does than on her individual performance. But as the game action unfolds, her all-around All-Star talents are on display. Late in the first quarter, Adrienne leaps towards the basket to make a layup, ending a long dry spell for the East. Almost immediately afterwards she makes two free throws and then another layup. Late in the second quarter, Adrienne leaps into the air in an attempt to block the shot of a West player. The crowd roars as Adrienne goes flying to the floor from the momentum of her effort.

In spite of the efforts of East players like Adrienne Goodson and Valerie Still, the West builds up a large lead, ending the half ahead 54-27. It's hardly a nail-biter type of game, and West coaches Lin Dunn and Maura McHugh seem to be enjoying watching the game action unfold just as the spectators are. Lin smiles from the bench and applauds her team's efforts. She appears much more relaxed than she usually is during Portland Power games. But relaxed doesn't mean unenthusiastic. "I'm honored to be part of the All-Star weekend," Lin comments just before the game. "I love coaching players at this level, and the best thing about this one is everybody wins. No matter what the score is, it's for fun. It's to showcase women's basketball."

The ABL All-Star game certainly is a "showcase." As much a celebration as a basketball game, it's a ceremonial mid season marker for the ABL's second season. A pause to celebrate talent and achievement—of the women in the league and of the league itself. In the ABL's second season, average attendance is up 20 percent so far, and the 15,213 fans who attend a January 3rd game in Hartford, Connecticut set a new league record for attendance. The nationally televised All-Star game is one more sign that the ABL, and also women's pro basketball, is alive and well.

"The calibre of this year's All-Star roster is a reflection of the outstanding level of talent we have in the ABL," Gary Cavalli comments in mid-December. "When you look beyond this All-Star list, you'll find another 10 to 12 outstanding players who could easily have made this All-Star team." He mentions several players, including Val Whiting and Katy Steding, both of whom were on last year's West All-Star team. Actually, many players from teams throughout the league are here for the all-star weekend, some simply to watch the game and enjoy the chance to socialize with other players. Others take part in the three-point shootout and the first ever ABL slam-dunk contest.

Jennifer Jacoby was scheduled to defend the three-point shooting title she earned last year. However, she won't be able to do so for medical reasons. On Saturday, after the preliminaries of the three-point and dunk contests, Jennifer lifts up her T shirt to reveal a line of surgical tape covering a recent surgical incision. The operation to remove part of a kidney, due to her recurrent problems with kidney stones, means she will have to miss the rest of the ABL season. After two knee reconstructions and several "scopes," Jennifer's knees are another problem area, and this may be her final year in the ABL. "I want to be able to walk by the time I'm 30, 35 years old," Jennifer says in mid-December. Yet in spite of her physical problems, Jennifer seems in good spirits, glad to be at Disney World for the All-Star celebrations.

Coaches and general managers, like Lisa Boyer, Kelly Kramer, and Linda Weston, are all in attendance at the All-Star weekend. They're here partly on business because the trade deadline is only a few days away. But they're also here just to enjoy the event. As Kelly Kramer puts it, "The players, the coaches, are real competitive, but . . . we're also a family when we all get together. . . . It's nice to be able to spend some time together away from the court."

Linda and Kelly have both enjoyed their teams' winning records this season. However, Lisa Boyer is in a less fortunate situation. After the Rage's near miss at a championship last year, this year Lisa's team is in last place in the Eastern Conference. Throughout the league, Lisa comments after a road game in Portland, "The benches are much much stronger and somebody's gotta lose." There are only nine teams in the league. "But everybody expects everybody to win." It's a remark that says a lot about the pressures on both players and coaches in a still very new, still fairly small league.

One of Lisa Boyer's players, Kirsten Cummings, who's also here for the All-Star weekend, has dealt with pressures of her own. She's faced the double challenge of coming back from last year's knee surgery and this year's surgery for a foot problem. The rehabilitation, she says after the same road game, has "been really hard and long." But she's optimistic about her chances of helping her team later in the season. "I definitely have a role on the team," she says. "I have no doubt in my abilities." And in fact by early January, in the last two games before the All-Star weekend, Kirsten comes off the bench to play significant minutes.

Katy Steding is also optimistic. "I'm feeling my age," she jokes about turning thirty in December. More seriously, she assesses her own performance and that of her team. "From worst to first in one year, less than a year, is pretty dang good," Katy says about her team. In mid-December, the Power own the best record in the Western Conference. For herself personally, Katy is upbeat as well. "I feel like I'm someone the team can count on," Katy says. As if to illustrate her point, during a January 3rd game against Atlanta, Katy puts on a shooting show, making four out of seven three-point shots.

In the same game, Falisha Wright shows how far she has come from the undrafted, replacement player she was last year. She hits a trio of three-point shots. The very next day, in a game against New England, Falisha's nine assists and no turnovers tie an ABL record held by Olympian Jennifer Azzi. "I'm having fun. I'm having the time of my life," Falisha says. The smile on her face, when she's introduced as the starter at point guard, conveys the same message. Although Falisha undergoes surgery on a torn meniscus shortly before the All-Star game, she'll be back on court soon.

Due to new players and a different playing rotation, Stacey Ford is less of a presence on court, but she can still make a solid contribution. In a January 4th game, Stacey comes off the bench and scores 10 points in a little over four minutes. Lisa Harrison, who started last season as a self-described "has been," is having a strong second season. In a hotly contested double overtime game in mid-December, Lisa's jump shot ties the game at the end of the first overtime. As the end of the second overtime period comes to a close, Lisa's steal, jump shot and foul shots help Portland to a six point win over Seattle.

In the same game, Val Whiting is a force on court for the Reign.

She hits a turnaround jumper to tie the score at the end of regulation and makes the first basket of the second overtime. Val is having a strong season individually. By the All-Star game, she's among the league leaders in scoring, rebounding, blocked shots, and steals. On January 6th, the 25 points Val scores against New England are a career-high for her. However, Val's new team is struggling.

Seattle's poor record—the worst in the ABL—affects everyone on the team, but perhaps especially the coach. In early December, after a home loss to Columbus, TV cameras reveal the stress on Jacquie Hullah's face as she walks off the court. A *Seattle Times* article a few days later questions how long Jacquie will remain coach of the Reign. She feels the pressure, Jacquie tells a reporter after a Sunday game which ends up as another defeat for the Reign, but she needs to keep her focus on coaching the team.

The very next day, Jacquie no longer needs to do that. She and her assistant coach have been fired. Jacquie "was perhaps doomed from the start," a writer from the *Seattle Times* comments, because due to the team makeup she was forced to use three or four rookies as her starting players. Brian Agler, head coach of the league-leading Columbus Quest, expresses a similar opinion, telling a reporter that starting four inexperienced players "makes a big difference." A trade which would alter the Seattle lineup doesn't seem possible. In the end, whatever the reason or reasons, Jacquie Hullah's preseason comments about the lack of job security for pro coaches have come true in her own case.

After the first game with their new coach, a loss to the Power in Portland, Seattle players sit around the visitors' locker room in warmups, snacking on donuts and muffins. Christy Hedgpeth, who played such an important role in helping to start the ABL, remained on the bench during the game. She admits that coming back from last season's injury, and not playing very much, has been hard. "It's gonna take me a while to get back to . . . playing the way I know I can," she says. For her and her teammates, the Reign's losing streak has also been difficult. About the coaching change, Christy describes Jacquie Hullah as "a great person" who was "committed" to the team, but adds that "a change needed to be made, and they didn't want to trade any players, so they changed the coach."

Christy hopes the Reign will make a fresh start, a point of view that is undoubtedly seconded by teammate Kate Paye, whose mid-December basketball statistics include 21 steals and a solid .364 shooting percentage from three-point range. Christy is similarly upbeat about the ABL as compared to the WNBA. "We have a lot better talent. We have a lot better quality of play," she asserts. "You look at a WNBA game and our game and there's just no comparison." But she adds a note of caution. After the WNBA's successful first season, Christy thinks that they are more than ever a serious competitor to the ABL.

In Long Beach, Trisha Stafford is a reserve player for the StingRays, the ABL's newest team. By the All-Star break she's averaging just over fifteen minutes and would like to be on court more. Yet she can certainly come in and make an impact. In a late December game against Portland, the close shot Trisha hits with only 5.6 seconds remaining gives her team a narrow one point win. A major plus for Trisha this year is playing in the Los Angeles area where friends and family and members of her father's church can come and watch. "I can't beat that," she says. "People that actually watched me grow up playing the game." However, Trisha is unsure where her future as a pro basketball player will lie.

In San Jose, Trisha's former teammate, Shelley Sandie, is having an easier time this season as compared to coming in mid-season last year. Among other accomplishments, by the All-Star break she's the league leader in free throw percentage. "I'm just enjoying playing basketball," Shelley says enthusiastically. "It's a lot of fun being in the league." If Shelley has the opportunity, she definitely wants to play in the ABL for another few years.

Across the country from California, Tara Davis' new basketball home is with the New England Blizzard. She made the team as a tryout player after letting ABL teams know she was available and considering an offer to play in Greece. Living away from her home in Seattle is "definitely different" for Tara, but she describes it as a "great experience." She's only playing very limited minutes, but she's pleased her team is winning games, hopeful her own role will expand, and appreciative of the chance to play for NBA legend KC Jones, whom she calls a "great coach."

Sheila Frost of the Portland Power has also played limited minutes this season. But she's received a special invitation to the All-Star weekend. Along with four other players, Sheila takes part in the ABL's first ever slam-dunk contest. It's an event that many see as slamming home a point about women's basketball.

"Women can't dunk." That's a big part of the rap against

women's basketball. With no flashy, high-flying, rim-rattling dunks, the women's version of the sport is said to be boring as compared to the men's game. But women do dunk—in some flashy and creative ways—at the 1998 ABL All-Star celebration.

The dunk contest, like the three-point shooting contest, begins on Saturday. Sheila Frost from the Power, and Linda Godby from the Reign, two of the league's tallest players, are both ready to dunk for the enthusiastic crowd who are here to watch something new and different in women's basketball. That new and different isn't easy. In the preliminary round, one contestant fails to dunk at all and there are a number of missed dunks. But there are also high-flying moves which inspire cheers and applause from the crowd.

In the preliminary round, Linda Godby misses her first attempt but makes a solid dunk on her second try. The crowd cheers. In the third round of dunks, she shoots the ball towards the basket, but isn't able to dunk it down. It's a mistake she makes up for right away with a more straightforward dunk. She ends up with enough points to place her among the three finalists.

Sheila Frost competes with battle scars—a black eye and twelve stitches on her forehead from a collision with a teammate in practice. She only scores points on one of her dunks, not enough to move on to the final competition. But what she gives up in points, she easily makes up in effort, creativity, and crowd-pleasing showmanship. Before her final dunk attempt, Sheila raises her arms to encourage a response from the audience. Then she jumps high enough to hang from the rim. When the ball misses its target, Sheila grabs her own rebound as she continues to hang from the rim. "Come on, Sheila! Put it in there," Lin Dunn shouts. Sheila hangs on a little longer and does exactly that.

On Sunday, at halftime of the All-Star game, the finals of both the slam-dunk contest and the three-point shootout are held. The lopsided score of the game itself—the West ends up winning 102 to 73—doesn't make for a sweaty palm, glued-to-your-seat experience. But very few fans leave the arena as three-point finalists Katie Smith and Dawn Staley shoot the lights out from long distance, with Dawn emerging as a close winner. Shortly afterwards, the dunk contest get underway.

Linda Godby runs up to the hoop with long, light-footed strides. She misses twice but each time follows a miss with a solid, workmanlike dunk. After her first successful dunk, she goes down on one knee, raising her arms and smiling at the crowd.

Kara Wolters of the New England Blizzard, at 6'7" the tallest player in the league, also plays to her audience. She puts on a blindfold for her first attempt but quickly converts it to a headband, in a basketball version of slapstick comedy. Before her second successful dunk, she puts a hand to an ear to encourage cheers from the crowd.

But it's Sylvia Crawley from the Colorado Xplosion who really comes up with an unforgettable performance. She makes a flashy first dunk with her legs stretched apart. Then she goes for the ultimate in showmanship with her second dunk. It's that second dunk which brings the crowd to its feet and inspires ABL players like Adrienne Goodson, Natalie Williams, and Linda Godby to hug and congratulate Sylvia.

Sylvia prepares for her last dunk methodically. She walks up to the basket, steps ten paces away from it, then waits as her mother, Marie, secures a black blindfold over her eyes. Suddenly it seems quiet in the arena. The Martin Luther King Pep Squad girls are watching rather than cheering. Perhaps there should be a dramatic drum roll to mark the moment.

Sylvia Crawley doesn't disappoint her audience. She runs up to the hoop, running lightly and gracefully in spite of the blindfold. Then she soars to the basket for a perfect dunk.

Appendix: Sources

Most of the material for this book came from the one or more interviews I conducted, in person or by telephone, with each of the people profiled in the book. ABL team media guides from the first and second seasons and official ABL statistics provided useful information about basketball achievements and particular games. What I've listed below are additional sources.

Chapter One

For a history of attitudes towards and achievements in American women's sports, including a history of women's basketball, *Coming on Strong: Gender and Sexuality in Twentieth-Century Women's Sport* by Susan K. Cahn (Cambridge, Massachusetts: Harvard University Press, 1994) was an extremely helpful source. *Playing Nice: Politics and Apologies in Women's Sports* by Mary Jo Festle (New York: Columbia University Press, 1996) provided essential information regarding women's basketball and women's sports since the 1950's, including material on Title IX. *A Century of Women's Basketball: From Frailty to Final Four* by editors Joan S. Hult and Marianna Trekell (Reston, Virginia: National Association for Girls and Women in Sport, 1991) gave useful material on the history of women's basketball, as did the the overview of women's basketball included in *At the Rim: A Celebration of Women's Collegiate Basketball* (Charlottesville, Virginia: Thomasson-Grant, 1991). My understanding of Title IX was also assisted by the Oregonian article of April 30, 1997 entitled "Women Athletes and Title IX," which supplied information on changes in female participation in sports.

My interview with Barbara Bell, about her mother Grace Sullivan Bell, gave me information on a basketball and sports pioneer, as did the newspaper accounts of games involving Bell from the University of Oregon newspaper during 1921-25.

For the history of previous professional basketball leagues in the United States, *Playing Nice* by Mary Jo Festle was the most comprehensive source. My interview with Cathy Aiken helped me learn about the LPBA, another league, as did articles in *The Phoenix Gazette* and *The Arizona Republic* from 1980. *ABL Courtside*, volume one, number two, included a brief account of Hazel Walker's Arkansas Traveller's written by Jay Jackson.

ABL Courtside, volume one, number two, by Dean Jutilla, supplied a brief history of the ABL and also gave league logos. *Venus to the Hoop* by Sara Corbett (NY: Doubleday, 1997) included some helpful history of the ABL and the WNBA, and also assisted my understanding of the U.S. National Team and 1996 Olympic Team, members of which were involved in the founding of the ABL, and included a helpful description of a players' only meeting about the ABL.

Several *Oregonian* articles also gave information about the founding of the ABL: "Portland is on the Blueprint for Women's Pro Basketball" by Abby Haight; "For ABL, the time is now—or at least tonight," also by Abby Haight on 10/18/97; and an account of the first ABL press conference from 9/27/95. The *Sports Illustrated* commentary on Steve Hams is from the October 9, 1995 issue, volume 83, number 16.

Chapter Two

My interviews with Katy Steding's mother, Patti Huntley; her former high school coach, Gary Lavender; her college and Olympic coach, Tara VanDerveer; and her Portland Power coach, Lin Dunn, helped give me insights into Katy Steding's life. Additionally, a number of print sources were useful. *The Lake Oswego Review* included articles on Steding's high school games. The Stanford Women's Basketball guides from 1987-88, 1988-89, 1989-90, and the *Stanford Sports Annual* from 1990-91 were all informative. "Steding as she goes" from the *Stanford Daily* by Mark Rogowsky on 3/2/90 gave useful information about her college career, as did the February 19, 1987 *Stanford Daily* article by Ed Stackler. The *Sports Illustrated* article by Hank Hersch, "The Cardinal rules," from April 9, 1990, volume 72, number 15, covered the 1990 NCAA championship game, and the

Stanford Women's Basketball 1990 NCAA Champions included numerous helpful articles.

Many *Oregonian* articles have covered Steding's sports career. Among these are "A Forced Timeout" from July 18, 1993; "A Step Back in Time—Katy Steding returns to Lake Oswego as an assistant coach" by Wade Nkrumah on 2/12/91; "Lake Oswego's Steding a starter for Stanford" by David Austin on 1/7/87; "A Steding Influence" by Steve Hunter on 3/1/95; "Call leads to spot on Spanish roster for Steding" by Abby Haight on 11/2/93; and "Experience a Priority for Women's Hoop Team" by Abby Haight on 6/12/92.

For events during and leading to the 1996 Olympics, *Venus to the Hoop* by Sara Corbett provided helpful information as did *Shooting from the Outside* by Tara VanDerveer with Joan Ryan (New York: Avon Books, 1997). The following *Oregonian* articles about Katy Steding's involvement with the Olympics and the U.S. National Team were also useful: "For U.S. Women, there's more at stake than gold" by Dwight Jaynes on 7/22/96; "The race is over for Portland's Steding" by Abby Haight on 7/20/96; "U.S. seeks tougher opponents" by Abby Haight on 1/15/96; "A tour de force" by Abby Haight on 4/8/96; "Steding's surge is decisive" from 7/22/96; and "This final victory is a statement" by Dwight Jaynes from 8/5/96. Also helpful were *Sports Illustrated* articles by Alexander Wolff: "The Home Team" from 5/29/95, volume 82, number 21, and "Road Show" from 7/22/96, volume 85, number 4.

Oregonian articles on ABL games involving Steding include "Power comeback falls one shot short in Richmond" from 2/3/97; "Dreadful start derails Power in Atlanta" from 2/16/97; "Power ends losing skid, and there is much rejoicing" by Jason Quick from 12/6/96. Jason Quick's profile of Steding, "Power's reluctant hero," from 12/15/96 was informative and thought provoking.

Chapter Three

The journal Christy Hedgpeth wrote for *ABL Sports Online*, describing a January road trip with the Reign, was extremely helpful. During my interviews with numerous other players, I also came to understand more about how valuable a role Christy Hedgpeth had played in encouraging players to join the ABL.

Chapter Four

The Stanford Basketball Guide – 1991-92 provided useful information on Val Whiting. For Whiting's childhood basketball experiences, the *Seattle Times* article by Steve Kelley, "Whiting marshalls skills for the Reign," from 10/15/97 was useful. For the ABL All-Star game on December 15, 1996, the Fox SportsChannel broadcast provided insight into Whiting's performance. Descriptions about Val Whiting's pre-season car crash were contained in an October 17, 1996 article by Steve Kettmann in the *San Francisco Chronicle*; an *Alameda Times Star* article by Michelle Smith from 9/27/96; a *Contra Costa Times* article by Chuck Barney from 10/17/96; and a *Daily Ledger Post Dispatch* article by Chuck Barney on 10/17/96. *Seattle Times* articles about Seattle Reign games including Linda Godby are by Steve Kelley on 1/24/96 and Blaine Newnham on 10/28/96. Also the broadcast of a January 19, 1997 game between Seattle and San Jose, televised on Fox SportsChannel, was helpful.

Chapter Five

The brief impressions about Jacquie Hullah I received from a few of her players helped with my profile of Hullah. Additionally, the following *Seattle Times* articles were helpful: "Life in the ABL/ on the road with the Reign" by Glenn Nelson from 10/21/96; "Peak experience—Hullah adapts to challenges, opportunities of young league" by Dick Rockne from 10/16/96; "Seattle Reign/A team in turmoil" by Glenn Nelson on 2/20/97; and an article by Les Carpenter on 1/18/97. An *Oregonian* article by Jason Quick, "Power knocks Seattle out of playoff race" describes Hullah in relation to some Reign players. And for information on Hullah's positive comments to her players, I drew from the Dana Squires article, "No 'quit' in this coach" in the December, 97/January, 98 issue of *Women's Sports Northwest*.

For the section on Lin Dunn, several players' comments were helpful. Useful *Oregonian* articles include "New coach hopes to get Portland players cooking" by Jason Quick on 1/3/97; and "No more tattoos, but Dunn wants another winner" on 10/16/97, also by Jason Quick, which provided very useful background information on Dunn.

Chapter Six

For the section on Adrienne Goodson, the article by Vic Dorr Jr. for the *Richmond Times-Dispatch*, "Goodson on the go for Rage," of 2/8/97, provided helpful information about Goodson's background. *Richmond Times-Dispatch* accounts of games involving Goodson are

"Goodson's shot lifts Rage over Blizzard," on 11/17/97; "Rage over-comes sluggish start" by Vic Dorr Jr. on 12/1/96; "Staley, Goodson drive Richmond past Colorado," by Vic Dorr Jr. on 11/23/97; "Goodson leads Rage over San Jose 83-69," on 1/6/97; and "Goodson leads Rage past Glory" on 2/12/97. During the playoff finals, the Fox SportsChannel broadcasts of the first finals game held on 3/2/97 and the second finals game, held on 3/4/97 were quite helpful. I was also assisted by articles about Goodson's involvement in the playoffs: an account of the first finals game by Vic Dorr Jr. in the *Richmond Times-Dispatch* on 3/3/97 and an article by Valerie Lister, "Rage tops Quest 75-62 to even series" in *USA Today* on 3/5/97.

Chapter Seven

The quotation from Kirsten Cummings about following one's heart comes from the 1996-97 media guide for the Richmond Rage. For my account of Cummings' preseason injury, I was assisted by Diane Pucin's article, "Player endures, overcomes adversity" for the *Philadelphia Inquirer* on 11/26/97.

With Trisha Stafford, the Fox Sports broadcast of the January 19, 1997 game between Seattle and San Jose was helpful. The San Jose Lasers media guide for the 1996-97 season supplied the quote by Denise Curry on coach Jan Lowrey.

Chapter Eight

For the section on Coquese Washington, Elaine Carter's obser-vation of fans waiting for autographs was helpful. The *Willamette Week* profile of Coquese from December, 1996 supplied overall back-ground information as well as information about her relationship with children in Flint, Michigan.

For Falisha Wright, an *Oregonian* profile of Wright, "Making the fast track," by Jason Quick on 2/8/97, supplied very helpful infor-mation about Falisha's honors, statistics, and achievements, her back-ground, and the assistance she gave teammate Michelle Marciniak. Another *Oregonian* article by Jason Quick, "Power's 79-76 overtime victory frustrates the Reign," on 2/10/97 provided the quote by Lin Dunn about Wright growing up on the court that night.

For Lisa Harrison's profile, the Fox Sports Northwest broadcast of the game between Portland and Seattle on December 5, 1996 was extremely helpful. The *Oregonian* article, "Harrison's career gets a new start," on 10/13/96 by Jason Quick gave me an additional perspective on what it was like for Harrison to return to basketball.

Chapter Nine

With Shelley Sandie, the Fox broadcast of a game between San Jose and Seattle on 1/19/97 was useful, as was the description of the competition between the U.S. and Australian Olympic teams contained in *Venus to the Hoop* by Sara Corbett.

The profile of Debbie Black, "The Tasmanian Devil," by Dean Jultilla in *ABL Courtside*, volume one, number two provided good background information. Game accounts involving Black in the *Rocky Mountain News* include "Black returns to inspire Xplosion in 96-74 victory" by Alan Pearce on 11/4/96; "Xplosion gets win, but Sheetz is injured" by Tony Jackson on 12/4/96; and "Quadruple-double lifts Xplosion back to .500" by Alan Pearce on 12/9/96.

Chapter Ten

For statistics from Kate Paye's first ABL season, the *Seattle Reign Preseason Prospectus, 1997-98*, was very helpful. The following *Seattle Times* articles were useful: "Reign captures victory, wins fans" on 10/28/96 provided a description of the opening home game; "Paye brightest of Seattle stars" by Dick Rockne on 10/28/96 described Paye's performance in the opening home game; "Reign now 7-0 at home" by Dick Rockne on 12/7/96 describes a December 6th game; and also useful was "Reign keeps hope alive with victory— Paye's basket is winner for Seattle" on 2/1/97. Also, the Fox Sports broadcast of the February 1, 1997 game against Colorado helped with my Paye profile.

For the section on Jennifer Jacoby, in addition to my interview with her, the Portland Power media guide for the 1996-97 season was quite useful, as was the Fox broadcast of the three-point shootout during the All-Star game. Additionally, I used the *Oregonian* article by Jason Quick, "Power gives Dunn a debut worthy of ovation," on 1/3/97 which described Jacoby's changed role.

For Natalie Williams, the brief biographies of 1998 All-Star players provided by the ABL gave the information about *Sports Illustrated* picking her as one of the five best women players. For very helpful background information on Williams, I referred to the *Sports Illustrated* article by Sally Jenkins, "Twin Killer," from the February 22, 1993 issue, volume 78, number 7. The description of Williams' return to action and leap towards the basket comes from the *Orego-

nian article by Jason Quick, "Power ends losing skid, and there is much rejoicing," on 12/6/96. Jason Quick's comments on Williams in "Power beats Laser to snap two-game losing streak," also in the *Oregonian*, on 1/17/97 were also helpful. The description of the sign asking Williams to stay in Portland is from another Jason Quick article, "Williams scores 30 as Power wins finale," in the *Oregonian* on 1/21/97.

Chapter Eleven

For Tara Davis, the *Seattle Reign Preseason Prospectus 1997-98* supplied some statistical information. The Fox Sports broadcasts of January 19, 1997 and February 1, 1997 games showed Davis in game situations. General information about Davis's strengths as a player came from the 1997-98 media guide for the New England Blizzard.

Chapter Twelve

For background information on Lisa Boyer, I drew on a May 15, 1996 article in *The Journal* from Ogdensburg, New York, "Boyer takes challenge of coaching," compiled by Dave Shea and Steve Heaton. A *Richmond Times-Dispatch* article by Vic Dorr Jr. on 9/5/96, "Rage will major in communications" supplied some of Boyer's preseason thoughts. During the playoffs, the Fox telecast of games on March 2, 1997 and March 11, 1997 were quite helpful, as was an article by Vic Dorr Jr. in the *Richmond Times-Dispatch*, "Columbus captures game 1," which gave Boyer's comments on that loss.

Chapter Thirteen

For Valerie Still, several newspaper articles provided material: "Full-court pressure—Columbus Quest player juggles motherhood, basketball career" by Aaron Portzline in the *Columbus Dispatch* on 12/12/96 and "Quest's Still lonely on road but ABL life enriches roles as mother, wife, player" by Valerie Lister for *USA Today* on 1/17/97. The *Richmond Times-Dispatch* article by Vic Dorr on 1/13/97 provided the quotation about Still as a renaissance woman. The Fox Sports broadcasts of the playoff finals games on 3/2/97 and 3/11/97 were invaluable.

Chapter Fourteen

The quote by Gary Cavalli about "bigger and better" came from a Fox Sports telecast of the last finals game on 3/11/97. The information on top draft picks came from the 1997 American Basketball

League Draft 5/5/97 compiled by the ABL. The information on DeLisha Milton Days came from an *Oregonian* article by Jason Quick, "Making a real impact" on 5/5/97. LaTicia Morris and Kedra Holland-Corn's comments about the ABL were in "ABL's soft sell draws stars away from WNBA" by Jason Quick on 4/26/97 in the *Oregonian*. Quick's article "ABL touts infusion of cash and flash" on 4/25/97 supplied useful information about the ABL's finances. An ABL press release from 4/24/97 gave information about new coach Angela Beck, and the ABL web site supplied info about K.C. Jones. *The Seattle Reign Preseason Prospectus 1997-98* supplied information about ABL attendance, and various short accounts in the *Oregonian* during the summer of 1997 supplied attendance figures for WNBA games. The *USA Today* article by Valerie Lister on 9/18/97, "McCray leaves Quest in lurch," provided Valerie Still's comments on Nikki McCray's move to the WNBA. A brief interview with the ABL's Dean Jutilla provided some general information about the league for this chapter, as did my interviews with Gary Cavalli, Steve Hams, and Linda Weston.

Useful magazine articles included "Up in the Air" by John Leland in the September 1st, 1997 issue of *Newsweek*; and "One on One" by Carla Fried, which provided a great deal of information on the ABL vs. the WNBA, as well as first and second team players from both leagues, from the Fall, 97 issue of *Sports Illustrated Women/Sport*. Information on the new television package for the ABL came from an ABL press release from 9/9/97 and includes the quote about the TV package by Gary Cavalli. Tara VanDerveer made her comments on the future of women's pro basketball at a reading/signing for her new book on September, 10, 1997 in Beaverton, Oregon.

The *Oregonian* account of Katy Steding's performance in an exhibition game, "Resurgent Steding shines in Power win," was by Jason Quick and appeared on 10/6/97. The quote of Lin Dunn about the discrimination she has encountered came from "No more tattoos, but Dunn wants another winner" by Jason Quick in the *Oregonian* on 10/16/97.

Epilogue

The quote from Gary Cavalli about talent in the league and other players who could be All Stars came from an ABL media release on December 17, 1997. I found the information about Falisha Wright tying Jennifer Azzi's record in a Game-Day Report on the Portland

Power from the *Oregonian* on 1/8/98. The information on Stacey Ford's scoring on January 4th, 1998 came from "Jacoby may miss shooting event" by Jason Quick in the *Oregonian* on 1/5/98. For my description of Lisa Harrison's performance in the December 14, 1997 double overtime game, I was assisted by the Fox Sports broadcast on the same date.

Regarding Jacquie Hullah's firing, the Fox Sports broadcast of a December 4, 1997 Seattle Reign game gave me a glimpse of Hullah walking off court. A *Seattle Times* article was also helpful: "Hullah's reign in Seattle over" by Bob Sherwin on 12/9/97. Also, Christy Hedgpeth's comments provided another perspective.

The description of Trisha Stafford's game-winning shot came from "Power's struggle continues with loss" by Jason Quick from the *Oregonian* on 12/29/97. The quote of Lin Dunn's encouraging words to Sheila Frost, in the slam dunk contest, came from "Even the misses were hits," by Jason Quick from the *Oregonian* on 1/18/98.